THE LAST CAMPAIGN

✦

THE LAST CAMPAIGN

ROBERT F. KENNEDY

AND 82 DAYS

THAT INSPIRED AMERICA

✦

THURSTON

CLARKE

HENRY HOLT AND COMPANY

NEW YORK

Henry Holt and Company, LLC
Publishers since 1866
175 Fifth Avenue
New York, New York 10010
www.henryholt.com

Henry Holt® and ®® are registered trademarks
of Henry Holt and Company, LLC.

Distributed in Canada by H. B. Fenn and Company Ltd.

Lyrics to "Clack Clack / The Oldest Living Son Medley"
and "Lincoln's Train," courtesy of John Stewart.

Library of Congress Cataloging-in-Publication Data

Clarke, Thurston.
    The last campaign : Robert F. Kennedy and 82 days that inspired
America / Thurston Clarke.—1st ed.
        p. cm.
    Includes index.
    ISBN-13: 978-0-8050-7792-6
    ISBN-10: 0-8050-7792-8
    1. Presidents—United States—Election—1968. 2. Kennedy, Robert F.,
1925–1968. 3. United States—Politics and government—1963–1969. I. Title.
    E851.C63 2008
    973.922092—dc22   2007045880
    [B]

Henry Holt books are available for special promotions
and premiums. For details contact: Director, Special Markets.

First Edition 2008

Designed by Victoria Hartman

Printed in the United States of America

1   3   5   7   9   10   8   6   4   2

In memory of
Marlin Miller
and Wilton Pyle

Let us dedicate ourselves to what the Greeks wrote
so many years ago: to tame the savageness of man
and make gentle the life of this world. Let us dedicate
ourselves to that, and say a prayer for our country
and for our people.

—Robert F. Kennedy, speaking in Indianapolis
on April 4, 1968, two hours after the assassination
of Dr. Martin Luther King Jr.

Contents

· Part III ·

RED STATE PRIMARIES

· Part IV ·

THE WEST COAST

PROLOGUE

JUNE 8, 1968

In 1968, America was a wounded nation. The wounds were moral ones, and the Vietnam War and three summers of inner-city riots had inflicted them on the national soul, challenging Americans' belief that they were a uniquely noble and honorable people. Americans saw news footage from South Vietnam, such as the 1965 film of U.S. Marines setting fire to thatched huts in the village of Cam Ne with cigarette lighters and flamethrowers as women and children ran for safety, and realized they were capable of atrocities once considered the province of their enemies. They saw smoke rising over Washington, D.C., during the riots following the assassination of Martin Luther King Jr., soldiers with machine guns guarding the Capitol, federal troops patrolling the streets of American cities for the first time since the Civil War, and asked themselves how this could be happening in their City Upon a Hill.

Nineteen sixty-eight was an election year, and the presidential candidates all promised to win or negotiate an end to the Vietnam War and to pacify America's cities with new social programs, draconian law enforcement, or both. But only one candidate, Senator Robert F. Kennedy of New York, recognized the moral wounds and promised to heal them. Days after announcing his candidacy on March 16, he accused

President Lyndon Johnson's administration of abandoning "the generous impulses that are the soul of this nation" and said he was running
to offer "a way in which the people themselves can lead the way back to
those ideals which are the source of national strength and generosity
and compassion of deed."

During his campaign for the Democratic nomination, Kennedy told
Americans that they were individually responsible for what their government had done in their name in Vietnam and for what it had failed
to do at home for minorities and the poor. He said they could not ac-
quit themselves of this responsibility simply by voting for a new president and new policies. Instead, they would have to participate in the
healing process. Because Kennedy had managed his late brother's 1960
presidential campaign and served in his cabinet as attorney general, he
understood that following a crude and divisive campaign with a high-
minded presidency would be difficult, and healing a morally wounded
nation after running an immoral campaign would be impossible.
Because he understood this, his campaign is a template for how a candidate should run for the White House in a time of moral crisis.

Since 1968, the word *hope* has become the oratorical equivalent of
an American flag lapel pin, a de rigueur rhetorical flourish amounting
to a vague promise of better days. But the hope that Robert Kennedy
offered was specific: that Americans' belief in their integrity and decency could be restored. His assassination on June 5, eighty-two days
after he had announced his candidacy, represented not just the death
of another Kennedy or of a promising young leader, but the death of
this hope. This explains why the most dramatic display of public grief
for an American citizen who had never been elected to the presidency
unfolded on June 8, 1968, when a twenty-one-car funeral train, its en-
gine draped in black bunting, carried Kennedy's body from his funeral
in New York to his burial in Washington.

Trains carrying the remains of Presidents Abraham Lincoln and
Franklin Roosevelt traveled at a mournful pace, passing bonfires, bands,
and weeping crowds, and stopping for tributes. But Kennedy's train was
scheduled to travel nonstop and at a normal rate of speed. Crowds were
expected, but no one imagined that on a steamy Saturday afternoon two
million people would head for the tracks, wading through marshes, hiking

across meadows, and slithering under fences, filling tenement balconies, clambering onto factory roofs, standing in junkyards and cemeteries, peering down from bridges, viaducts, and bluffs, placing 100,000 coins on the tracks, waving hand-lettered GOODBYE BOBBY signs, and forging a 226-mile-long chain of grief and despair.

Political reporter Theodore White, one of the 1,146 passengers, wrote, "It was only, however, when the funeral train that was to bear him to Washington emerged from the tunnel under the Hudson that one could grasp what kind of a man he was and what he had meant to Americans." Once the train crossed into New Jersey, mourners jamming station platforms and spilling onto northbound tracks forced the engineer to reduce his speed. After a northbound express killed two people standing on the tracks in Elizabeth, the Penn Central halted all other traffic on the line and the funeral train continued to Washington at half speed. Inside the coaches, some of Kennedy's ten children played with balloons in the dining car while their mother, her black veil pulled back over her head, walked through the coaches, greeting mourners. Passengers ate in the dining cars, drank until the bar car ran dry, or remained determinedly sober. They laughed, cried, or sat in stony silence, found this impromptu wake distressing or a fitting tribute. But they all stared out the windows and saw their grief reflected in the faces of people whom they usually flew over or sped past.

Looking out those windows were many of the people responsible for the political and cultural life of the nation during the years since John F. Kennedy's inauguration: New York socialites and Massachusetts backroom pols, Hollywood celebrities and media heavyweights, star athletes and famous writers, architects and opponents of the Vietnam War, men who had served in John Kennedy's administration and might have served in Bobby's. There was Charles Evers, whom Bobby Kennedy had comforted after his brother, civil rights leader Medgar Evers, was assassinated in 1963, and who was now thinking about Bobby: "Where, dear God, is the man to take his place?" There was Coretta Scott King, whom Bobby had comforted after her husband was assassinated in April of that year, and Jackie Kennedy, who had told former White House aide Arthur Schlesinger that she feared "the same thing" that had happened to her husband would happen to

Bobby because "there is so much hatred in this country, and more people hate Bobby than hated Jack."

Passengers stared out the windows and saw men in undershirts, sport shirts, uniforms, and suits: crying, saluting, standing at attention, and holding their hard hats over their hearts. They saw women in madras shorts, housedresses, and Sunday dresses: weeping, kneeling, covering their faces, and holding up children as if telling them, "You look at Robert Kennedy, and that's the way you should lead your life." They saw people who were also mourning Martin Luther King Jr. and John F. Kennedy, although they may not have known it, and people who were weeping because they sensed that this signified the end of something, although they were not sure what. They saw some of the same derelict factories, creaky tenements, shuttered stores, and crime-battered neighborhoods that anyone traveling this route today still sees, but might not be seeing had Robert Kennedy lived.

Even after the air-conditioning failed and the food ran out, some passengers were saying, "I hope this train ride never ends," because they knew this was the last time that Bobby Kennedy would bring them together. They wept when high school bands played "Taps" as the train slid through stations at Trenton and New Brunswick, and when mourners in the Philadelphia and Baltimore stations sang Kennedy's favorite hymn, "The Battle Hymn of the Republic"; they wept when police bands played "The Star-Spangled Banner" and "America the Beautiful," and again when they passed diamonds where Little Leaguers stood at attention along the baselines, heads bowed and caps held over their hearts.

Because anyone who owned an American flag had flown it or brought it, they saw flags flying at half-staff in front of factories and schools, dipped by American Legion honor guards, and waved by Cub Scouts. Because anyone owning a uniform had worn it, they saw policemen in gold braid and white gloves, fire companies standing at attention next to their trucks, and veterans in Eisenhower jackets and overseas caps snapping salutes.

They saw the kind of white working-class backlash voters who had supported former Alabama governor George Wallace's 1964 candidacy for the Democratic nomination, and would vote again for

Wallace or Republican Richard Nixon in November, although until four days before many had planned to vote for Robert Kennedy. Today, these whites had not only turned out to mourn a politician who was an acknowledged champion of black Americans, and who had condemned an American war as "deeply wrong"; they had decided that the most fitting way to do this was to wear a uniform and wave a flag.

"Marvelous crowds," Arthur Schlesinger told Kenny O'Donnell, a former White House aide to John Kennedy who had been Bobby Kennedy's Harvard classmate.

"Yes," O'Donnell replied. "But what are they good for?"

But Adalbert de Segonzac of *France Soir* noticed that they were the same kind of people—he called them "small white people"—who had cheered Kennedy in the working-class towns of northern Indiana. They may not have been *good* for anything now, he thought, but they *proved* something, and he opened his article about the funeral train, "Robert Kennedy won the American election today."

Richard Harwood of the *Washington Post* saw "trembling nuns" and "adoring children," reported that blacks cried most, and concluded, "It may not have had the grandeur of the last train ride Abraham Lincoln took through the weeping countryside a century ago. But no one could be sure of that."

Not since Lincoln had black Americans embraced a white politician as passionately and completely. They, as well as many whites, feared that Robert Kennedy's assassination, like Lincoln's, had eliminated the only leader who could heal and unify a wounded nation. Some of the spectators who broke into "The Battle Hymn of the Republic" as the train passed through Baltimore and Philadelphia may have been making the Kennedy–Lincoln connection as well; those gathered at the Lincoln Memorial who flicked on lighters, held up matches, and sang "The Battle Hymn" as his cortege paused en route to Arlington certainly were. NBC commentator David Brinkley called Kennedy "the only white politician left who could talk to both races" and compared his assassination to Lincoln's, and as images of Kennedy's funeral train appeared on the television screen, another newsman read an account of Lincoln's funeral train, saying, "The people are lined up along the tracks . . . particularly black people. They have built bonfires for miles, and the train is proceeding within the parallel lines of bonfires. . . . And so the train bearing the body of Abraham Lincoln reached Washington."

After the accident at Elizabeth, the train traveled so slowly that its passengers noticed details about the people outside their windows. They saw a long-haired girl on a horse, five nuns standing on tiptoes in a yellow pickup truck, a crowd of young black militants with Afros holding up clenched fists, white policemen cradling black children in their arms, a family with a sign reading THE GEBHARTS ARE SAD, and five black boys in church clothes, each holding a rose. AP reporter Joe Mohbat and Jack Miller, a prosecutor who had served as chief of the Criminal Division in Bobby Kennedy's Justice Department, broke down and wept when the train passed a line of saluting schoolchildren, a reminder of John F. Kennedy Jr. saluting his father's casket. Gertrude Wilson of the *Amsterdam News* put her hands against the window and sobbed at the sight of a black woman in Baltimore clutching a hand-lettered sign that said HOPE.

Sylvia Wright of *Life* remembered a wedding party standing in a Delaware meadow. The bridesmaids held the hems of their pink and green dresses in one hand, their bouquets in the other. As the last car carrying Kennedy's coffin passed, they extended their arms and tossed their flowers against its side. After seeing this, and the solemn Boy Scouts, black women prostrate with grief, and brawny white men gripping tiny flags in ham-hock hands as tears rolled down their cheeks, Wright asked herself the question that has become the silent descant of most everything written or said about Bobby Kennedy: *"What did he have that he could do this to people?"*

ON THE TWENTIETH anniversary of Robert Kennedy's assassination, author Jack Newfield called it "a wound that hurts more, not less, as time passes." On its twenty-fifth anniversary, Judi Cornelius, a Native American woman who had arranged Kennedy's visit to her reservation, visited his grave at Arlington only to discover that, she said, "My heart ached just like it had two and a half decades earlier, and some wounds to [our] tender dreams never heal." On its thirtieth, former aide Peter Edelman told a reporter, "I had a dream for years that he [Kennedy] came back alive. Actually, I still do." And a year after that, *New York Times* reporter Anthony Lewis said, "The year after he died, I wrote a column about him. 'Time,' I wrote, 'does not diminish the sense that life without him is incomplete.' Thirty-one years later, I still feel that way."

What did he have?

Congressman John Lewis, who had been on Kennedy's campaign staff, asks himself "What would Bobby do?" before casting a difficult vote in the House of Representatives. Kennedy's former press secretary, Frank Mankiewicz, who had announced Kennedy's death to reporters at Good Samaritan Hospital in Los Angeles, saying, "Senator Robert Francis Kennedy died at 1:44 A.M. today, June 6, 1968. . . . He was forty-two years old," remembers him whenever he hears "The trumpet shall sound" aria in the *Messiah*, "because Bob Kennedy was the trumpet, and he's still sounding for me." Doug German, a young Kennedy volunteer in Nebraska, says he abandoned party politics afterward because "The music died for me." John Bartlow Martin, who wrote speeches for Adlai Stevenson and John Kennedy before writing them for Bobby, went into seclusion at his home in rural Michigan, writing in his diary, "It's over, the brief bright dream. Last time they let us have it for three years [JFK's presidency]. . . . Now I feel nothing but bleak despair. . . . [Before] there was the thought, 'well, there's always Bob: Now there isn't.'" Jerry Bruno, Kennedy's hard-boiled advance man, claims the politics were never the same for him, adding, "It was like all of our lives just stopped." *Life* photographer Bill Eppridge never asked to cover another campaign, and says, "When you get to the pinnacle what else is there? It would have been like going back and shooting weddings." And whenever Eppridge visits the Vietnam War memorial, he finds himself looking at the names of servicemen killed after January 15, 1969, when Kennedy might have been inaugurated, wondering how many would still be alive. Attorney Jim Tolan, who had prepared the way for—in political parlance, "advanced"—many of Kennedy's appearances that spring, leaves the room whenever images of him appear in a television documentary. "I fell in love with Robert

Kennedy, with his goodness," he says. "Listen, I *loved* that man." Associated Press correspondent Joe Mohbat, who spent more time in close physical proximity to him than any reporter that spring, lost his taste for journalism and became a lawyer. "I can still see him with his shirt sleeves rolled up, and his hairy muscular forearms," he says. "One lid covers more of one eye than the other—a kind of droopy lid—and there is an absolute intensity about him, even when he's joking. There will *never* be anyone like him. History won't allow it, the media won't allow it, the blogs won't allow it." He stops before adding in a choked voice, "You *really* want to know what Bob Kennedy was? He was fucking beautiful."

What did he have?

Those still mourning him usually mention Hugh McDonald, his twenty-nine-year-old assistant press secretary, perhaps because McDonald's grief was an extreme version of their own. He had dashed into the pantry of the Ambassador Hotel seconds after the shots and handed his suit jacket to bodyguard Bill Barry, who used it to stanch the blood flowing from the wound in Kennedy's head. McDonald wept as he removed Kennedy's shoes to make him more comfortable. Later, he wandered the corridors of the Ambassador Hotel and Good Samaritan Hospital, clutching a pair of size 8½ black shoes with arch supports, wearing a blank expression, and saying, "I've got his shoes . . . I've got his shoes." Because McDonald had been in charge of checking the credentials of those entering the room where Kennedy was speaking, he blamed himself for admitting the assassin. He suffered from shock and depression, ended up divorced, attempted suicide, and died in a Los Angeles rooming house in March 1978, ten years to the month after Robert Kennedy had announced his candidacy.

What did he have?

Director John Frankenheimer, who drove Kennedy to the Ambassador Hotel on the night of the assassination, developed a drinking problem that crippled his career for two decades. Olympic decathlon champion Rafer Johnson, who was steps away when Kennedy was shot, suffered months of paranoia, using public telephones and fictitious names to communicate with friends because he believed he was next.

Singer Rosemary Clooney, who was also at the Ambassador that night, insisted that Kennedy had survived and his death was an elaborate hoax. She suffered a nervous breakdown and was institutionalized. On the night of Kennedy's funeral, singer Bobby Darin remained by his grave in Arlington until dawn, sleeping on the ground and claiming to have experienced what he called a "metaphysical illumination" that had transformed him into a "new me, a better me . . . striving for only one thing: to help the world change toward goodness."

What did he have?

Many are haunted by Kennedy's phantom presidency. Two decades after his death, Ralph Bartlow Martin wrote, "I have no doubt at all that if nominated he [Kennedy] would have been elected. And if elected, a great President, maybe greater than his brother. But they would have killed him." As Kennedy lay dying, Jack Newfield told John Lewis, "I can feel history slipping through my fingers." Four decades later, Lewis says, "I thought that if this one man was elected president, he could move us closer to what many of us in the movement called 'The Loving Community.'" Former Kennedy aide Peter Edelman still believes that his presidency "would have influenced the tone and direction of American politics for decades." Edwin Guthman, who worked in the Kennedy Justice Department, writes, "To know anything about him is to know that had he lived and won in 1968, he would have been a great President." *Look* correspondent Warren Rogers told an interviewer in 1997 that his presidency would have left "a far more decent, a far gentler and less uncouth country than we are today," and the political commentator Mark Shields, who worked for him in the Nebraska primary, says, "I'll go to my grave believing Robert Kennedy would have been the best President of my lifetime."

Ask Shields, Mankiewicz, and other former Kennedy aides what his presidency would have meant, and you invariably hear the word *different*: "This would be an entirely different country," "Everything would be different," or words to that effect. Ask *how* things would be different, and you hear two narratives: one describing Kennedy's presidency and the other, its legacy.

Imagining his presidency is easy because, as even his enemies would concede, he meant what he said. So it is likely that he would have

negotiated a settlement to the Vietnam War soon after his inauguration, saving the lives of the two million Vietnamese and twenty
thousand American servicemen killed during the Nixon administration. Because he would not have bombed Cambodia, America would
have escaped the trauma of Kent State and Jackson State, and Cambodia would probably have escaped the murderous Pol Pot regime. The
Watergate would be just another apartment building, and America
would have avoided the disillusionment and cynicism following that
scandal. Had Kennedy won the presidency, young and minority Americans would have had a champion in the White House. The riots and
protests marking Nixon's first year would have been blunted, and
Kennedy might have convinced Americans that real "immorality"
meant poverty, racial discrimination, and an unnecessary war. Had
Kennedy beaten Nixon in 1968, both parties might not have
embraced—or at least not so readily—the sound bites, focus groups,
stage-managed appearances, screened questions, bogus spontaneity,
and other corrosive hallmarks of Nixon's successful campaign. And
had Kennedy won, then the guiding principle of Nixon's campaign as
spelled out in his secret 1968 manual—"The central point of scheduling is that the campaign is symbolic, i.e. it is not what the candidate actually does as much as what it appears he does [that matters]"—might
have been discredited rather than emulated.

Frank Mankiewicz defines what a Kennedy presidency would have
meant: "This would be a totally different country, not like it is today,
with the political machinery grinding against itself, sending off
sparks." But what *kind* of oil was Kennedy proposing to pour into the
jammed political machinery of the time? Might it still be effective?

What did he have?

The obvious answer to Sylvia Wright's question is that he had his
last name and his position as the oldest surviving brother of a beloved
and martyred president. But even this is insufficient to explain the intensity and longevity of the grief following his assassination, nor are
his youth, eloquence, and good looks, although they made his death
more heartbreaking. They are not enough because had he been assassinated or died of natural causes *before* running for president, or in the
early days of his campaign, it is inconceivable that two million people

would have turned out for his funeral train, or that there would ever have been such a train, or that his phantom presidency would remain so haunting. Had his assassination not been preceded by his eighty-two-day campaign, it is also inconceivable that 92 percent of the residents of Harlem would have claimed to be mourning him more than JFK, or that Norman Mailer would have admitted loving him "by five times more in death than life," or that at his funeral tears would have coursed down the cheeks of both Tom Hayden of the Students for a Democratic Society (SDS) and Mayor Richard Daley of Chicago, two men at opposite ends of the Democratic Party's political spectrum, or that more photographs of him would still be hanging in congressional offices than of any other former member of the House or Senate, or so it is said.

It is Robert Kennedy's campaign that explains the grief, reveals how he would have freed America's jammed political machinery, and answers Wright's question and its obvious corollary: What did he do during those eighty-two days?

His campaign explains why authorities assumed that his assassination would spark riots in black neighborhoods equal to those following the assassination of Martin Luther King Jr., why the Pentagon's new riot-monitoring unit, the Army Directorate for Civil Disturbances Planning and Operations, immediately went on a state of alert, and why almost twenty-five thousand California National Guard troops were readied to move into the ghettos. The military was not alone in forecasting a violent reaction. Two weeks earlier, Tom Wicker had written in the *New York Times*, "The people of the ghetto are volatile and suspicious and militant; if they believe Kennedy has been 'dealt out' by the Democrats their response could be angry and even violent." Many of Kennedy's black supporters had also expected the ghettos to explode as they had for Dr. King. They seemed almost embarrassed that they had not, and explained that their people had still been reeling from the King assassination and were too shattered to lash out again.

Kennedy's campaign also explains his popularity with black Americans, why some called him a "blue-eyed soul brother," why Charles Evers's reaction to his assassination was wailing, "My God! My God!

What are my people going to do?" and why John Lewis responded by, he says, "crying, sobbing, heaving as if something had been busted open inside," even though he had not wept for Martin Luther King Jr. His campaign explains why many of the same Midwestern farmers, factory workers, and white ethnics who would vote Richard Nixon, Ronald Reagan, and both Bushes into the White House, voted for Robert Kennedy in the Democratic primaries, and why Fred Papert, who managed his advertising campaign, is justified in believing that millions of Americans would have turned out for his funeral train, even if it had traveled through the Deep South or Far West, "all those areas where everybody thinks people are different, ultra-conservative, and reactionary."

One of the reporters covering Kennedy's campaign called it a "huge, joyous adventure." Revisiting it can also be a joyous experience because no credible candidate since has run so passionately or recklessly, or without the customary and ever-expanding carapace of consultants, pollsters, spinners, and question-screeners. Nor has anyone put poverty at the center of a presidential campaign, except John Edwards, excited minorities and the poor as much, been trusted as much by both blacks and working-class whites, or criticized the American people so brazenly. Try to imagine a mainstream politician saying, as Kennedy did in a *New York Times* essay, "Once we thought, with Jefferson, that we were the 'best hope' of all mankind. But now we seem to rely only on our wealth and power," or, as he did on *Meet the Press:* "I am dissatisfied with our society. I suppose I am dissatisfied with my country." You cannot because today's thin-skinned electorate would never tolerate such criticism.

Revisiting Robert Kennedy's campaign can be heartbreaking because it resembles a kind of slow-motion suicide, and because one knows who, and what, is coming next; not just the second assassination of a Kennedy, but Talking Points, Red and Blue States, *That depends on what the meaning of "is" is*, and *Bring 'em on!* Revisiting it is also tricky because he was at his best during those eighty-two days. Author Wilfrid Sheed, who worked for one of Kennedy's rivals for the Democratic nomination, Senator Eugene McCarthy of Minnesota, would later concede that Kennedy's campaign had been "what his life had been about all along, and that his death henceforth would serve principally to direct our eyes to it," adding, "For those few weeks at least, Bobby became a very great man, transcending his own nature and even some of our quibbles with it."

One of Kennedy's friends told biographer William Shannon, "You never know which Bobby Kennedy you're going to meet," and Shannon, writing about Kennedy while he was still alive, called him "rude, restless, impatient," but also "brilliant, inspiring, forceful." It was this second Bobby Kennedy who campaigned for the Democratic nomination that spring. Because Kennedy was at his best during his last campaign, one is tempted to highlight his missteps to avoid appearing too partisan. Hays Gorey of *Time* said that some reporters covering the campaign did just that, admitting, "At some point it sank in on most of us that there was something real and good and decent about the candidate. Yet we had to regard his every move as suspect or we weren't being good reporters."

Bobby Kennedy was no saint. He had a quick temper, and he could be cruel to those he disliked or who had disappointed him. He had worked for Senator Joseph McCarthy's notorious Senate Permanent Subcommittee on Investigations in 1954 and retained an affection for McCarthy longer than was seemly. He had been a tough and merciless interrogator while serving as chief counsel to a Senate committee investigating the penetration of labor unions by organized crime, and a demanding and hard-boiled manager of JFK's 1960 presidential campaign. One of JFK's aides told *Washington Post* reporter Richard Harwood that there had been a "good Bobby and a bad Bobby" in 1960, and the bad one resembled "a petulant baseball player who strikes out in the clutch and kicks the bat boy." But Harwood noted that that side of Bobby Kennedy was not in evidence in 1968. Instead, "What came out most . . . was his gentleness," he said. JFK adviser Ted Sorensen remembered the Bobby Kennedy of the 1950s being "militant, aggressive, intolerant, opinionated, somewhat shallow in his convictions . . . [and] more like his father than his brother [JFK]," but believed that by 1968 he had transformed himself, abandoning his hard line on the Cold War, repudiating the Vietnam War, and becoming deeply troubled by poverty and racial injustice.

While serving on these Senate committees in the 1950s and as his brother's attorney general and principal adviser in the early 1960s, Bobby Kennedy had become acquainted with the government's darkest secrets. He knew about President Kennedy's adulteries and America's involvement in the coup resulting in the assassination of South Vietnamese president Ngo Dinh Diem. He had investigated and interrogated union bosses corrupted by the Mafia, approved and encouraged CIA attempts to assassinate Fidel Castro, authorized wiretaps on Martin Luther King Jr.'s telephones in the mistaken belief that two of his associates were Communists, and turned a blind eye to attempts by FBI chief J. Edgar Hoover to intimidate and discredit King. But because he knew all this, he also knew more about the inner workings of the government and the White House than any presidential candidate in history, and he ran for that office with eyes wide open, understanding the risks he was assuming and hatreds he was unleashing by becoming the second Kennedy in a decade to seek it.

Although he had only served in the Senate for three years, he was more qualified to assume the presidency than John Kennedy had been in 1960. He had been an excellent attorney general—some thought the best in history—and had served as a kind of assistant president, witnessing the Bay of Pigs debacle firsthand, playing a pivotal role in resolving the Cuban Missile Crisis, conducting clandestine negotiations with Soviet diplomats, and supervising the CIA. Since his brother's assassination in Dallas he had become more contemplative and sensitive, and felt more guilty over his role in embroiling America in the Vietnam War, and his brother's choice of Lyndon Johnson as vice president. There was also, for him, the possibility that something he had done—perhaps his obsession with eliminating Fidel Castro, or the enemies he made by pursuing mobsters and corrupt union officials—had prompted his brother's assassination.

REVISITING ROBERT KENNEDY'S campaign has never been more timely. In 1968, young men who could not afford to pay for college were drafted and died in disproportionate numbers in Vietnam. Four decades later, poor young men and women volunteer for military service to earn the money for college tuition and die in disproportionate numbers in Iraq. In 1968, as now, an unpopular president was waging a controversial war that had divided Americans and poisoned the nation's relations with its allies. What Kennedy said about that war could be said verbatim about Iraq:

> For it is long past time to ask: what is this war doing to us? Of course it is costing us money . . . but that is the smallest price we pay. The cost is in our young men, the tens of thousands of their lives cut off forever. The cost is in our world position—in neutrals and allies alike, every day more baffled and estranged from a policy they cannot understand.
>
> There is a failing of generosity and compassion. There is an unwillingness to sacrifice.
>
> We cannot continue to deny and postpone the demands of our own people while spending billions in the name of the freedom for others.
>
> We have an ally in name only. We support a government without supporters. Without the effort of American arms, that government would not last a day.
>
> The front pages of our newspapers show photographs of American soldiers torturing prisoners.

During his campaign, Kennedy spoke of a nation where "the affluent are getting more affluent and the poor are getting poorer," a situation that the late journalist David Halberstam summarized in a sentence that could have been written four decades later: "The rich were getting richer in America and the poor were getting poorer and by and large the rich were white and the poor were black." In 1968, riots following the assassination of Dr. Martin Luther King Jr. highlighted the chasm between white and black Americans. Thirty-seven years later, Hurricane Katrina had a similar effect. On November 15, 2005, some former passengers on Kennedy's funeral train gathered with several hundred others at the Capitol for a "memorial commemoration" of Robert Kennedy's eightieth birthday. (Had he been celebrating in person, he would have been a year younger than former presidents Jimmy Carter and George H. W. Bush). One searches in vain for similar events marking the landmark birthdays of presidents such as Franklin D. Roosevelt and John F. Kennedy, but if anyone considered it unusual to be marking Robert Kennedy's eightieth birthday thirty-seven years after his death, they remained silent. Instead, the unspoken assumption was that his presidential campaign had never mattered so much, and the unspoken question hovering over John Kerry, Hillary Clinton, Barack Obama, and others offering tributes was which one had the courage to raise the issues that he had, and campaign as he did.

Following speeches and the presentation of the annual Robert F. Kennedy Human Rights Award, a video was screened showing the devastation in New Orleans following Hurricane Katrina. Its only sound track was a speech that Kennedy had delivered at the University of Kansas on March 18, 1968, two days after announcing his candidacy. And so, as black residents of New Orleans waded through their flooded streets, Kennedy could be heard saying, "I have seen these other Americans—I have seen children in Mississippi starving. . . . I don't think that's acceptable in the United States of America." As they stood on rooftops, waving at helicopters, he said, "If we believe that we, as Americans, are bound together by a common concern for each other, then an urgent national priority is upon us. We must end the disgrace of this other America." As they milled outside the convention center, he said, "But even if we act to erase material poverty there is another great task. It is to confront the poverty of satisfaction—a lack of purpose and dignity—that inflicts us all. Too much and too long we seem to have surrendered community excellence and community values in the mere accumulation of material things."

The stars may never be aligned as they were in 1968, and Americans may wait decades for another year as pivotal, or for another eighty-two days that become the axis upon which such a pivotal year turns. Or perhaps not. There are things that Robert Kennedy did and said during his campaign that only the brother of a martyred president could have done and said, but there are others that another candidate could easily do and say, if the American people demanded them. John Nolan, who scheduled many of Kennedy's appearances that spring, believes, "What he did was not really that mystical. All it requires is someone who knows himself, and has some courage."

PART I

✦

EARLY
DAYS

ONE

NO CHOICE

MARCH 16–17, 1968

Two months after John F. Kennedy's assassination, Robert Kennedy traveled to Asia on an itinerary that had originally been planned for JFK. During the trip, he visited a girls' school in the Philippines where the students sang a song they had composed to honor his brother. As he drove away with CBS cameraman Walter Dombrow, he clenched his hands so tightly that they turned white and tears rolled down his cheeks. He shook his head, signaling that Dombrow should remain silent. Finally he said in a choked voice, "They would have loved my brother." Dombrow put his arm around him and said, "Bob, you're going to have to carry on for him." Kennedy stared straight ahead for half a minute before turning to Dombrow and nodding. It was then, Dombrow said, that he knew Bobby would run for president, and realized how much he loved him.

A deep, black grief gripped Robert Kennedy in the months following his brother's assassination. He lost weight, fell into melancholy silences, wore his brother's clothes, smoked the cigars his brother had liked, and imitated his mannerisms. Eventually his grief went underground, but it sometimes erupted in geysers of tears, as had happened in the Philippines. He wept after seeing a photograph of his late brother in the office of a former aide, wept when asked to comment on the Warren Commission report, and wept after eulogizing JFK at the 1964 Democratic convention with a quotation from Shakespeare's *Romeo and Juliet:* "When he shall die, take him and cut him into little stars, and he will make the face of heaven so fine that all the world will be in love with the night and pay no attention to the garish sun."

During his brother's thousand-day presidency there had been no policy differences between them; whatever John Kennedy wanted for the country was what Bobby wanted. After his brother's assassination, Bobby became determined to continue acting in his spirit. Even when he took up issues such as poverty that had never ranked high on JFK's agenda, he tried to persuade himself that his brother would have approved. After discovering that several days before his death, JFK had written POVERTY in a bold hand on a doodle, Bobby had it framed and displayed it on his office wall. No matter that JFK had been a fanatical doodler, or that there was no other evidence that he had been planning to make poverty a second-term priority, Bobby considered the doodle proof that his brother would have approved of him becoming what Arthur Schlesinger later called the Tribune of the Underclass.

Kennedy was still mourning his brother and endeavoring to live for him when he ran for the U.S. Senate from New York in the autumn of 1964, telling a friend that he wanted to ensure that the hopes JFK had kindled around the world did not die, and saying in his victory statement that he had won "an overwhelming mandate to continue the policies" of President Kennedy. During the campaign, he retraced the route his brother had taken across upstate New York in 1960, passed out the *PT 109* tie clasps that commemorated his heroism, and autographed copies of JFK's book, *Profiles in Courage.* He looked down at crowds filling the streets surrounding his hotel in Buffalo and said, "They're here for him; they're not for me." When a friend congratulated him on his victory he replied, "If my brother was alive, I wouldn't be here. I'd rather have it that way."

At first, it appeared that his presidential campaign would be another homage to his brother. He announced his candidacy on March 16 in the Caucus Room of the Old Senate Office Building, the same room that his brother had used for the same purpose. He stood in the same spot and began with the same sentence: "I am today announcing my candidacy for the presidency of the United States." After saying that he was running to "close the gaps that now exist between black and white, between rich and poor, between young and old," he concluded with a passage that made him sound like his brother, perhaps because it had been contributed by Ted Sorensen, his brother's former speechwriter: "I do not lightly dismiss the dangers and the difficulties of challenging an incumbent President. But these are not ordinary times and this is not an ordinary election. At stake is not simply the leadership of our party and even our country. It is our right to [the] moral leadership of this planet."

Some advisers had urged him to excise this passage from his speech, arguing that it was the kind of New Frontier hubris that had ensnared America in Vietnam. *Washington Post* reporter David Broder would call it "the nostalgic rhetoric of the earlier Kennedy era." Only later did it prove to have been a prescient summary of where America stood on March 16, 1968.

Kennedy's "right to moral leadership of this planet" line turned out to be closer to the truth than even he, or Ted Sorensen, realized at the time. At stake was not so much Americans' moral leadership, but their belief that they were worthy of such leadership. The same March 17, 1968, *New York Times* front page carrying the headline "Kennedy to Make Three Primary Races: Attacks Johnson" also contained a dispatch from South Vietnam reporting that U.S. troops had killed 128 enemy soldiers during an operation in Quang Ngai Province. Only after Kennedy was dead and Nixon had become president was it revealed that sixteen hours before Kennedy had announced his candidacy and pledged to restore America's moral authority, American soldiers commanded by Lieutenant William Calley had massacred over five hundred South Vietnamese civilians in the Quang Nai hamlet of My Lai.

On the day that Kennedy announced his candidacy, it was by no means obvious that 1968 would become such a watershed. Except for the January Tet Offensive by Communist forces in South Vietnam, the year's momentous events would all occur after Kennedy's March 16 announcement, with many of the most shocking unfolding during his campaign. Had you told anyone in the Senate Caucus Room that morning that during the next eighty-two days President Johnson would decline to seek a second term, Martin Luther King Jr. and Robert Kennedy would

both be assassinated, and America would suffer its worst racial disturbances since the Civil War, they might have believed that some of those
things might happen, but not all, nor in such quick succession.

After concluding his announcement, Kennedy took questions rang-
ing from skeptical to hostile. His response to the charge that his decision to enter the race on the heels of Senator Eugene McCarthy's
success in the New Hampshire primary was "opportunistic" was so
unconvincing that it elicited muffled laughter. When asked how he
would disentangle America from Vietnam, he said that he favored "de-
escalating" the war by negotiating with all parties to the conflict and
insisting that the South Vietnamese assume more of the burden of
combat, leaving "less of the effort . . . in the hands of the United States
government and American soldiers."

As he left the Capitol, supporters screaming his name grabbed at his
clothes and leaped in the air to see him, much like his brother's supporters had in 1960. Anyone witnessing this and hearing the New Frontier
echoes in his announcement would have been justified in assuming that
his campaign would be an extended tribute to his brother. Instead,
March 16 would be the end rather than the beginning of such a tribute,
and during the next three months he would run on issues his brother had
seldom raised and sometimes in a manner his brother would have found
undignified.

Richard Nixon, who had lost the presidency to JFK in 1960, watched
Kennedy's announcement from a hotel room in Portland, Oregon. John
Ehrlichman, one of several aides in the room with Nixon, later wrote,
"When it was over and the hotel-room TV was turned off, Nixon sat
and looked at the blank screen for a long time, saying nothing. Finally,
he shook his head slowly. 'We've just seen some very terrible forces un-
leashed,' he said. 'Something bad is going to come out of this.' He
pointed at the screen, 'God knows where this is going to end.' Meanwhile, Kennedy was telling Nicole Salinger, the wife of press secretary
Pierre Salinger, "I'm sleeping well for the first time in months. I don't
know what's going to happen, but at least I'm at peace with myself."

Following his announcement, Kennedy flew to New York and
marched in the St. Patrick's Day parade. Supporters of Senator Eugene
McCarthy shouted, "Coward!" and "Opportunist!" Conservative Irish-

Americans who supported President Johnson and the war yelled, "Go back to Boston!" and "Get a haircut, ya bum!" A middle-aged man broke through police lines and screamed insults in Kennedy's face. A student from a local Catholic college told a reporter, "I swear to God, if he didn't have twenty cops around I'd punch him in the mouth."

The hostility shocked Jim Stevenson of *The New Yorker*, who noted that "ruthless and opportunistic," the words commonly pinned on Kennedy by his enemies, were the slogans of the day. Kennedy held his right hand close to his chest, offering a tentative wave. But when he looked up and saw Jackie and John Kennedy Jr. waving from their apartment window, he smiled and threw his arms into the air.

He invited Stevenson to join him in his apartment at UN Plaza after the parade. Stevenson felt uneasy about monopolizing him on such an important day. But once they were seated in a bedroom overlooking the East River, Kennedy, in his shirtsleeves and cradling a drink, began speaking, and Stevenson realized that he simply wanted to celebrate. Stevenson noted that although Kennedy was "riding on the exuberance of at last making an important decision," he was also "wary."

Stevenson traveled with Kennedy during the early weeks of the campaign. Some of his observations appeared in *The New Yorker*; others are in an unpublished manuscript. Instead of the mop-haired and buck-toothed Bobby of the political cartoonists, Stevenson painted a more nuanced portrait, describing a face in which there was "almost too much going on in too many directions in too little space," and where "the nose hooks outward; the teeth protrude; the hair hangs down; the ears go up and out; the chin juts forward; the eyelids push down." His expression was tough, Stevenson noted, but the toughness was directed inward and represented "a contempt for self-indulgence, for weakness." Stevenson also detected a fundamental sadness, not a sentimental one denoting self-pity, but "a resident, melancholy bleakness."

When Kennedy returned to Washington that evening, no one met him at National Airport, and he joked to reporters that "even my driver has deserted me." But he was obviously distressed and said, "Our hero returns, and a huge throng turned out to greet him. It took the police to hold them back."

The next morning he appeared on *Meet the Press* and was asked if he would support President Johnson if Johnson became the nominee. Instead of dodging the question or finessing it by saying that of course he planned on winning the nomination, he gave an answer certain to anger Democratic Party bosses who controlled the nomination process and considered loyalty a virtue trumping all others. If Johnson continued pursuing the same policies, Kennedy said, then he would have "grave reservations" about supporting him. "I'm loyal to the Democratic Party," he added, "but I feel stronger about the United States and mankind generally."

Throughout the weekend, Kennedy and aides placed calls to Democratic senators, governors, and party leaders. They had hoped for endorsements, or at least promises to remain uncommitted until Kennedy could win some primaries. Instead, many of the recipients of these calls urged him to withdraw.

Liberal Democrats feared that he and McCarthy would split the antiwar movement. Conservative and moderate Democrats feared he would divide the party and put Nixon in the White House. Even Averell Harriman, Douglas Dillon, and General Maxwell Taylor, who had served in the JFK administration and were godfathers to Bobby's children, refused to support him. Senator George McGovern of South Dakota said he was glad he was running, but would remain neutral. The chairman of the Democratic Party in Alabama predicted that his campaign would draw no more attention than "an intra-party dispute in Czechoslovakia," and the Washington attorney heading Citizens for Johnson and Humphrey doubted that Kennedy could persuade Senator McCarthy's supporters "that he's neither ruthless nor an opportunist." Mayor James Tate of Philadelphia, an influential machine politician, accused him of having a "wise guy attitude," and said, "If John F. Kennedy had not been President, Robert Kennedy would still be counsel for some Senatorial committee."

Mayor Richard Daley of Chicago was the boss of bosses in 1968. Not only did he control the votes of the Illinois delegation, but the convention was being held in his city that year, making him the most influential Democratic leader in the nation. When asked if Kennedy could win the nomination, he bellowed, "No!" and compared him to Judas Iscariot, saying, "Even the Lord had skeptical members of His party. One betrayed him, one denied him, and one doubted him." Several days later, reporter Jimmy Breslin asked Kennedy how important Daley was to his chances of winning the nomination. "He's the whole ball game," Kennedy replied.

Daley's reaction was mild compared to that of hard-core Kennedy haters such as William Loeb, editor of the Manchester *Union Leader*, who had previously called him "the most vicious and dangerous leader in the United States today." Senator Hugh Scott [R] of Pennsylvania declared that "the election of Bobby Kennedy as President would, indeed, endanger the fundamentals of the democratic system," while the Greek military junta, believing he endangered their totalitarian system, ordered newspapers to limit their coverage of Kennedy's campaign and stop publishing his photograph.

With the exception of Franklin D. Roosevelt, no twentieth-century American politician had attracted such a large, diverse, and bitter company of enemies as Robert Kennedy. He was hated because of what he had done, what his brother had done as president, and what it was feared he would do if he won that office. Union leaders hated him because he had exposed corruption in their ranks and sent Teamsters head Jimmy Hoffa to prison. The business community had not forgiven him for sending FBI agents barging into corporate offices looking for evidence of price fixing during the 1962 "Steel Crisis." White southerners loathed him because his Justice Department had enforced school desegregation, and liberals distrusted him because he had worked for Joe McCarthy. The right-wing columnist Westbrook Pegler, who had also been a ferocious critic of FDR and the New Deal, welcomed the possibility that, as he put it, "Some white patriot of the southern tier will splatter his [Kennedy's] spoonful of brains in public premises before the snow falls," and at a meeting of senior FBI agents, J. Edgar Hoover's deputy Clyde Tolan remarked offhandedly, "I hope somebody shoots and kills the son of a bitch."

PRESIDENTIAL PRIMARIES WERE less important in 1968 than they have since become. There were fewer of them, and fewer that counted. Instead, party leaders wielded considerable influence over the selection of delegates and their convention votes, effectively control-ling the nomination. Nevertheless, a strong showing in several crucial primaries could create a bandwagon effect within the party leadership. This had happened in 1960, when John Kennedy had defeated Hubert Humphrey in the West Virginia Democratic primary, proving that a Catholic candidate could beat a Protestant in a heavily Protestant state, and that his religion would be less of an obstacle than previously assumed.

In 1968, Robert Kennedy had to defeat Senator Eugene McCarthy [D-Minn.], who was also running as an anti-Johnson, antiwar candi-date, and President Lyndon Johnson in every primary that he still had time to enter, and hope that a strong showing would convince the party apparatchiks that he had a better chance of defeating Richard Nixon, the likely GOP nominee, in November. The first primary he could en-ter was in Indiana on May 7, then came Nebraska and the District of Columbia on May 14, Oregon on May 28, California and South Dakota on June 4, and New York on June 18. Kennedy and his advisers were concerned that some party leaders might pledge their delegations to Johnson during the seven weeks between Kennedy's announcement and the Indiana primary. Kennedy believed that to persuade them to remain uncommitted he had to demonstrate his popularity by appear-ing before large and enthusiastic crowds at rallies, airport welcoming ceremonies, and motorcades in both primary and nonprimary states. It was a tricky strategy because if his crowds were too frenzied, they might frighten moderate Democrats and party leaders, but if they were small and unresponsive, party leaders would probably stick with Johnson. Further complicating this strategy were Kennedy's own shortcomings as a campaigner. Although he had been involved in politics since 1951, and had been a skilled manager of his older brother's campaigns, he had only run for public office once, in the 1964 New York Senate race. In that campaign, he had proven himself to be a clumsy and uninspiring speaker, stammering and speaking in a monotone, prone to long si-lences, and uncomfortable before enthusiastic crowds, seemingly unable to shake his post-Dallas melancholy.

When Kennedy flew to Kansas City on the evening of March 17 to launch his presidential campaign, no one could be sure that he would draw the kinds of crowds and ignite the kind of enthusiasm that would persuade Democratic leaders to remain uncommitted. He had decided to deliver his first campaign speech at Kansas State University (KSU) only because he had already agreed to give a lecture there in a series honoring former Kansas governor and Republican icon Alf Landon. It was not a state where, given more time, he would have chosen to launch his campaign. Richard Nixon had trounced JFK in Kansas in 1960, and it had only voted for a Democratic presidential candidate once since 1916. Among the previous Landon lecturers had been Republican governors Romney of Michigan and Reagan of California. They had drawn large crowds, but when Martin Luther King Jr. spoke on the campus in January, university officials gave him the cold shoulder, his audience was small, and the manager of a local radio station warned his counterpart at the campus station that he would be doing Kansans "a disservice" by broadcasting King's words.

Before heading to La Guardia Airport to board a flight to Kansas City, Kennedy called campaign aides Jim Tolan and Jerry Bruno. They had been in Kansas for several days preparing the ground and, according to Bruno, "becoming more nervous by the hour" because they knew that if Kansas was a disaster, the entire campaign could be derailed. Kennedy reached them at the Topeka offices of the state's Democratic governor, Robert Docking. He told them he was worried that McCarthy's supporters would heckle him, conservative students would boo him, the press could report it all, and his campaign would be finished in a day. "You guys better do well tomorrow," he said, "because the eyes and ears of the world are on those two stops."

Four years of planning had preceded John F. Kennedy's bid for the presidency. Robert Kennedy had a few days.

There had been no time to put together a campaign organization, so on the eve of his announcement he told Fred Dutton, an astute attorney in his mid-forties who had worked in his brother's White House, "I'd like to have you travel with me. I hope you don't mind." Dutton agreed, and during the next several months he would become Kennedy's de facto campaign manager and trusted confidant, plotting strategy, refereeing disputes between other aides, and seldom leaving his side.

There had been no time to order campaign buttons, so press secretary

Frank Mankiewicz scooped some leftovers from the Senate campaign out of a drawer and brought them to the airport.

There had been no time to charter a plane, so Kennedy was taking a scheduled United Airlines flight that left late because he had insisted on stopping at the gate to greet his fellow passengers who, if they happened to represent a cross-section of the country, were either delighted or infuriated by his candidacy.

Most of Kennedy's campaign flights would be jolly affairs marked by singing, drinking, and practical jokes. But his first one was uncharacteristically tense, and the haze of cigarette smoke, droning engines, night sky, and suspicion among some in the Kennedy entourage that they were embarking on an enterprise that might end very badly, evokes a squad of paratroopers preparing to jump into a countryside of uncertain loyalties, where they may be hailed as liberators or shot before hitting the ground.

Ethel Kennedy had left from Washington a few hours before on a different flight and would join her husband at the Kansas City airport for the short hop to Topeka. After losing her parents and brother in plane crashes, she was a nervous flier and liked to travel with friends she called "pals" or "sparklies" who distracted her during flights and helped with her grooming and wardrobe. None of her top four "pals" had been available at such short notice, so she had recruited Rene Carpenter, the estranged wife of astronaut Scott Carpenter. Carpenter threw some clothes in a bag, filled a thermos with gin and tonics, and hurried to the airport. But today she found Ethel less concerned with crashing than with how these conservative midwestern Kansans would treat her husband, and during the flight she and Carpenter traded jokes in dark humor. "Do you think they'll boo him?" Ethel asked. "Will they hate him?" She never posed the next question, the one that was probably running through the minds of others accompanying Robert Kennedy to Kansas that afternoon: "Will they kill him?"

Anyone walking up the aisle of Robert Kennedy's flight would have seen rows of seats occupied by people whom author Victor Navasky in his book *Kennedy Justice* called "honorary Kennedys," men and women linked to the Kennedy family through friendship, marriage, work, and political alliances, and willing to put their careers and private lives on hold while they helped a Kennedy win an election. The "honorary Kennedys" joining Bobby's campaign fell into five groups: men like Edwin Guthman and John Seigenthaler who had worked for him in the Justice Department; current Senate aides, such as Jeff Greenfield and Adam Walinsky; Pierre Salinger, Kenny O'Donnell, and Ted Sorensen, who had served in JFK's campaign and White House; "Teddy's people," whose first loyalty was to Ted Kennedy; and personal friends like mountaineer Jim Whittaker and pro football star Roosevelt (Rosey) Grier. The Honorary Kennedys differed from the usual network of friends, former aides, and political advisers who join a presidential campaign because many had only worked in Kennedy campaigns and their loyalty to the Kennedy family was more personal than ideological. Adam Walinsky, for example, had never been a great fan of JFK and had not worked in his 1960 campaign. While Walinsky was serving in the Justice Department's Office of Legal Counsel, the venerable pacifist A. J. Muste embarked on a peace march from Quebec to Florida, where he planned to take a boat to the U.S. Navy base at Guantánamo Bay. The Justice Department's internal security division had decided to seek an injunction to prevent him from completing the march. The attorney general was required to sign an affidavit supporting it, but when Walinsky presented it to Kennedy he said, "Let me get this straight. You want me to prevent an 83-year-old man from marching 800 miles for peace? Fuck it. I don't think he's a threat to the security of the United States. I'm not going to sign this." Walinsky was impressed that Kennedy was not only reading the papers coming across his desk, but making humane and intelligent judgments on them.

During the flight to Kansas City, Kennedy told the Honorary Kennedys and reporters gathered in the aisle around his seat, "I didn't want to run for President. But when he [Johnson] made it clear the war would go on, and that nothing was going to change, I had no choice." But since he clearly had the political choice of holding his nose and supporting Johnson's reelection, as many other antiwar Democratic senators intended to do, what he really meant was that he had no moral choice.

The question of whether he should challenge Johnson for the Democratic nomination in 1968 had been the subject of frequent and passionate debates among Honorary Kennedys and family members for the six months preceding his decision. By the fall of 1967, Arthur Schlesinger, Ethel Kennedy, and most of his young Senate staffers were urging him to run. They argued that Johnson was vulnerable, the Democratic Party was already split over the war, and that if Kennedy stood on the sidelines, students and antiwar activists would support another candidate, and he might never win them back. Soon after the 1966 election, Adam Walinsky, the most outspoken of Kennedy's Young Turks, had sent him a memorandum titled "Gratuitous advice." In it, Walinsky called Lyndon Johnson a lame-duck president, predicted he would lose the 1968 general election, and warned Kennedy that "he who stands with LBJ now goes into eclipse—perhaps irretrievably." Walinsky concluded that although Kennedy's chances for unseating Johnson were not good, he had to try anyway because the chances of him or any Democrat beating an incumbent Republican in 1972 were even worse, and because, Walinsky wrote, "I believe you should be President. And I believe you should speak out about the war."

Ted Kennedy, Ted Sorensen, and other former JFK White House aides, men whom Robert Kennedy described to *New York Times* reporter Anthony Lewis as "most everyone whom I respect," were strongly opposed to him running. They argued that he could not win, that party and union leaders were certain to back Johnson, and that a Kennedy candidacy risked being viewed as another chapter in the long-running Kennedy–Johnson feud, rather than an honest difference over policy. They also pointed out that if Republicans won the White House in 1968, the Democratic leadership would blame Kennedy and oppose giving him the nomination in 1972. Some were afraid that, as Jackie Kennedy had said to Arthur Schlesinger, "the same thing that happened to Jack" would happen to Bobby, although they knew Bobby well enough not to voice these fears to him. In 1996, Ted Kennedy admitted to biographer Adam Clymer that he had feared Bobby might be assassinated. "We weren't that far away from '63 [when JFK was killed]," he said, "and that was still very much of a factor."

Kennedy was concerned that if he ran, an increasingly unstable Lyndon Johnson might "wag the dog," provoking an international crisis or even starting a war to upstage his candidacy. In late 1967, as Kennedy was completing *Thirteen Days*, his account of the 1962 Cuban Missile Crisis, he had told Adam Walinsky, "You know, we had fourteen people in that room [the Cabinet Room in the White House], and if any one of six of them had been President, we would have had a nuclear war." (In the book, he wrote about these fourteen men: "Some, because of the pressure of events, even appeared to lose their judgment and stability.") During the same conversation, he said, "The problem is that if I run against Johnson, I don't know what he's going to do." Secretary of Defense Robert McNamara, who had also served in JFK's administration and was opposed to Bobby running in 1968, stoked his fears, perhaps on purpose, by recounting conversations during which Johnson had spoken about possible, and frightening, countermoves against North Vietnam and China. The fear that Johnson's obsessive hatred for him might prompt him to act irrationally had also inhibited Kennedy's criticism of his Vietnam policies. "I'm afraid that by speaking out I just make Lyndon Johnson do the opposite," he once told reporter Jack Newfield. "He hates me so much that if I asked for snow, he would make rain, just because it was me [asking]."

The fact that Bobby's brother and wife, Ted and Ethel Kennedy, were on opposite sides of the debate contributed to his indecision. Ted Kennedy was a more cautious and canny politician than Bobby, and more inclined to adhere to Senate and party rules and customs. He was so certain that entering the race in 1968 would be a mistake that he enlisted other senators in his campaign, even approaching Senator George McGovern in the Senate gymnasium and imploring him to discourage Bobby. Ethel Kennedy was equally determined that he should run, and enlisted the family Christmas card in her campaign. On the inside was a photograph of an antique car onto which she superimposed photographs of herself and the children holding signs saying SANTA CLAUS IN '67. The back carried a small photograph of Bobby. He had a sly grin on his face, and a cartoon balloon over his head said, "Would you believe Santa Claus in '68?"

One might have thought that Ethel Kennedy, who knew that during her husband's term as attorney general the telephones at Hickory Hill, the Kennedys' home in McLean, Virginia, had rung with threats such as "We know where your kids go to school and we know how they get there" and "Do you know what hydrochloric acid can do to your eyes?" would be the last person to want him to run. But she was almost as complicated as he was: recklessly frank yet guarded, canny and guileless, brash and sensitive, an observant Catholic who threw wild parties and hobnobbed with celebrities. Perhaps she wanted him to run because she imagined it would be great fun, a kind of nonstop Hickory Hill party, or because she was competitive with Jackie and considered it her turn to be First Lady, or because she believed her husband's fate was in God's hands. More likely, it was because she understood him better than anyone, believed in him more, was convinced he would be a great president, and knew he would never forgive himself if he sat out the race.

The debate within the Kennedy camp had continued through the fall and winter. But two events occurring at the end of November made his candidacy virtually inevitable. The first was his November 26 appearance on *Face the Nation* during which he characterized the argument that Americans were fighting to prevent communism from threatening the mainland as "immoral," saying, "Do we have the right here in the United States to say that we're going to kill tens of thousands, make millions of people, as we have, refugees, kill women and children, as we have? . . . I very seriously doubt whether we have that right." Then, continuing to frame the issue in moral terms, he said, "When we use napalm, when a village is destroyed and civilians are killed. . . . This is a moral obligation and a moral responsibility for us here in the United States." A panelist asked why, if he felt this way, he believed that Johnson should run for a second term. Because there was no honest answer to this question, Kennedy hedged and dissembled. During a private meeting with Kennedy six weeks later, the influential columnist Walter Lippmann pointed to the same conundrum, telling him, "If you believe that Johnson's reelection would be a catastrophe for the country—and I entirely agree with you on this . . . the question you must live with is whether you did everything you could to avert this catastrophe."

In fact, Kennedy needed only to reread his own words to be reminded that framing his opposition to the Vietnam War in moral terms, yet refusing to challenge Johnson for the nomination, was a prima facie case of moral cowardice. In a new introduction to *Profiles in Courage* written just weeks after his brother's death, he had declared that "President Kennedy was fond of quoting Dante that 'the hottest places in hell are reserved for those who, in a time of great moral crisis, maintain their neutrality.'" In the postscript to his book *To Seek a Newer World* [1967], he had called it "thoughtless folly" to attempt "to solve problems and take action unguided by ultimate moral aims and values," adding that "only those who dare to fail greatly can ever achieve greatly," and had quoted Aristotle that "at the Olympic games it is not the finest and strongest men who are crowned but those who enter the lists . . ." How could someone who had written these words not run against Johnson?

The second event guaranteeing Kennedy's candidacy came on November 29, when Senator Eugene McCarthy of Minnesota declared that he would challenge Johnson for the Democratic nomination on an antiwar platform. McCarthy's announcement was curiously half-hearted, as if even he recognized that his candidacy was quixotic. At a press conference afterward he appeared to be encouraging Kennedy to enter the race, saying, "There would surely be nothing illegal or contrary to American politics if he or someone else were to take advantage of what I'm doing."

Kennedy considered McCarthy lazy and pompous and had probably not forgiven him for delivering a passionate speech at the 1960 convention nominating Adlai Stevenson, the last-ditch candidate of everyone hoping to deny the nomination to John Kennedy. After learning that McCarthy had entered the race, he told George McGovern, "Eugene McCarthy is *not* competent to be President," adding wistfully, "he's going to get a lot of support. I can tell you right now, he'll run very strong in New Hampshire. I'm worried about you and other people making early commitments to him because it may be hard for all of us later on." As he spoke, McGovern imagined him thinking, "My God, *I* should have done this. Why didn't I move earlier?"

He continued agonizing over his candidacy during the Christmas holidays. Just after the New Year, he announced to close friends and advisers that he had decided to wait until 1972, telling them, "The support just isn't there. People will think it's a personal vendetta between me and Johnson." In a January 4 speech in San Francisco he declared that he expected to support Johnson despite their disagreements over Vietnam. He reaffirmed this during an off-the-record conversation at a press breakfast on January 30, saying that he would not oppose Johnson "under any conceivable circumstance." The next day, Communist forces launched coordinated attacks on South Vietnamese cities and military installations. The Tet Offensive, as it was called because it commenced on Tet, the Chinese lunar new year, proved to be a military defeat but a psychological victory for the Communists, and persuaded many Americans that the Johnson administration's optimistic pronouncements about the war had been ill-founded or intentionally disingenuous. When Kennedy said in Chicago nine days later that Tet had "shattered the mask of official illusion with which we have concealed our true circumstances, even from ourselves" and that "total military victory is not within sight or around the corner," he was voicing a conclusion reached by a majority of Americans.

A second event pushing Kennedy into the race came on February 19, when the National Advisory Commission on Civil Disorders, headed by Governor Otto Kerner of Illinois, issued its report on the riots that had convulsed Detroit, Newark, and other American cities during the summer of 1967. Kerner's report warned that America was becoming "two societies, one black, one white—separate but unequal," and called for "a commitment to national action—compassionate, massive, and sustained, backed by the resources of the most powerful and the richest nation on earth." Johnson disagreed and refused to meet with commission members or accept a bound copy of their report. Kennedy complained to friends that this signaled that Johnson was "not going to do anything about the war and he's not going to do anything about the cities, either."

Kennedy continued painting himself into a corner on Vietnam by charging in a March 7 Senate speech that escalation had failed in Vietnam, leaving Americans to face their responsibility for the suffering of the Vietnamese people. "Are we like God of the Old Testament," he asked, "that we can decide, in Washington, D.C., what cities, what towns, what hamlets in Vietnam are going to be destroyed?" Arthur

Schlesinger believed that Kennedy had decided that America would have to withdraw unilaterally from Vietnam, although he could not say so publicly. During a conversation in early March between Averell Harriman and William Walton, a Kennedy friend and opponent of the war, Harriman had told Walton, "Your friend Bobby is not for cut-and-run as you are." When Walton repeated the conversation, Bobby said, "Little does he know."

Frank Mankiewicz believes that once Kennedy had condemned the Vietnam War in strong moral terms it became impossible, morally and politically, for him not to run. After Kennedy had leveled a particularly bitter attack on the war during a speech in Chicago in February, Mankiewicz told him, "I don't know how you can say those things about the major enterprise in which your country's engaged and then continue to support that leadership." Kennedy did not dispute this. As Mankiewicz saw it, his denunciation of the war had made it impossible for him to campaign for Johnson, yet if he failed to support him, or ran against him and lost, party leaders would be furious, and unlikely to support him in 1972. Adam Walinsky made the same argument, asking Kennedy, "What are you going to do if you *don't* run? Who will you support?"

The consensus of Kennedy's friends and advisers is that he had decided to enter the race by mid- to late February or early March. Mankiewicz believes he may have decided by mid-February, around the time he published an essay in the *New York Times* warning, "We seem to have fulfilled the vision of Yeats: 'Things fall apart; the center cannot hold: / mere anarchy is loosed upon the world.'"

Edwin Guthman, who had served as his press officer in the Justice Department, learned that he had decided to run when Kennedy called to ask whether Guthman thought he should accept an invitation to fly to Delano, California, on March 10 and join Cesar Chavez, the head of the United Farm Workers of America, in ending a monthlong fast affirming Chavez's commitment to nonviolence. After advising Kennedy to go, Guthman asked if he was going to run. "I think I have to," he replied. "If I don't, I'll have to support Gene McCarthy, and I can't do it in good conscience. A lot of people are still against it. The Democratic Senators who are up for reelection will be upset, but Tet has changed everything, and if I don't go now and make an effort in the primaries, I think I'll be nothing."

Guthman pointed out that supporting Chavez might cost him the support of some white voters in the California primary. "I know," Kennedy replied, "but I like Cesar."

During the flight to California, Kennedy told his aide Peter Edelman, "I'm going to run; now I have to figure how to get McCarthy out of it." When he met Guthman while changing planes in Los Angeles he told him he had decided to wait until after the March 12 New Hampshire primary. A few hours later, he broke the news to Chavez, saying, "Yeah, I think I'll run. Maybe I'll run. Yeah, I think I'm going to run."

McGovern urged Kennedy to wait until after the March 12 New Hampshire primary before declaring his candidacy. Otherwise, McGovern warned, he might divide the antiwar vote by siphoning off a large number of write-in votes that would otherwise go to McCarthy. Kennedy agreed and postponed his announcement. On March 12, McCarthy won 42 percent of the popular vote. Johnson scored 49 percent, but the results were a humiliating repudiation of a sitting president, and a stunning victory for McCarthy.

Less than twenty-four hours later, a reporter asked Kennedy for his reaction. Instead of dissembling, Kennedy said, "I am actively reassessing the possibility of whether I will run against President Johnson." Most in the Kennedy camp believed that he had blurted out what was on his mind, and immediately regretted having answered so honestly. Reporter Jack Newfield called it "a classic political blooper that he would never live down, or adequately explain away," adding, "In a few careless seconds he [Kennedy] resurrected the sleeping stereotype of himself as a ruthless political opportunist." McCarthy's supporters were scathing. Columnist Murray Kempton of the *New York Post* spoke of Kennedy's "rage at Eugene McCarthy for having survived on the lonely road he dares not walk himself," and said he had "confirmed the worst things his enemies have ever said about him." Mary McGrory wrote that at a moment when McCarthy seemed to have captured the allegiance of the nation's youth, Kennedy had "moved with the ruthlessness of a Victorian father whose daughter has fallen in love with the dustman."

Robert Kennedy made small talk by asking questions. It was a way to avoid unwanted intimacies and collect information. He listened intently, and was interested in the answers, but people sometimes imagined that because he was seeking their advice, he had not already reached a decision on a particular issue. And so during the three days between his "reassessing my position" comment and his announcement, he appeared to be debating whether or not to run, when in fact he had already decided. While driving to an event on Long Island with Sylvia Wright on March 15, he asked her if she thought he was crazy to run. "My brother thinks I'm crazy," he said. "He doesn't like this. He doesn't go along. But then, we're two different people. We don't hear the same music. Everyone's got to march to his own music." And hours before declaring his candidacy he told advisers who were still begging him to change his mind, "I've got to try it, even if I fail. "I'd [kill] . . . myself inside if I let myself act like a hypocrite."

As he was reviewing his announcement the next morning he complained to Ted Sorensen that one passage made no sense, adding, "Not that anything we are doing today makes sense anyway." Sorensen was reminded of what JFK had said after Bobby had jumped off a sailboat into frigid waters off the coast of Maine: "It either showed a lot of guts or no sense at all, depending on how you looked at it."

Challenging Johnson made little political sense. The last time a party had denied a sitting president renomination had been in 1884, when Republicans nominated James G. Blaine over President Chester Arthur, and Blaine had gone on to lose the general election. The only kind of sense that Kennedy's decision made was moral sense. By charging that the tactics being employed by the Johnson administration in Vietnam were immoral, and that the war had inflicted grave wounds on the national soul, he had made it impossible for him to support Johnson while maintaining his honor. Forced to choose between Johnson and honor, he chose honor.

It was understandable, but wrong, that after Kennedy's March 13 comment about reassessing his options his decision would be criticized as ruthless and opportunistic. In fact, it was brave and principled: brave because unlike McCarthy who had nothing to lose by challenging Johnson, he was risking his political future, and principled because he was following the dictates of his conscience rather than the realpolitik calculations of his late brother's advisers. The fact that he was challenging Johnson on moral grounds would indelibly mark his campaign, determining the issues he would raise and how he would raise them, the compromises he would and would not consider, and the two speeches that he would deliver in Kansas on March 18.

TWO

"HE'S GOING ALL THE WAY"

MARCH 17–18, 1968

Kennedy was last to disembark in Kansas City. After waving from the doorway and slipping a hand into the pocket of his suit jacket, a JFK mannerism, he started down a flight of metal stairs. Ethel Kennedy, Rene Carpenter, and Governor Docking stood below with reporters, policemen, and students from a local Catholic college. It was a small but acceptable crowd, given that Kennedy was only staying long enough to board Docking's private plane. While he was still on the stairs, the doors of the terminal flew open and over a thousand people, led by a vanguard of young women screaming "Bobby!" dashed across the tarmac. After they pinned him against the bottom of the stairway he laughed and, delighted by their enthusiasm, said, "Help me change American foreign policy." When he finished he told them they had just heard his first campaign speech, adding, "Now, let's all clap."

Reporters called it a turnout worthy of a general election, and evidence of a "subterranean longing for change," but it was less spontaneous than it seemed. Herb Schmertz, who would later become known for the Mobil Oil essays he placed in advertisements on the Op-Ed pages of the *New York Times*, had brought in a busload of trainee TWA flight attendants and announced Kennedy's imminent arrival over the public address system. Unlike most Kennedy staffers, Schmertz believed in the Vietnam War, and still does. When asked why he worked for Kennedy, he offers some breezy explanations, such as "Campaigns attract the most beautiful women" and "You know, you don't necessarily have to agree with your candidate on everything" before offering the real Honorary Kennedy reason: "Ah, well, the things you do for your friends."

Three thousand people greeted Kennedy in Topeka. He walked slowly along a fence bordering the runway, staring intently at the faces, and leaning back as he shook hands, to prevent someone grabbing his hair or clawing his cheeks. Then he climbed onto a metal stairway and shouted, "We don't have to accept the division of races and ages."

In the ballroom of the Ramada Inn he addressed a thousand party foot soldiers who had contributed to Docking's reelection campaign, and had undoubtedly read that day's editorial in the *Topeka Capital-Journal* warning that President Johnson would punish anyone supporting Kennedy. Despite the huge airport crowds, Kennedy appeared nervous and fell back on JFK, saying, "In 1960 . . . the American people and mankind looked to John Kennedy," and reminding them that his brother had chosen to make one of his final campaign stops in Kansas. A band played "When Irish Eyes Are Smiling" while these clubhouse Democrats pulled out cameras and hundreds of flashbulbs exploded, freezing Kennedy in their harsh white light.

As he left, he asked Jim Slattery, who headed a Kennedy for President club at nearby Washburn University, "How am I doing here?"

Slattery told him he was doing well but then, remembering that Kennedy had just urged everyone to work for him in their "villages and hamlets," added, "But you ought to know that we have villages and *towns* in Kansas." Kennedy was in such high spirits that he threw back his head and laughed.

Back at the governor's mansion Kennedy and Docking sat alone in Docking's study. They wore bathrobes, and ate roast beef sandwiches, and drank the Heineken that Docking had laid in because he knew it had been John Kennedy's favorite beer. Docking had already told reporters that the Kansas delegation was uncommitted, although it would be unusual for it not to support an incumbent president on the first ballot. Docking's late father, who had preceded him as governor, had been a minor-league Honorary Kennedy and an early JFK supporter who had been rewarded for his loyalty with a position at the Export-Import Bank. But despite this, and despite having witnessed an impressive demonstration of Bobby's popularity at the Ramada Inn, culminating in a mob of prominent Kansas Democrats yanking the buttons off his coat and shirt (now being sewn back on in the next room by Rene Carpenter), Kennedy did not press Docking to support him or keep the Kansas delegation uncommitted.

Fred Dutton, Kennedy's de facto campaign manager, was socializing with Docking's aides in another room. He was not surprised to hear later that Kennedy had failed to capitalize on this opportunity to solicit Docking's support. He knew that although Bobby had performed the usual political horse-trading for his older brother, he found it impossible to do it for himself. Offering Docking a quid pro quo or reminding him of the favors his brother had done for his father were, according to Dutton, "the kind of things Bob just couldn't do."

One often hears this phrase applied to Bobby Kennedy. Those using it usually mean that these were not things that he preferred not to do, they were things that he found impossible. Columnist Stewart Alsop was struck by his "curious inability to talk about himself," and believed he was "absolutely incapable" of doing what was second nature to most politicians. John Nolan remembers his inability to smile on demand—"he just couldn't"—and by the way he would look down at his speech or at the floor when an audience applauded, waiting for the moment to pass.

Kennedy also found it difficult to explain to audiences *why* they should vote for him, and was notoriously reluctant to discuss his feelings. During his Senate campaign, a reporter had asked him, "What was your reaction when . . ." and "How did you feel when . . ." and he had to tell her, "I just don't do very well with questions like that."

He also resisted saying anything that sounded unlike him. When a State Department official briefing him before a trip to South America suggested some diplomatic lines he might use to deflect awkward questions about human rights violations by the Brazilian government, he snapped, "I don't talk like that," adding, "As I see it . . . you can abolish political parties and close down the Congress and take away the basic freedom of the people and deny your political opponents any rights at all and banish them from the country and you'll get a lot of our money.

But if you mess around with an American oil company, we'll cut you off without a penny. Is that it?"

So instead of interrogating Governor Docking about the loyalties of the Kansas delegation, or hinting that he might be rewarded for his support with a position in a future Kennedy administration, he asked him how Kansans felt about Vietnam, and whether he thought an anti-war speech would be better received at Kansas State or the University of Kansas. He concluded by saying, "What I'm going to say isn't very popular," an extraordinary thing for a presidential candidate to say, and mean, hours before delivering his first campaign speech.

Docking's response must have been discouraging because before turning in, Kennedy called Adam Walinsky, who was fine-tuning the speech he would deliver at Kansas State. "Listen, we've got to make sure not to be too extreme," he told him. "You know these people are very conservative." Walinsky urged him to relax. The KSU students might have conservative parents, he said, but they were as radical and opposed to the war as students elsewhere. "How do you know that?" Kennedy asked. "Well, I mean they just *talk*."

The Kennedys and Rene Carpenter spent the night in adjoining rooms on the second floor of the governor's mansion. The next morning, Ethel knocked on Carpenter's door and whispered, "Can you *please* help Bobby?" She explained that he was having breakfast alone with the Dockings while she was still doing her hair. Knowing what this meant, Carpenter threw on some clothes and dashed downstairs. Bobby was sitting at the end of a long table, staring silently at his plate, picking at his food. Making small talk was something else he could not do. "I mean, he simply *could not* do it," Carpenter says. "So I began chattering away and saved the day."

As she and Ethel drove to the campus, they joked about how they would survive when the conservative KSU students attacked their car. "I'll pretend I'm you," Carpenter said. "I'll throw my body over yours," Ethel promised. "I'll take the bullet."

KENNEDY ATE A second breakfast at the Student Union, where he told a group of university officials and student leaders, "Some of you may not like what you're going to hear in a few minutes, but it's what I believe; and if I'm elected President, it's what I'm going to do."

Before leaving for the field house he stopped in the men's room and stood at a urinal next to Dan Lykins, head of KSU Collegians for Kennedy. Lykins tried making small talk. Kennedy cut him off and asked, "What kind of a reception do you think I'll get?"

"There's more antiwar sentiment here than people think, and my gut feeling is that people loved your brother."

"But what kind of a reception will *I* get?"

"McCarthy has some support, but I think they'll give you a standing ovation."

"I hope you're right," Kennedy said grimly.

The rally was held in the Ahearn Field House, a hulking stone structure with exposed steel rafters and a dirt ring to accommodate live-stock shows and rodeos. Because Kennedy had attracted a record-setting crowd of 14,500, students stood in stairwells, sat cross-legged on the basketball court and under the press tables, and perched on the rafters and scoreboard, dangling their legs in space. Their signs said BOBBY IS GROOVY! and KISS ME, BOBBY, or they said GENE FOR INTEGRITY and TRAITOR!

The Kennedys walked onto the dais with Kansas State president James McCain, Governor and Mrs. Docking, and former governor Alf Landon. The students jumped up, cheering, stamping their feet, and scuffing up clouds of dust that dimmed the light and hung like smoke. They cheered because Kennedy was youthful and handsome, John Kennedy's brother, and he reminded them of happier times. Seventeen-year-old Kevin Rochat, the son of a KSU professor, cheered because he thought everything had gone wrong since JFK's assassination, and only his brother could make it right. Ralph Titus, who managed the university radio station, believes these conservative students cheered him because Vietnam had made even them uneasy.

Kennedy edited his speech during the introductions, sometimes glancing up to study the students in the front rows, as if he was changing the text according to their expressions. He saw girls in long skirts who had never worn makeup, and short-haired boys in neckties who were brave enough to leave their prairie towns, but not to burn their draft cards. George Embrey of the *Columbus Dispatch*, who had once been stationed at nearby Fort Leavenworth, considered it a typical KSU basketball crowd of students leavened by some adults from neighboring towns. The only difference was a large contingent of plainclothes officers who had turned out in response to death threats.

Kennedy looked so nervous and vulnerable that Jim Slattery had a sudden urge to climb onto the platform and hug him. "Come on! Come on!" he thought, "You're my guy!" Kennedy began by mistakenly thanking "Governor and Mrs. Landon" for their hospitality last night. When he stopped to correct himself his voice cracked and those near the stage noticed his hands trembling and his right leg shaking.

After praising Landon's distinguished career, he said, "I am also glad to come to the home of another Kansan who wrote, 'If our colleges and universities do not breed men who riot, who rebel, who attack life with all their youthful vision and vigor then there is something wrong with our colleges. The more riots that come on college campuses, the better [the] world for tomorrow.'"

The audience quieted and Landon and the dignitaries exchanged worried glances. Docking wore a quizzical "Where is he going with this?" expression.

Later that spring, after students at Columbia had occupied university offices and race riots had convulsed 119 American cities, no politician—perhaps not even Kennedy—would have uttered these words on a college campus. But by March 1968, students had already picketed military recruiting centers, marched on the Pentagon, and burned draft cards, making this a risky way for Kennedy to open his first campaign speech. Had there been talk radio and twenty-four-hour news cycles, this sound bite might have destroyed his candidacy in a matter of days.

After a pause, Kennedy identified the author of the quotation, saying, "The man who wrote these words was that notorious seditionist, William Allen White—the late editor of the *Emporia Gazette*—and one of the giants of American journalism." White had been a close friend of Landon's, and an icon to Kansas Republicans. All eyes now went to Landon, waiting for his reaction. If there was a moment when Kennedy's campaign hung in the balance, this was it.

Landon slapped his knee and guffawed, and the field house erupted in laughter and applause. Kennedy continued, saying, "He [White] is an honored man today; but when he lived and wrote, he was often reviled on your campus as an extremist—or worse. For he spoke as he believed. He did not conceal his concern in comforting words; he did not delude his readers or himself with false hopes and illusions. It is in this spirit that I wish to speak today."

He told the KSU students that their country was "deep in a malaise of the spirit," and suffering from "a deep crisis of confidence"—the kinds of phrases that no politician has dared utter since President Carter was pilloried for speaking of a national "crisis of confidence" during his notorious "malaise" speech, in which he never used the word *malaise.*

He opened his attack on President Johnson's Vietnam policy with a confession and an apology. "Let me begin this discussion with a note both personal and public," he said. "I was involved in many of the early decisions on Vietnam, decisions which helped set us on our present path."

He acknowledged that "the effort may have been doomed from the start" and admitted that the South Vietnamese governments that his brother's administration had supported had been "riddled with corruption, inefficiency and greed," adding, "If that is the case, as it well may be, then I am willing to bear my share of the responsibility, before history and before my fellow-citizens. But past error is no excuse for its own perpetuation. Tragedy is a tool for the living to gain wisdom. . . . Now, as ever, we do ourselves best justice when we measure ourselves against ancient tests, as in the *Antigone* of Sophocles: 'All men make mistakes, but a good man yields when he knows his course is wrong, and repairs the evil. The only sin is pride.'"

His apology elicited the loudest cheers of the morning, perhaps because these students appreciated hearing an adult admit to a mistake, or because they, too, had once supported the war and Kennedy's mea culpa made it easier for them to admit that they, too, had been wrong.

He framed his opposition to Vietnam in moral terms, telling them, "I am concerned—as I believe most Americans are concerned—that the course we are following at the present time is deeply wrong. . . . I am concerned—as I believe most American are concerned—that we are acting as if no other nations existed, against the judgment and desires of neutrals and our historic allies alike."

He reminded them that events had made a mockery of the Johnson administration's desperate optimism: "Every time—at every crisis—we have denied that anything was wrong . . . and issued more confident communiqués. Every time, we have been assured that this one last step would bring victory. And every time the predictions and promises have failed and been forgotten."

He urged them to consider "the young men we have sent there; not just the killed, but those who have to kill; not just the maimed, but also those who must look upon the results of what they do," and to consider "the price we pay in our own innermost lives, and in the spirit of our country." This was why, he said, "war is not an enterprise lightly to be undertaken, nor prolonged one moment past its absolute necessity."

At first he seemed tentative and wooden, stammering and repeating himself, too nervous to punctuate his sentences with gestures. But with each round of applause he became more animated. Soon he was pounding the lectern with his right fist, shouting out his words, and concluding his litanies of the Johnson administration's catastrophic and immoral war policies with, "I don't think we have to accept that here in the United States of America!" "I think we can do better in this country!" and "I think that's unacceptable!"

Rene Carpenter watched the students in the front rows. Their faces shone and they opened their mouths in unison, shouting, "Yeah! Yeah! Yeah!"

Hays Gorey of *Time* called the electricity between Kennedy and the KSU students "real and rare" and said that "a good part of it is John F. Kennedy's, of course, but John Kennedy himself couldn't be so passionate, and couldn't set off such sparks."

Kevin Rochat was close to weeping because Kennedy was so direct and honest. He kept telling himself, "My God! He's *saying* exactly what I've been *thinking*!"

Jim Slattery, who would later be elected to Congress from Kansas, reread the KSU speech during the second Iraq war and decided it was so powerful "because Kennedy was talking about what was *right*!"

Kennedy concluded by saying, "Our country is in danger: not just from foreign enemies; but above all, from our own misguided policies—and what they can do to the nation that Thomas Jefferson once told us was the last, best, hope of man. There is a contest on, not for the rule of America but for the heart of America. In these next eight months we are going to decide what this country will stand for—and what kind of men we are."

He raised his fist in the air so it resembled the revolutionary symbol on posters hanging in student rooms that year, promised "a new America," and the hall erupted in cheers and thunderous applause.

As he started to leave, waves of students rushed the platform, knocking over chairs and raising more dust. They grabbed at him, stroking his hair and ripping his shirtsleeves. Jim Tolan was almost crushed against a wall, and Herb Schmertz was left with a lifelong phobia of crowds. University officials opened a path to a rear exit, but Kennedy waved them off and waded into the crowd. Stanley Tretick of *Look* magazine stood on the platform, photographing the melee and shouting, "This is Kansas, fucking *Kansas*! He's going all the way. He's going all the fucking way!"*

Kennedy left the field house standing on the backseat of a convertible. Kevin Rochat thrust out his hand as he passed. Instead of the bone-crushing handshake he had expected, Kennedy's grip was soft and gentle. By the end of the day Jim Slattery had signed up one thousand students to work for Kennedy in the Nebraska primary. Hays

---

*It was Richard Nixon, however, who went all the way. On September 16, 1970, four months after Ohio National Guard troops killed Kent State students protesting the bombing of Cambodia, he delivered his own Landon Lecture at KSU, then considered one of the few campuses in the nation where his appearance would not trigger a riot. Again, Governor Docking and Alf Landon sat on the dais, and many of the same students who had heard Robert Kennedy must have been in that audience, too. The Young Republicans had organized the seating this time, and had packed the front rows with Nixon supporters. Nixon appeared wearing an oversized purple-and-white Kansas State tie, and opened with five minutes of paeans to KSU athletic teams, followed by a jeremiad against student radicals. When protesters who had been exiled to the balcony began chanting antiwar slogans he said, "My text at this point reads, 'The voices of a small minority have been allowed to drown out the responsible majority.' That may be true in some places, but not at Kansas State!" At this, his supporters kicked and hit the protesters with umbrellas and security guards ejected them from the field house. When Nixon declared that it was time for responsible faculty members and students to "stand up and be counted," most of this audience of more than fifteen thousand—a few hundred more than had heard Kennedy—gave him a standing ovation. Perhaps some were applauding the presidency instead of its current occupant, or were embarrassed by the protesters, but it proved that this really was a fairly conservative campus.

Gorey encountered a man in his seventies who was as enthusiastic as the students. "I think he'll be President," he told Gorey.

One reporter would call the Landon lecture "the first indication that we were about to embark on something unlike anything we had ever experienced." Cries of "Holy shit!" and "What the hell are we in for?" echoed through the press bus as it pulled away from the campus. But once the excitement had ebbed, John J. Lindsay of *Newsweek* said, "Listen, I'm not sure we're going to like how this turns out."

Tolan and Bruno had planted an editorial in the University of Kansas newspaper criticizing its students for being "conservative and apathetic." It had the desired effect of swelling the audience at the Allen Field House to twenty thousand, the largest in university history. Kennedy's reception was even more raucous than at Kansas State. Witnesses spoke of "roaring students" and "raw emotion let loose." Reporter Jack Newfield described it as "emotion beyond reason, cheering until saliva ran, clapping until hands hurt," and *New York Post* columnist Jimmy Breslin believed it indicated that "the day when a politician can survive with slogans may be gone."

At Kansas State, Kennedy had explained how Vietnam had wounded the national soul. At the University of Kansas, he told students that they could heal their country by ending the disgrace of poverty and hunger among their fellow citizens. The first speech had contained the diagnosis; the second, the remedy.

Adam Walinsky had hurriedly inserted some of the best-received lines from Kansas State into the speech, and Kennedy repeated the White quotation about encouraging riots on college campuses, and said that Vietnam threatened the "national soul." But most of his speech concerned the plight of what he called "the other Americans." He spoke about "children in the Delta area of Mississippi with distended stomachs, whose faces are covered with sores from starvation," and "Indians living on their bare and meager reservations . . . with so little hope for the future that for young men and women in their teens the greatest cause of death is suicide," and "people of the black ghetto, listening to ever-greater promises of equality and justice, as they sit in the same decaying schools and huddle in the same filthy rooms, warding off the cold and warding off the rats."

After declaring that ending the suffering of these other Americans should be "an urgent national priority," he questioned one of the sacrosanct tenets of American political discourse, that economic growth, consumption, and the American dream were inextricably linked. "Too much and too long, we seem to have surrendered community excellence and community values in the mere accumulation of material things," he said. "Our gross national product, now, is over eight hundred billion dollars a year, but the GNP—if we should judge America by that—counts air pollution and cigarette advertising, and ambulances to clear our highways of carnage. It counts special locks for our doors and the jails for those who break them. It counts the destruction of our redwoods and the loss of our natural wonder in chaotic sprawl. It counts napalm and the cost of a nuclear warhead . . . and the television programs which glorify violence in order to sell toys to our children. Yet the gross national product does not allow for the health of our children, the quality of their education, or the joy of their play. It does not include the beauty of our poetry or the strength of our marriages; the intelligence of our public debate or the integrity of our public officials. It measures neither our wit nor our courage . . . it measures everything, in short, except that which makes life worthwhile. And it can tell us everything about America except why we are proud that we are Americans."

Walinsky had not expected this to be an applause line and was surprised when the students cheered. Kennedy seemed oblivious to their reaction, and Walinsky decided that after months of indecision, he was concentrating more on his own liberation than on how audiences were reacting to it.

In prepared speeches and impromptu remarks throughout his campaign, Kennedy would continue to describe the sufferings of poor Americans and assail the GNP as a measure of national worth. As in Kansas, these passages received loud applause. Walinsky believes they were effective because audiences recognized that they were what he calls "an authentic expression of Kennedy's life as a political figure and as a human being." Kennedy's riff on the GNP was more than a clever bit of speechwriting, it was a summary of causes he had championed during his years as a U.S. senator. Everything in it reflected his demonstrated interests, including the reference to "the beauty of our poetry," an appropriate concern for someone who read, marked, and memorized verse.

Before returning to the Kansas City airport, the Kennedy press corps stopped for a quick restaurant meal. Jimmy Breslin asked a table of reporters, "Do you think this guy has the stuff to go all the way?"

"Yes, of course he has the stuff to go all the way," John Lindsay replied. "But he's not going to go all the way. The reason is that somebody is going to shoot him. I know it and you know it. Just as sure as we're sitting here somebody is going to shoot him. He's out there now waiting for him. . . . And, please God, I don't think we'll have a country after it."

There was a stunned silence. Then, one by one, the other reporters agreed. But none asked the most heartbreaking question, whether Kennedy himself knew it.

Riding in a convertible had left Kennedy chilled, and he began the flight back to Washington huddled in his late brother's topcoat. He became increasingly talkative, describing to reporters the expressions he had seen on the faces of individual students. "Could you really *see* them from where you were standing?" Jimmy Breslin asked. "I saw them. I saw every face in the building," he said, closing his eyes and shaking his head. "Did you ever see anything like it? You can hear the fabric ripping. If we don't get out of this war, I don't know what these young people are going to do. . . . It's very dangerous."

He exclaimed to others stopping by his seat, "I feel free! I feel like a man again!" and told Jim Tolan, "You know, I didn't like myself for what I was doing and saying before, saying I would support Johnson."

One of Kennedy's favorite authors was Ralph Waldo Emerson. He had marked three passages in the copy of Emerson's essays that he kept on his desk at home in Hickory Hill. One declared, "If the single man plant himself on his instincts, and there abide, the huge world will come round to him." Kennedy was about to discover if Emerson was right.

THREE

"BOBBY AIN'T JACK"

MARCH 21–31, 1968

Three days after leaving Kansas, Kennedy embarked on a ten-day, thirteen-state, cross-country trip that Frank Mankiewicz began calling the "Free At Last Tour." Before the tour, Kennedy had been inhibited by conflicting advice from advisers and friends; during it, he was impulsive, made the important decisions himself, and traveled without an entourage of consultants, managers, pollsters, and media advisers, and unencumbered by months of calculation and compromise—without everyone and everything that drains spontaneity and moral clarity from a campaign.

He started in Alabama and Tennessee on March 21, then spent a day in upstate New York before heading west for three days in California, followed by stops in Oregon and Washington, and Red States Idaho, Utah, Colorado, Indiana, and New Mexico. The itinerary was designed to place him before a succession of large and enthusiastic audiences, and to demonstrate to the machine politicians who controlled the nominating process that his popularity spanned race, class, and geography. The press had a crucial role to play in this strategy because the Democratic leaders would be influenced by what they read in national newspapers like the *New York Times* and *Washington Post*.

Kennedy's aides cast his going-into-the-streets strategy as a virtue rather than a necessity, with one telling *Saturday Evening Post* reporter David Wise on March 24, "We take the position that the old rules don't apply. America is in flux, everything is changing. The old way of delegate hunting doesn't apply. We're going to the people. And we're going to win." In other words, Kennedy was employing some New Politics techniques in an attempt to impress practitioners of the Old Politics, campaigning in the streets to influence backroom wheeling and dealing.

In *Bobby Kennedy and the New Politics*, author Penn Kimball defined a New Politician as a candidate who relied on a personal organization instead of party machinery, employed sophisticated media techniques, sought to consolidate rather than divide voters, and stressed style over issues. The campaign Kennedy launched a month after the publication of Kimball's book had two of these characteristics: his reliance on the Honorary Kennedys, and his attempt to reassemble the New Deal coalition of minorities and working-class whites. Otherwise, his media campaign was rudimentary, and instead of style, he stressed issues such as Vietnam, poverty, and race. Instead of New Politics, he would practice an improvisational "Jazz Politics," one of spontaneous and exuberant riffs requiring a performer who was comfortable in his own skin and unafraid to play without a score.

Many of the tour's venues had the brick-wall simplicity of a jazz club. There were no elaborate stages distancing Kennedy from an audience, and no backdrops wallpapered with slogans summarizing his message. Even in 1968, this was considered such a departure from the norm that, after Kennedy's appearances in Seattle, the political reporter of the *Post-Intelligencer* would write, "Gone is the bunting-bedecked platform, the rostrum with its fancy seal, the flags and ever-present swarm of dignitaries. . . . America is changing. The traditional ways are Exit, friend."

Even when Kennedy stuck to a prepared speech, his words sounded improvised. Adam Walinsky and Jeff Greenfield wrote many of his speeches on the fly, in hotel rooms or on planes, sometimes supplying him only with file cards of talking points. He often raced through a prepared speech only to spend twice as long responding to questions. He sometimes turned his answers into lengthy riffs on the nobility of sacrifice, the unfairness of student deferments, and the indecency of poverty. He improvised, for example, on his plea that Americans "learn the harsh facts that lurk behind the mask of official illusion with which we have concealed our true circumstances [in Vietnam], even from ourselves," telling an audience in San Jose, "We can no longer differ on reality; we can no longer deceive ourselves," and students in Los Angeles, "I am on the side of those who are not afraid to recognize past error, who refuse to blindly pursue bankrupt policies which will rend us from our friends and drain us of our treasure, in the fruitless pursuit of illusions long since shattered."

He turned audiences into sidemen, bantering with them, interviewing them, and conducting polls, inviting students at Brigham Young University to vote on solutions to the Vietnam War. After "escalation and the dispatch of an additional 20,000 soldiers" received the loudest cheers, he asked in an innocent voice, "Have you signed up yet?"

Some students at the University of Nebraska booed when he said, "Our real power lies not in guns, bombs, and napalm, but in exemplary action at home and abroad," and booed again when he said he favored halting the bombing of North Vietnam. He lost his temper and snapped, "Unless we kill every one of them, including the women and children and their supporters, you are going to have to deal with them." Vietnam was not World War II, he said, it was a political struggle that posed a moral question: "Do we have the right to destroy all the people in Vietnam to save it?"

If a crowd was cold, he said, "Clap!" They laughed and clapped, and were his. He used interruptions or hostile questions as a pretext for telling a joke, and chipping away at his reputation for being ruthless. Chimes rang out from a tower at San Jose State and he said, "Ronald Reagan, I'll get even with you." Someone asked sarcastically if he thought having the name "Kennedy" gave him an advantage, and he agreed, adding that "Robert" was also an advantage. A student in Oregon shouted, "At least McCarthy was on time!" and he shot back, "Yeah, but I'm worth waiting for." When a baby began crying and its mother stood up to leave, he said, "Please don't leave!" explaining that if she did people would say that he had "ruthlessly" thrown a baby out of the hall.

His jazzy politics were perfect for the sixties. Like the Beatles, he seemed to be making it up as he went along and his campaign had a Magical Mystery Tour quality.

When cameraman Walter Dombrow slipped into a motorcade crowd and yelled, "Sock it to 'em, Bobby!" Kennedy shouted back, "Catch me, Walter," jumped into his arms, then climbed back into his car and yelled, "Charge!" When a hippie who had been jogging alongside his car handed him his draft card, he calmly autographed it and handed it back. A boy on a motorcycle pulled alongside and, taking his hands off the handlebars, pulled a camera from his pocket and tried to snap a photograph. Kennedy grabbed the camera and handed it to an aide, who took a picture and passed it back to the boy. Later, a reporter who witnessed the episode wrote that the boy could have been reaching for a gun.

ON MARCH 21, the first day of the tour, Kennedy delivered a speech to students at the University of Alabama in Tuscaloosa, where he had once sent federal marshals to enforce the registration of black students. He told them he had come to the South because he believed that "any who seek higher office this year must go before all Americans: not just those who agree with them, but those who disagree; recognizing that it is not just our supporters . . . but all Americans, who we must lead in the difficult years ahead." At a time when Americans were "divided by a difficult, costly war abroad," a presidential campaign had to be more than a matter of "courting and counting votes," he said, and would be a failure if it left Americans as divided as when it began.

That afternoon, he asked ten thousand students gathered in Vanderbilt's Memorial Gymnasium, "Who is it that is trying to divide the country?" He answered, "It is not those who call for change, it is those who make present policies . . . who have removed themselves from American tradition, from the enduring and generous impulses that are the soul of this nation."

His remark that "every dictatorship has ultimately strangled in the web of repression it wove for its people, making mistakes that could not be corrected because criticism was prohibited" led Richard Harwood of the *Washington Post*, a gruff former combat marine who had embarked on the tour as a Kennedy skeptic, to complain that by comparing the Johnson administration to a dictatorship, he had come close to crossing "the line of acceptable political discourse." But in another article Harwood called audiences at Tuscaloosa and Nashville "large and generally enthusiastic," and reported Kennedy receiving a "warm ovation"—the kind of observations Kennedy needed to impress Mayor Daley and other Democratic Party bosses.

Harwood would serve as a bellwether for Kennedy's relationship with his press corps. He had grown up poor in Tennessee, enlisted in the Marine Corps at seventeen, fought in the Pacific, and initially distrusted Kennedy for everything that he was not: rich and privileged. Within weeks of joining the campaign, he had changed his mind, and saw a man who was reaching out to the poor and would fulfill the promises he was making to them.

Before arriving in California on March 23, Kennedy had stuck to university campuses. John Nolan, who scheduled many of these appearances, believes he did this more for "inner reasons" than political ones, because he was desperate to win back the "A students," the smart, politically aware ones who had idolized JFK and embraced the New Frontier, but were now supporting Eugene McCarthy. But it was also true that a college campus was the only place where a politician could count on drawing a large weekday audience.

Proof that Kennedy's appeal extended beyond the campus came when he flew into San Francisco on March 23 and a thousand people mobbed him at the airport. He climbed onto a ticket counter and, in a voice resembling JFK's, delivered some trademark JFK lines, saying, "I come here to ask for your help!" and, "I think we can do better!" But then, perhaps realizing what he was doing, he distanced himself from the New Frontier, adding, "We have new problems and we have new answers."

He flew on to Stockton in the San Joaquin Valley, where Mayor Joseph Doll welcomed him by proclaiming, "I know that God is on your side!" Kennedy was embarrassed, but put Doll down gently, saying, "As long as I have God, I hope I have some delegates to go with Him. Or that when He gets to Chicago, He'll bring some with Him."

His motorcade into Stockton was like dozens to come. He stood on the backseat of a convertible, waving, studying faces, and memorizing the signs. Inside the car, aides knelt on the seat and floor, their arms wrapped around his waist and legs to prevent him from being pulled into the crowd. Photographers and cameramen followed in a second convertible, standing on bumpers and hanging from doors so it resembled a tank bringing an infantry platoon into battle. Gangs of children ran alongside, screaming "Bobby!" and flinging open their arms to embrace him. Whenever he stopped, hundreds of outstretched arms encircled him so that in photographs taken from above he appeared to be a bud in the center of an exotic flower. People stole his cuff links and handkerchiefs, pulled his hair, and left his hands scratched and bleeding. He emptied his pockets afterward and crumpled notes covered his lap like confetti. They begged him to attend graduations, visit sick children, and know that prayers were being said and candles lit.

The crowd at the Stockton courthouse contained a large contingent of Chicanos and reminded *The New Yorker*'s Jim Stevenson of the one that had mobbed the Beatles at Carnegie Hall. (The pictures that *Life* photographer Bill Eppridge took of audiences listening to Robert Kennedy and the Beatles are eerily similar. In both, young men and women stare up at a stage, faces shining, mouths open, and eyes glazed over in rapture.) Kennedy dispensed with the usual "I know you are proud to live in Stockton" boilerplate and, at a time when many Americans were defining "indecency" as long hair, drugs, sex, and a lack of respect for the older generation, he said: "Decency is at the heart of this whole campaign. . . . Poverty is indecent. Illiteracy is indecent. The death, the maiming of brave young men in the swamps of Vietnam . . . that is also indecent. And it is indecent for a man to work with his back and his hands in the valleys of California without ever having hope of sending his son on to college. This is also indecent." America had once been "the kind of country that stood for decency and for justice, for confidence and for hope," he said. "But now sometimes it seems we have become something else."

Later that afternoon, an audience of middle-class white Californians screaming "Bobby!" almost crushed him against a wall at Sacramento's Florin Shopping Center. He told them the same thing he had said to Stockton's Chicanos: "It is indecent for a man on the streets of New York City or Cleveland or Detroit or Watts to surrender the only life that he has to despair and hopelessness." Then he expanded on the "indecency" of the Vietnam War, saying, "While the sun shines in our sky, men are dying on the other side of the earth. Which of them could have come home and written a great symphony? Which of them could have come home to cure cancer? Which of them might have played in a World Series or given us the gift of laughter from the stage?"

In San Jose that evening, it took him thirty minutes to push his way to a platform through a crowd of fifteen thousand filling a downtown park. After speculating on the lost contributions of the Vietnam dead, calling poverty and illiteracy "indecent," and decrying the divisions in American society, he told the predominantly working-class audience, "Every day 10,000 of our fellow human beings starve elsewhere in the world," and called it "monstrous" that Americans bought eight million new cars every year while most people in the world could not afford shoes—an impolitic thing to say to people who may have been dreaming of owning their first new car.

The next day, traffic on roads leading to the Monterey airport was backed up for seven miles, and thousands of people dashed onto the runway after he landed. As he was saying, "We have seventy million TV sets, but I travel to the Delta in Mississippi and I see children starving," he noticed a little girl being crushed against a chain-link fence. He held up his hands for quiet, then waded into the crowd and picked her up.

This was one of many occasions when he would demonstrate a peripheral vision that was both real and metaphorical, enabling him to speak about people living on the peripheries of society while also noticing the angry woman, bewildered child, or wheelchair-bound man on the periphery of an audience. He noticed a woman fall and scrape her knee as his motorcade passed and invited her into his car. He saw a young man sitting in front of a farmhouse in a wheelchair and stopped and spoke with him for several minutes before pressing a *PT 109* tie clasp into his hand, leaving him in tears. "Did you see their eyes?" he asked Roger Mudd of CBS after his car had inched through crowds lining roads outside Detroit. "Did you see their faces?" he asked after driving through Watts, and went on to describe the expressions of the children who had chased his car. "The big thing about them is they listen," he said about Hoosiers after campaigning in Indiana.

"You see this face way in the back of the crowd and he's listening. He's not off in space. That means the people you're talking to don't want generalities . . .'It's nice to be in Indiana, I'm a nice fellow, please vote for me.' They don't want that. You have to tell them something."

Kennedy's peripheral vision meant that he also seldom missed an enemy. After noticing angry faces in a crowd in Kokomo, Indiana, he told newsman David Brinkley, who thought his reception there had been good, "They *hate* me in Kokomo!"

He read and remembered the signs, but it was not the SOCK IT TO ME BOBBY! and ALL THE WAY WITH RFK ones that he wanted to discuss but the ones saying, WHERE WERE YOU IN NEW HAMPSHIRE? RUTHLESS ROBERT, and ALL HAIR NO BRAINS.

From Monterey he flew to Los Angeles, where a crowd screaming "Bobby!" chased him through the airport. His motorcade was "one of the wildest political demonstrations ever given a political figure," according to the *Los Angeles Times*, "uproarious, shrieking and frenzied," and "a spectacle without parallel in the American experience."

In Watts, people hung from the branches of live oaks and stood on car roofs, denting them. He began by telling one street-corner audience what it wanted to hear, saying, "The Commission on Civil Disorder has told us what we should have known long ago: that racial injustice, racial deprivation, racial exploitation, is a national issue. It infects our great metropolitan areas as much as it does the South." But then he followed this with a law-and-order message. "And I tell you here in California the same thing I told those in Alabama with whom I talked. The gulf between our people will not be bridged by those who preach violence, or by those who burn or loot."

At another street corner he said, "I want hatred and prejudice to disappear from this country. I pledge to you that when a young man goes to Vietnam to fight, when he comes back to the United States he will be treated with justice." A member of the audience hearing this told reporter David Wise that he was voting for Kennedy, "not just for Watts. I'm not just pullin' for Watts, I'm pullin' for the whole country. I'd like somebody to pull the country out."

At a downtown rally ten thousand Chicanos cheered when he criticized the government for spending $36 billion in Vietnam but refusing to fund school lunches. In Griffith Park, people perched on floodlight pylons and spilled from the amphitheater onto surrounding hillsides. During a speech at its outdoor Greek Theater, he spoke of "islands of blacks afraid of islands of whites. Islands of Northerners bitterly opposed to islands of Southerners," and charged that "for almost the first time, the national leadership is calling upon the darker impulses of the American spirit—not perhaps deliberately, but through the actions and the example it sets—an example where integrity, truth, honor and all the rest seem like words to fill out speeches rather than guiding beliefs."

His press corps had arrived at the Greek Theater late and in a bad mood after one of their buses became lost on the freeways. They turned on Kennedy afterward, criticizing what became known as the Darker Impulses speech. *Time* accused him of "demagoguery." Robert Donovan wrote in the *Los Angeles Times* that "when a war becomes a flaming political issue, the line between debate and demagoguery becomes a thin one." Richard Harwood wondered if the frenzied crowds were encouraging him to employ rhetorical devices "bordering on the demagogic." After Kennedy and King had been assassinated and My Lai exposed, the Darker Impulses speech would seem to have been a rather tame diagnosis of the situation and, when compared to the kind of political rhetoric that has since become commonplace, it seems even tamer.

Author Theodore White, who was chronicling the 1968 presidential election for his *The Making of a President* series, wrote that Kennedy's campaign would reach such "a terrifying frenzy" in minority neighborhoods like Watts that sharing a car with him could be a frightening experience. But even watching his motorcades on television frightened some middle-class whites, who saw images confirming the charge that he was a rabble-rouser and demagogue. What television could not convey, however, was that unlike a genuine demagogue, Kennedy believed what he was saying. He was also courting many of the dangers faced by a demagogue who stirs up strong emotions in a crowd, yet was taking none of the security measures that demagogues adopt to protect themselves.

The Darker Impulses speech and the frenzied crowds had also made some of Kennedy's advisers uneasy. Pierre Salinger was distressed by what he called "a terrible strident tone" in the speeches and called him from Washington to complain. Dutton took Harwood aside and told him, "It's too bad we had to open this show on Broadway instead of New Haven," and pointed out that John F. Kennedy had time to eliminate his oratorical excesses. Frank Mankiewicz worried that the crowds were becoming so physical and hysterical that some reporters were beginning to fear for their lives, imagining themselves crushed in a stampede or pushed off an auditorium balcony. Kennedy responded to the criticism by trying to dampen the frenzy and soften his attacks on the Johnson administration.

After leaving California, he spent three days hopping across Oregon, Washington, Idaho, Utah, Colorado, and Nebraska, finally stopping in Indianapolis on the evening of March 28 to file petitions entering his name in the May 7 Indiana primary. Afterward, he met in his hotel room with Mike Riley, the young attorney heading his Indiana campaign, and Bill Schreiber and Louis Mahern, volunteers who had collected signatures for the petitions.

Mahern was shocked by Kennedy's appearance. After a week on the tour, his hands were swollen, red scratches ran up his arms, and he was suffering from laryngitis. As Mahern briefed him on the political situation, Kennedy fixed him with such a piercing stare that Mahern imagined him seeing to the back of his skull. He asked Mahern in a hoarse whisper if he had experienced any problems collecting the necessary signatures to put him on the ballot in each of Indiana's congressional districts. Mahern said it had been easy, even in overwhelmingly Republican districts. He thought people in Washington did not understand how much Johnson was detested, even in Indiana.

The ease of collecting signatures for the Indiana petitions was the only concrete good news to emerge from the tour. Despite the large and enthusiastic crowds, Kennedy had not received the endorsement of a single influential Democrat. The reaction of Dale Tooley, chairman of the Denver Democratic Party, was typical. After Kennedy had drawn eighty-five hundred people to the Denver Arena, and tens of thousands had lined the route of his motorcade, Tooley told reporters that "experienced political activists were seldom swayed by an address or an appearance." Even reporter Jack Newfield, usually a Kennedy enthusiast, seemed to agree with Tooley's assessment, and speculated in the *Village Voice* that Kennedy might not crack the "totalitarian arithmetic" of the coming Democratic convention.

Still, Kennedy probably persuaded some Democrats to remain uncommitted until he could prove his strength in the primaries. And it was during the tour that reporters covering him for the first time realized that the stereotypical ruthless and opportunistic Bobby Kennedy was at odds with the shy and witty man they were coming to know, and that Kennedy came to believe that the crowds had come to cheer him more than to remember his brother.

It was difficult for Kennedy to escape his brother's shadow. Whenever he crossed the Arlington Memorial Bridge he saw the flame marking his brother's grave; whenever he rose to speak in the Senate he faced men who had heard his brother speak in this same chamber, and were undoubtedly comparing them. He came the closest to leaving his brother behind when he left Washington and pursued issues that he was making his own, traveling to Poland in the spring of 1964, speaking to students in South Africa in 1966, and visiting Indian reservations and migrant labor camps throughout his years in the Senate.

During the first week of his campaign he had sometimes evoked JFK, telling the airport crowd in Topeka, "When it was a question of whether or not we were going to get the country moving again, the American people and mankind looked to John F. Kennedy," and students at Kansas State, "You are the people, as President Kennedy said, who have the least ties to the present and the greatest ties to the future." He used the same line again at Vanderbilt, prompting a Nashville newspaper to headline its story, "RFK Visit Here Recalls Late Brother's Talk."

His advisers feared that by mentioning his brother so frequently he was courting a backlash. Arthur Schlesinger sent a memorandum warning that although there was "tremendous nostalgia" for John F. Kennedy, there was also "great potential resentment against anything which might appear an exploitation or manipulation of that nostalgia." As if to prove Schlesinger's point, columnist Murray Kempton, who had idolized JFK, wrote, "There is such a thing as evocation of the great dead, and there is also such a thing as the exploitation of corpses. Senator Kennedy seems appallingly far from recognizing the difference."

Kennedy complained that it was impossible for him not to evoke his late brother. He spoke with the same accent, was running for the same office, traveling with the same aides, being covered by the same journalists, and stopping in the same towns. Signs proclaiming CALL THE ROLL AT THE ROUND TABLE—CAMELOT WILL COME AGAIN and NEW IMAGE IN '68—BACK TO CAMELOT greeted him in Sacramento, and after he left the city, a headline proclaimed that "Kennedy in Sacramento. Echoes Brother's Lines." A supporter warmed up an audience in Mishawaka, Indiana, by shouting, "We loved John F. Kennedy when he was President, and we will love Bobby." A front-page story in Davenport, Iowa, began, "It was on a Tuesday in October, 1960, that Kennedy's brother, John F., drew an estimated 10,000 persons into the streets jutting off the corner of East Second and Main Streets. . . . R.F.K. will also address an outdoor rally at the same intersection."

It was also impossible for him not to be reminded of JFK.

He autographed his late brother's books and accepted gifts of quilts and paintings bearing his image. Politicians who had welcomed JFK to their towns in 1960, and who still wore the *PT 109* tie clasps that he had given them and that memorialized his World War II torpedo boat, now welcomed Bobby to the same auditoriums and courthouse squares. He addressed a rally at John F. Kennedy Square in Detroit, where his brother had launched his 1960 campaign, and drove down John F. Kennedy avenues and expressways. Whenever he sat in the backseat of a convertible, he reminded spectators of Dallas.

He recognized his brother's former campaign workers attending a rally in Portland. He opened a campaign office in a black neighborhood of Omaha where a crayoned sign in the window said KENNEDY WHITE BUT ALRIGHT / THE ONE BEFORE, HE OPENED THE DOOR. He was introduced at one Omaha rally as "a man who brings with him the memory of a happy time," and at another in Indiana, by an attorney who said, "A few years ago, a young man named Kennedy . . . began to capture the hearts and minds of a great number of people throughout Jackson County. . . . [Now] another young man named Kennedy stands here again at this same spot and begins to capture the hearts and minds of people throughout Jackson County." He was introduced as "The Honorable John F. Kennedy" in Salt Lake City, and in Grand Rapids cheerleaders chanted "JFK in '68! JFK in '68" until one horrified girl clapped her hands over her mouth.

The confusion was understandable. He and his late brother shared family traits, and those resulting from the natural tendency of younger siblings to imitate older ones. Both were impatient men who jiggled their legs and tapped their teeth, made small talk by asking questions, seldom carried cash, and were fond of sports. They both liked reporters and celebrities, maintained year-round tans, took frequent showers, wore as many as five clean shirts a day, and were monomaniacal about their favorite foods—clam chowder for Jack, chocolate ice cream drenched in chocolate syrup for Bobby. They both memorized poetry, saved quotations in notebooks that they inserted into their speeches, and delivered litanies of deplorable conditions punctuated by refrains of "We can do better!" and "I don't think that's acceptable!" They prized civic virtue over consumption and comfort, and believed Americans wanted to be more than shoppers and consumers. Bobby attacked the GNP as a measure of worth and happiness, while Jack referred to the "contest between the comfortable and the concerned" and sometimes quoted in his speeches a line from T. S. Eliot's *The Rock*, "And the wind shall say: 'These were decent people, their only monument the asphalt road and a thousand lost golf balls.'" Jack told Americans to "Ask Not," Bobby urged them to prize "personal excellence and community values" over the "accumulation of material things."

Both were nervous public speakers who rushed their words, could be stiff when delivering prepared speeches, and were better speaking extemporaneously. The judgment of one biographer, that when John Kennedy answered questions "all agreed he was invariably sharp, sparkling, and supremely confident," also described Bobby.

Both disarmed their critics with self-deprecating humor, although Jack's wit was more practiced and Bobby's more spontaneous. After nominating Bobby to be his attorney general, Jack had joked about giving him "a little legal experience." When Bobby groused about being the butt of this joke, Jack said, "In politics you've got to make fun of your vulnerable points in order to make people laugh with you. If you poke fun at yourself, then you get the people on your side," advice that Bobby took to heart in his own campaigns.

Friends who had admired Jack's urbanity and charm found Bobby brash and surly. Southerners who had hated Jack, hated Bobby even more. Liberals who had never forgiven Jack for failing to cast a vote censuring Senator Joseph McCarthy were even less likely to forgive Bobby, who had worked for McCarthy. Bobby's candidacy galvanized all the "Kennedy-haters" whom he now faced without the martyr's halo that was, for the moment, protecting his brother's reputation.

After witnessing the mob scene at the park in San Jose during the tour, newsmen covering Bobby discussed the differences between the two brothers. A photographer said that despite having traveled extensively with Jack Kennedy, he never felt he really *knew* him. Bobby, however, was much warmer, and his emotions were much closer to the surface. A reporter thought that John Kennedy had been more charming than Bobby, but also more detached, and sometimes a little cynical. Another said that the big difference was that the crowds wanted to touch JFK, but they wanted to grab Bobby.

Friends of both men used words like *cool* and *passionate* to distinguish them. According to Ben Bradlee, Jack Kennedy was always in control of his emotions, while Bobby often lost his cool, but in a good way, becoming passionate about injustice. Arthur Schlesinger called JFK "a cool man of reason," while Bobby, he said, was "passionate, blunt, and abrasive." He thought that JFK accepted reality, while RFK rebelled against it; JFK was "a realist disguised as a romantic," Bobby "a romantic disguised as a realist." John Bartlow Martin, who wrote speeches for both, said that JFK sometimes made fun of his public statements in private, while Bobby, who believed what he was saying, never did. "Jack also gave the impression of decisive leadership," Martin said. "Bob seemed less sure he was right, more tentative, more questioning, and completely honest about it." Pierre Salinger, who served both as press secretary, observed that "John Kennedy had this very easy way with people but was hard as nails inside, and Bob Kennedy had a tough exterior and he was really soft inside." JFK had been "a tremendous man," he said, but Bobby was "a revolutionary" who had "wanted to change the very fabric of life in this country."

As the Free At Last Tour continued, Bobby Kennedy distanced himself from his brother. When a man waving a BOBBY AIN'T JACK! sign confronted him in California, he muttered, "I'm not trying to be." He avoided mentioning President Kennedy, even when referring to achievements such as the Cuban Missile Crisis, Test Ban Treaty, and the Peace Corps. He seemed to discount the space program, one of his brother's signature issues, telling an audience in California, "I think that it's important that we enable a man to walk on the moon. But I think it is more important that we be able to walk safely in the streets of our nation's capital and our other cities at night." He added that if forced to choose between cutting the space program or welfare payments, he would choose cutting back on space. He told students in Ogden, Utah, "The answers of the New Frontier are not necessarily applicable to the problems of the future," and promised to do "a better job of solving the problems of this generation than the New Frontier did in solving the problems of the previous generation." He made the same point at Brigham Young University, arguing that New Deal and New Frontier policies were unsuited to the present, saying, "We must seek new guidelines for the future, not be bound by the past."*

He continued distancing himself from the New Frontier during an interview with the British television personality David Frost in Portland on the evening of March 25, telling Frost, "We're living in a different time," and saying he was concerned about "what *can* happen in 1969, not what happened in 1963." He called the New Frontier "part of my life that is past," admitting, "Until November 1963, my whole life was built around President Kennedy." After Dallas, however, "I had to play a different role, because what had existed for me then didn't exist."

---

*Kennedy had first sensed that the New Frontier was dated while campaigning for Democratic congressional candidates in 1966. "It's really very different from 1960," he told Peter Edelman. "All of those people who looked like they were having a tough time in 1960 now have cars. They can get to the rallies, you can schedule the rally in the parking lot of a shopping center and they're all very comfortable. You get the sense talking to them that the major thing they are worried about is any threat to that comfort." He added that if he could talk to them face-to-face he thought he could make them less comfortable.

The New Frontier veterans who had campaigned for JFK in 1960 and served in his administration—men like Kenny O'Donnell, Ted Sorensen, and Pierre Salinger—spent much of the campaign working in Bobby's Washington headquarters, while Dutton, Mankiewicz, and his younger Senate aides, who had a better grasp of how the country had changed since 1963, traveled with him. The more time he spent in their company, and the less with his brother's former advisers, the more he separated himself from the New Frontier. "You've got to be patient with some of these older people," he told Jim Tolan. "You know, people from the '60s and the President's campaign don't appreciate the phenomenon that's taken place."

Tolan believes that Kennedy underwent a major catharsis during the tour, struggling at first to decide whether the crowds were cheering for what his brother had done or for what he was promising to do, and finally deciding they were there for him. For Tolan, the defining moment came on March 26 as he and Kennedy were walking across the University of Washington campus to an auditorium. Suddenly, someone reached from the crowd following them, pulled off Kennedy's *PT 109* tie clasp, and ran. In the autumn of 1965, Kennedy and Tolan had been campaigning in the Bronx for the Democratic candidate for mayor when a boy had tried to remove Kennedy's *PT 109* clasp. He grabbed the boy's hand and, looking into his eyes and speaking in a soft voice, said, "Please don't take that, my brother gave it to me." Afterward, he put away the original clasp, wore a copy, and traveled with a box of spares to replace the ones he lost to crowds.

But that afternoon in Seattle, Kennedy had left his spare clasps in his hotel room. When he and Tolan reached the door to the auditorium he asked Tolan if he could borrow his *PT 109* clasp.

"I can't do that, Bobby," Tolan said.

Kennedy gave him a puzzled look. Finally, Tolan said. "Okay, I'll lend it to you. But I want it back."

Kennedy stared at him blankly for several seconds. Finally, a smile crossed his face and he said, "Okay, I get it. My brother gave it to you, right?"

"No, Bobby," Tolan replied, pausing for effect. "*You* did."

Kennedy nodded slowly several times, and his smile became a broad grin.

The Free At Last Tour ended with a two-day swing through New Mexico and Arizona. On March 31, Kennedy returned to New York from Phoenix. When the pilot announced they were approaching John F. Kennedy International Airport, AP reporter Joe Mohbat turned to Kennedy and said, "It must be quite something to land at an airport named for your brother."

"I wish it was still called Idlewild," he replied.

PART II

✦

"PROPHETS GET SHOT"

FOUR

THE ERA OF GOOD FEELINGS

MARCH 31–APRIL 4, 1968

As Robert Kennedy's plane was approaching the airport named to memorialize his late brother, President Johnson delivered a televised address during which he deprived him of his two principal issues: the unpopular Vietnam War, and the unpopular president who was stubbornly waging it.

Johnson announced that he was suspending bombing raids against North Vietnam and would seek a negotiated settlement to the war, measures Kennedy had been advocating. Then, quoting from John F. Kennedy's inaugural address, he said, "Yet, I believe that now, no less than when the decade began, this generation of Americans is willing to 'pay any price, bear any burden, meet any hardship, support any friend, oppose any foe to assure the survival and the success of liberty,'" adding that, "Since these words spoken by John F. Kennedy, the people of America have kept their compact with mankind's noblest cause"—the implication being, of course, that Robert Kennedy had not.

He concluded with the most genuinely surprising news ever conveyed in a presidential address, telling Americans, "I do not believe that I should devote an hour or a day of my time to any personal partisan causes or to any duties other than the awesome duties of this office—the Presidency of your country. . . . Accordingly, I shall not seek, and will not accept, the nomination of my party for another term as your President."

As soon as Kennedy's plane arrived at the gate, New York State Democratic chairman John Burns ran on board, shouting, "The president is not going to run! The president is not going to run!" Kennedy, stunned, fell back into his seat, asked Burns to repeat himself, then said, "You must be kidding." He and aides had discussed the possibility that Johnson might withdraw, but no one believed it was likely, or might happen so soon. Kennedy turned to *Los Angeles Times* reporter Richard Daugherty and asked if he should make a statement. Daugherty, a former Hollywood press agent, said, "You didn't actually hear what he [Johnson] said, so a wise course might be to have no comment at all for now."

As Kennedy walked through the gate Dutton murmured, "No comment . . . No comment . . ." An elderly woman waving a Kennedy poster screamed, "You're our next President! You're our next President! You're our next President!"

Perhaps as a reward for his advice, Daugherty was allowed to ride into Manhattan with Kennedy. He was undoubtedly hoping for an exclusive interview. Although he later described the atmosphere in the car as "crackling with excitement," Kennedy spent most of the ride staring silently out the window, speaking only once to say, "I wonder if he'd have done this if I hadn't come in?"

It was assumed at the time that Johnson had decided not to seek reelection because he realized that he had lost the confidence of party leaders after his poor showing in New Hampshire, and expected to suffer another humiliating setback in the April 2 Wisconsin primary. Later, it came out that he had feared that a second term might kill him, and had told Vice President Humphrey that the men in his family died young from heart disease. It also came out later that on March 18, the same day that Kennedy had been speaking in Kansas, Johnson had met to assess the war with a group of nine retired military officers and statesmen known informally as the Wise Men. The group was weighted with hawks and at its meeting in November had recommended staying the course in Vietnam. But on March 18, the Wise Men stunned Johnson by concluding that the war was unwinnable, and bombing the North and increasing American troop strength in the South would have no appreciable effect on its outcome. Their pessimistic assessment, the New Hampshire results, and Johnson's concerns about his health had undoubtedly all contributed to Johnson's decision, but Kennedy's suspicion that his own entry into the race had been the deciding factor turned out to be correct. After leaving the White House, Johnson told historian Doris Kearns Goodwin, "And then the final straw: the thing I feared from the first day of my Presidency was actually coming true. Robert Kennedy had openly announced his intention to reclaim the throne in the memory of his brother. And the American people, swayed by the magic of the name, were dancing in the streets."

Kennedy told reporters gathered outside his UN Plaza apartment building that he would issue a statement in the morning. Upstairs, an impromptu celebration was already under way. Many of Kennedy's friends and aides believed that party leaders would begin lining up behind him this evening. A few weeks earlier, Frank Mankiewicz had told Hays Gorey of *Time* that if Johnson withdrew, his delegates would go to Kennedy "in a day," and he still believed that. Kennedy's hard-nosed Senate aide Joe Dolan circulated through the apartment saying, "We can sew it [the nomination] up tonight." As John Burns left the building he told newsmen, "My personal feeling is that it means Kennedy is the next President."

Kennedy was more circumspect. He called the celebrations "premature," told Ethel to serve scotch instead of champagne, to avoid the sound of popping corks, and asked aide Milton Gwirtzman to help him dampen the euphoria. When mountaineer Jim Whittaker called with congratulations, Kennedy replied, "It isn't that easy."

Future Wisconsin governor Pat Lucey was a Kennedy volunteer in Indiana. When he heard the news, he thought, "That's it! Bob is going to be the nominee." Louis Mahern remembers the Indiana staff feeling a euphoria "bordering on giddiness." He had watched Johnson's speech in his room at the Marott Hotel in downtown Indianapolis. Ted Kennedy was next door, eating a chicken sandwich. When Johnson dropped his bombshell, Ted whooped in amazement and chunks of chicken flew across the room. He burst into Mahern's room, holding the remains of the sandwich. They tried to call Bobby's apartment, but after getting a busy signal decided to go to Mike Riley's downtown law office so they could use his multiple phone lines to call the prominent Democrats who they expected would be jumping on the Kennedy bandwagon.

They spent three hours calling conservative Midwestern senators and big-city bosses, Southern senators who hated Bobby, Northern governors who admired him, and Johnson loyalists who were hoping that Vice President Humphrey would now enter the race. They called Mayor Daley several times, and each time his aides refused to disturb him. Everyone was polite but noncommittal. Not a single governor or congressman was ready to endorse Bobby. (Within the next several days Senators Joseph Tydings [D-Md.] and Stephen Young [D-Oh.] had come out for Kennedy—scarcely the avalanche of support that many Kennedy aides had expected.) As they were returning to the Marott through downtown Indianapolis, Ted Kennedy kept saying, "What startling developments! What startling developments," and as they passed a brightly lit Dunkin' Donuts, he exclaimed, "This has been an amazing year! What more could possibly happen?"

Bobby was making similar calls, treading carefully, saying, "This obviously creates a changed situation," "I'd like to have your consideration," and, "I just hope that you don't make any commitments until I have a chance to talk to you personally." Not one influential Democrat endorsed him, and the next morning's headlines said, "Withdrawal Opens Race to Humphrey" and "Administration Supporters Now Looking to Humphrey."

The fruitless calls confirmed Kennedy's complaint that, as he told Ted Sorensen later, "I'm the only candidate who has ever united business and labor, liberals, Southerners, party bosses, and intellectuals. They're all against me." Perhaps it had been rash to place these calls so late that they woke some of their recipients, and unseemly to have made them so soon after Johnson's speech. But one could say in Kennedy's defense that he had simply succumbed to the euphoria sweeping America that evening. Members of the antiwar movement and male college students facing the draft were the most jubilant, but even middle Americans viewed Johnson's withdrawal as proof that their political system worked. The next day, editorials praised Johnson for his wisdom and courage, the stock market soared, and there was an intense moment of national happiness not unlike that following President Kennedy's inauguration, although that one had lasted several months while this would end in four days. The most dramatic manifestation of the happiness occurred on its last day, April 4, when Lyndon Johnson attended the investiture of Archbishop Cooke at St. Patrick's Cathedral. When he had visited the cathedral in December for Cardinal Spellman's funeral, the congregation had been silent and cold, but this time he received a standing ovation.

THE NEXT MORNING, Robert Kennedy held a previously scheduled press conference at the Overseas Press Club. He began by reading aloud the obsequious telegram that he had just sent to President Johnson. It praised Johnson's withdrawal as "truly magnanimous," and "respectfully and earnestly" requested a meeting to discuss how they could work together in the interest of national unity. He then read a prepared statement praising Johnson for his "courage and generosity of spirit." One reporter described him as "dazed." More likely, he was uncomfortable and embarrassed. Asked what issues he would stress now that Johnson was out of the race and Vietnam seemed on its way to being settled, he suddenly came alive, saying in a strong and confident voice: "the crisis of our cities, the tension among our races, the complexities of a society at once so rich and so deprived."

A few hours later, Jim Stevenson rode with him to a meeting in Brooklyn. After flipping through some magazines, exchanging a few words with the other passengers, and waving at a cabbie on the East River Drive who had shouted "Give it to 'em, Bobby!" Kennedy spent the rest of the trip staring out the window. "He abandons, piece by piece, the outside world—puts away the magazines, the cigar is forgotten, the offer of gum is unheard, and he is utterly alone," Stevenson wrote. "His silence is not passive; it is intense, and it is interesting to watch Kennedy's face—only half seen—as he does nothing, is alone with himself. His face, close-up, is structurally hard: there is no waste, nothing left over and not put to use; everything has been enlisted in the cause, whatever it may be."

The cause on April 1 was the obvious one of adjusting to the new political landscape. Words like *rudderless* and *floundering* have been used to describe Kennedy's campaign between March 31 and April 4. "It's hard to get it all going again," he complained in private. "Here you were in a fight you knew was right. Then in one night it was gone." When his Senate aide Carter Burden drove him to the airport for a flight to Philadelphia on April 1, Kennedy struck Burden as strangely subdued and Burden had the impression that he believed that Johnson's withdrawal might rob his campaign of its emotion and fun.

Losing Vietnam as an issue troubled Kennedy the most. He told his friend the columnist Art Buchwald that he had been counting on it to win the nomination, and was now in "a lot of trouble."

Throughout his brother's administration, Kennedy had supported the increase in U.S. financial and military support to the government of South Vietnam. By November 1963 the number of American military advisers in Vietnam had risen to over sixteen thousand, but JFK had refused to bomb North Vietnam or send American ground combat forces into battle in the south. In March 1965, President Johnson abandoned this cautious policy. Bobby had viewed Johnson's escalation as a departure from JFK's strategy, and during a private meeting at the White House in April urged him to reverse course and suspend the bombing. In July, he had given a speech voicing his first public criticism of Johnson's policy, declaring that "victory in a political war is not won by escalation, but by de-escalation" and that "the essence of counter-insurgency is not to kill, but to bring the insurgent back into the national life." By the winter of 1968, he was calling for negotiations, a suspension of the bombing, and the South Vietnamese troops shouldering more of the fighting. In public, he opposed an immediate withdrawal of U.S. forces, but privately he told newsmen who had covered combat operations in Vietnam, "When I'm President, we're out of Vietnam, immediately. You guys won't have to go back."

Reminders that Kennedy had suddenly lost the Vietnam War as an issue filled his daily press digest. The *Baltimore Sun* praised Johnson's peace initiative as "a move of major consequence" and the *Chicago Sun-Times* said Hanoi's response warranted "cautious optimism."

Kennedy reacted to the news by falling back on what Jack Newfield called "the old politics of blarney and accommodation." At a late afternoon rally in Camden, New Jersey, on April 1, he made a blatant pitch for Johnson's supporters, praising him lavishly for having sacrificed personal considerations "to win the peace for which all men yearn." At a Democratic dinner in Philadelphia on April 2, he offered encomiums to Mayor James Tate, a boss who was in Hubert Humphrey's pocket and had recently called Kennedy a "wise guy." He praised Tate's accomplishments in a speech echoing JFK's historic "Ich bin ein Berliner" oration, saying "Let them come to Philadelphia!" instead of "Let them come to Berlin!" Despite the groveling, neither Tate nor the other machine politicians sharing the dais with Kennedy endorsed him.

During a White House "unity meeting" on April 3, Kennedy congratulated Johnson on a "magnificent" speech. But when he tried saying, "You are a brave and dedicated man, Mr. President," the words were so contrary to what he believed—he had once called Johnson "mean, bitter, vicious—an animal in many ways," who "lies continuously, about everything"—that they stuck in his throat and he had to repeat them. If one had to choose the lowest, most dishonest moment of Bobby's campaign, this would be it.

No one can know what Kennedy was thinking as he stared silently out of those car windows during these four days. But he was too astute a politician not to realize that the two issues he had lost—the Vietnam War and the Johnson presidency—had also been difficult ones for him: Vietnam, because no matter how frequent and heartfelt his mea culpas, he could never escape his responsibility for America's initial involvement in the conflict; and Johnson, because his own brother had chosen him to be his running mate. But he was also astute enough to appreciate that Johnson's departure had suddenly freed him to do what he had promised when announcing his candidacy—"propose new policies" rather than "oppose one man."

During the press breakfast in January when he had declared that he would not challenge Johnson under any "foreseeable circumstances," he had also told reporters, "If someone could appeal to the generous spirit of Americans to heal the race question, [then] this is what the campaign should be about." Now with Johnson and the war off the table, he could do just that. In fact, the campaign that he relaunched on April 4 would be another Free At Last Tour since, freed at last from Vietnam and

Johnson, he could concentrate on race, poverty, and sacrifice. These issues, ones he had championed in the Senate, were more important than a single wounded presidency or calamitous war. They engaged him so deeply because he had learned about them through experience instead of briefing papers, through his heart rather than his mind.

He had become an advocate for Native Americans after visiting their forlorn reservations as a U.S. senator and discovering that their school libraries lacked books about Indian history and culture. He had become a hero to Chicano farmworkers after participating in hearings held by a Senate subcommittee on their attempts to form a union. He began championing the urban poor after tramping through tenements in Harlem and Bedford-Stuyvesant, questioning gang members in Harlem, and meeting a young Puerto Rican girl whose face had been disfigured by rat bites. He became determined to improve the living conditions of migrant laborers after touring a camp outside Rochester, New York, where the workers and their families lived in abandoned school buses lacking running water or toilets. In one bus he had found a dozen children lying on filthy mattresses, their stomachs bloated by malnutrition. Before leaving, he announced that he was going to sponsor legislation to prohibit camps like this one. As he was being driven away, he told aide Jerry Bruno, "This is why you go into politics, because you can use your position to help people in trouble," and Bruno saw tears welling in his eyes.

He added Third World poverty to his causes after visiting South America in November 1965. By the time he reached Brazil's impoverished northeast, he had already been moved by the suffering he had seen in Peru and Chile. After attending mass in Salvador on the second anniversary of his brother's assassination, he walked through a seaside slum where the stench from open sewers was so nauseating that his Brazilian security detail retreated to their cars. At a community center named for his late brother he told an audience of barefoot children, "President Kennedy was most fond of children. Can I ask you to do a favor for him? Stay in school, study hard . . . and then work for your city and Brazil." Then, during a four-hour motorcade through the jammed streets of Natal, he kept shouting, "Every child an education! Every family adequate housing! Every man a job!"

His most shattering encounter with poverty came when he traveled to the Mississippi Delta in April 1967 on a congressional subcommittee investigating reports of starvation among black sharecroppers thrown out of work by the mechanization of the cotton industry. After listening to a day of testimony, he visited the homes of destitute blacks in Cleveland, Mississippi. Reporters remained outside the shacks at his request, so there are no press accounts or photographs, only the recollections of aide Peter Edelman and Marian Wright of the NAACP Legal Defense Fund, who accompanied him inside.

In a windowless shack reeking of mildew and urine he came upon a mother and six children. A malnourished two-year-old girl with a distended stomach lay sprawled on the floor, surrounded by roaches and playing listlessly with a grain of rice. He knelt down and began stroking her hair and murmuring, "Hello . . . Hi, baby . . ." Realizing that she was too weak with hunger to respond, he gathered her into his arms and began rocking and kissing her. (Marian Wright admitted that she could not have picked up that filthy child, and it was then, she decided, that Kennedy was "for real.") Moments later, a little boy toddled into the room. Kennedy sat next to him on a grimy bed. As he rubbed the boy's distended stomach tears streamed down his cheeks. Kennedy's active moral imagination meant that his response to suffering like this went beyond pity and outrage. It meant, according to Cesar Chavez, that Kennedy "could see things through the eyes of the poor." And so he imagined *himself* living in one of those tenements, abandoned school buses, or Appalachian hollows, and even more important for a man who loved and prized children, he imagined his own children bitten by rats, attending the crummy reservation schools, or starving in Mississippi.

Kennedy returned to Virginia to find his children at the dinner table. "In Mississippi a whole family lives in a shack the size of this room," he said. "The children are covered with sores and their tummies stick out because they have no food. Do you *know* how *lucky* you are? Do something for your country."

The next morning he met with Secretary of Agriculture Orville Freeman and demanded that the Department of Agriculture begin immediately distributing food stamps for free, instead of requiring the destitute to purchase them for a nominal sum that was beyond their reach. Then he flew to New York and stopped at the apartment of his aide Carter Burden. When Burden's wife, Amanda, opened the door, he grabbed her by the shoulders and said, "You don't know what I saw! I have done nothing in my life! Everything I have done was a waste! Everything I have done was worthless!"

The starving children of Cleveland, Mississippi, shocked Robert Kennedy more than anything since his brother's assassination. He may have run for the Senate in 1964 to memorialize his brother and continue his legacy, but he entered the presidential race in 1968 to end the Vietnam War and the kind of suffering he had witnessed in Mississippi.

In the Senate, Kennedy had addressed poverty with the same ferocity that he formerly brought to the task of eliminating Fidel Castro. Because he had arrived at the issue of poverty through emotion instead of ideology, his proposals were nonideological. He was suspicious of welfare because he thought it robbed the individual of self-respect and a place in the community. He believed that the government could not improve inner-city neighborhoods without the participation of their inhabitants, that poverty programs should be designed and administered by community organizations, that jobs were crucial, and that the most effective way of creating them in poor communities was through a partnership between local people and private enterprise.

No Northern state appeared to be less promising for a campaign focusing on poverty and racial justice than Indiana, where Kennedy would contest his first primary. Its southern counties had sympathized with the Confederacy, and during the 1920s the Ku Klux Klan enrolled more members than in any other state. Since World War II, Indiana had lagged behind other Northern states in prohibiting discrimination in employment, housing, and public accommodation. Its cities had large populations of blue-collar workers from Eastern Europe and Appalachia who lived in close physical and economic proximity to blacks, felt threatened by their progress, and had given George Wallace 30 percent of the state's vote in the 1964 Democratic primary, his best showing in the North. John F. Kennedy had lost Indiana to Nixon by ten percentage points in 1960, and eight years later, only one of the state's hundred Democratic leaders who had backed JFK was endorsing Bobby.

Even more troubling, Bobby found himself in a three-way primary contest with Senator Eugene McCarthy and Governor Roger Branigin, a Harvard-educated attorney who played the Hoosier hick and had outfitted his campaign headquarters to resemble a country store. Branigin was running as a favorite son, and had initially entered the race as a stand-in for Johnson. He was now standing in for Johnson's vice president, Hubert Humphrey, whose candidacy had become a foregone conclusion. Branigin had won the statehouse by the largest plurality in Indiana history, controlled a patronage machine that forced twenty thousand appointed state officeholders to kick back 2 percent of their salaries to the Democratic Party, and enjoyed the support of the business community, the unions, all but one of ninety-two Democratic county leaders, and the conservative *Indianapolis Star*, whose headline declaring that Kennedy was "Unfit, Unshorn, Unwanted," was a preview of how it would cover the primary.

Branigin was presumed to be strong in rural areas and small cities, and McCarthy had a lock on the university towns and suburbs. Kennedy could count on black voters, but they only comprised 6 percent of the population. To win the primary he would have to win over the blue-collar whites who had supported Wallace—a tall order for someone viewed as the most popular leader among black Americans after Martin Luther King Jr. The state's Democratic congressmen had warned Kennedy that Branigin was certain to defeat McCarthy, and would probably beat Kennedy, too. One influential Hoosier supporter urged him to skip the primary and let McCarthy take the defeat. A poll taken just before Johnson withdrew showed Branigin leading with 42 percent, Kennedy with 35 percent, and McCarthy with 20 percent. A private poll commissioned by Kennedy at the beginning of April had him running slightly ahead of McCarthy and slightly behind Branigin.

Had Kennedy ducked Indiana, it would have been viewed as an admission that he could not appeal to working-class whites. He had to run, and because Indiana was his first primary, he had to win it. Yet he rejected two deals that would have appreciably improved his chances.

In late March, Ted Kennedy and David Burke met in a Chicago hotel with Gordon St. Angelo, Indiana's Democratic chairman. St. Angelo told them that he and Branigin's wife were trying to dissuade Branigin from running as a favorite son. Then, as Burke remembered it, St. Angelo implied that his arguments with Branigin would have more weight if Kennedy would agree to make St. Angelo the Democratic national chairman. St. Angelo's proposition was the kind of horse-trading that is common in primary politics, but Kennedy refused the deal, perhaps because St. Angelo was manifestly unqualified to serve as national chairman.

A second offer came from the Teamsters. A union official asked Ted Kennedy what the Teamsters "could expect" for their former president Jimmy Hoffa in exchange for their support. Hoffa was serving time in a federal prison after being convicted of multiple felonies by the Kennedy Justice Department. The official proposed that Kennedy ask the current attorney general, Ramsey Clark, to move Hoffa from the prison mattress factory to the prison farm so he could spend more time outdoors. When Ted Kennedy and David Burke relayed the offer to Bobby, who suspected Hoffa might have had a role in his brother's assassination, he said, "What you can do is, you go back to your fellow from the Teamsters and you tell him that I will not speak to Ramsey Clark. As far as I'm concerned Jimmy Hoffa can stay in the mattress factory forever. And if I'm ever elected President of the United States, he has a darn slim chance of ever getting out of jail."*

Kennedy's briefing papers described Indiana as an "anti-politician, anti-government, anti-taxation, anti-big-city, and anti-Catholic" state where the American Legion had its headquarters and the Ku Klux Klan had its national headquarters during the 1920s and was still active. The most encouraging memorandum came from John Bartlow Martin, who called his fellow Hoosiers "suspicious of foreign entanglements, conservative in fiscal policy, and with a strong overlay of Southern segregationist sentiment." But Martin also thought that they might support "a new and strong and hopeful leader in a time of trouble," and recommended that Kennedy "favor civil rights but oppose disorder." He reported that canvassers in Hammond, a white backlash

---

*In 1971, President Nixon commuted Hoffa's sentence and he was released from prison.

city in Lake County, had found former Wallace voters were leaning toward Kennedy. They knew he favored blacks, but considered him "a strong executive capable of controlling disorders."

Kennedy invited Martin to write speeches for him and accompany him to Indiana on April 4. When Martin boarded the chartered flight to South Bend he was shocked by the gray in Kennedy's hair and the lines in his face, and thought, "He has suddenly lost his boyishness."

During the flight, Kennedy told Martin that he wanted simple speeches, not like the ones that Martin had written for Adlai Stevenson. He asked him to write a foreign policy speech for his appearance at Louisiana State the next day, and Martin showed him a speech that he had already submitted to the campaign. Kennedy decided to use it and, moments after asking Martin to avoid Stevensonian speeches, said he particularly liked the passage quoting Adlai Stevenson that self-criticism was "the secret weapon of democracy." He told him to give the quotation to Jeff Greenfield with instructions to incorporate it into the speech he was delivering at Notre Dame. But because Martin did not know Greenfield by appearance, he handed the quotation to Adam Walinsky instead. Walinsky, incredulous that Robert Kennedy would want to quote Adlai Stevenson, left the passage out. Kennedy chewed Walinsky out afterward, an incident prompting Martin to observe, "This campaign promised to be like the others I'd been through." It was also a preview of the coming weeks, when Martin would spar with younger and more liberal aides over how much Kennedy should adjust his message to appeal to a conservative Hoosier electorate, a dispute presaging decades of similar sparring between liberals and centrists, and purists and triangulators within the Democratic Party.

ONE LOOKS FOR omens on a day like April 4, 1968, but the sound track recorded by the film crew accompanying Kennedy on his charter flight to South Bend contains only the routine conversations, clicking typewriter keys, and cheering airport crowds of any campaign flight. Instead, the omens were in Memphis, where Martin Luther King Jr. had told an audience at the Masonic Temple the day before, "Like anybody, I would love to live a long life. Longevity has its place. But

I'm not concerned about that now. . . . I'm not worried about anything. I'm not fearing any man," and they were in Indianapolis, where FBI agent Angelo Lano warned his superiors that the Kennedy rallies scheduled for April 4 "might be subject to some violence simply to embarrass Senator Kennedy." Lano also informed local police that a Jid Kaler of Detroit had called Kennedy headquarters in Washington on April 2 and threatened Kennedy's life. Kaler had spent the night of April 3 at a motel forty miles northeast of Indianapolis before vanishing.

While Kennedy was en route to South Bend, Mayor Richard Lugar of Indianapolis summoned Mike Riley to City Hall and demanded that he cancel a Kennedy rally scheduled for that evening, arguing that the neighborhood was too dangerous for police to guarantee Kennedy's safety. When Riley refused, Lugar threatened to order his fire department to lay hoses across streets to prevent automobiles from entering the area. "Then we'll tell people to walk," Riley replied. Lugar called a press conference and urged Kennedy to cancel the rally. Jim Tolan, who had advanced the event, was astonished to hear the mayor of an American city admitting that his police force could not protect a presidential candidate.

Kennedy launched his Indiana campaign with a speech at Notre Dame titled "Feeding America's Hungry." It was certain to be reported across the state, but contained nothing to appeal to the backlash whites or fiscal conservatives who were leaning to Branigin, nothing about Vietnam to appeal to potential McCarthy supporters, and no pandering to Hoosier pride, just a catalog of the sufferings of people living on distant Indian reservations and in distant sharecropper shacks.

Kennedy told the students, "This is the most affluent nation the world has ever known. This nation—our nation—has a food-producing capacity unrivaled in the history of the world. Yet, in the midst of our great affluence, children—American children—are hungry, some to the point where their minds and bodies are damaged beyond repair. I have seen, in the Mississippi Delta and on Indian reservations, children who eat only one meal a day—one meal of bread and gravy, or grits, or rice and beans." To end the disgrace of children "with bloated bellies and sores of disease on their bodies," he called for changes in the food stamp program, the emergency purchase and distribution of surplus food, and demanded that the government "fund the employment of men who cannot find work." If we cannot prevent our fellow citizens from starving, he said, "We must ask ourselves what kind of a country we really are; we must ask ourselves what we really stand for."

During the question period, he returned to his theme of national redemption through good works, of healing the wounds that Vietnam had inflicted on the national soul by eliminating hunger and poverty. He said, "It is for us to turn this country to a path of honor, not through arms or wealth or force [but] by finding our own satisfaction in the conduct of our country," and asked, "What other reason do we have really for [our] existence as human beings unless we've made some other contribution to somebody else to improve their own lives?"

He continued to Ball State University in Muncie on a smaller chartered plane, leaving most of his staff and press to fly on to Indianapolis. Ten thousand students packed the floor, balconies, and bleachers of the Ball State Gymnasium. They gave him a reception that a Muncie newspaper described as "frenzied," but was less so than the one at Kansas State, perhaps because Vietnam suddenly seemed less urgent.

He told them that with Vietnam seemingly "on the way to being settled," they needed to ask themselves, "What kind of help and how much should we give to the underdeveloped nations of the world?" and "What kind of programs can we develop to build a better America here at home for people who lead lives of desperation?"

For thirty minutes, in a speech that would be largely ignored because of what happened later that evening, Kennedy spoke more passionately about poverty than ever before. In his speech at the Greek Theater in Los Angeles on March 25, he had promised Americans a way to reclaim "the ideals which are the source of national strength and generosity and compassion of deed." At Ball State, he told them they would accomplish this by participating in an effort to lift their fellow citizens out of poverty.

An audiotape shows him pleading with the Ball State students as if his campaign, and their nation's future, depended on their becoming as outraged by poverty as he was.

He begged them to "decide what obligation we have to other people on the globe" and to examine "how we can help the millions of our fellow citizens who lead lives of hopelessness and poverty where, as Sophocles said, 'day follows day with death the only goal.'"

He told them that seven out of ten children died before their tenth birthday in Latin America, and that for many African children every living moment was filled with disease. He encouraged them to imagine themselves growing up as one of these children, saying, "These men and women and children that we hear about and that I'm talking about here, they're not statistics, they are human beings whom I have seen . . . each with a right to live a life of dignity and purpose just as much as you and I have."

He urged them to do something about the sufferings he had described. "What really is our purpose in life?" he asked. "For all the advantages we have, don't we have a major responsibility and an obligation to those who do not have those advantages? Don't we have a major responsibility? Not the government of the United States, but the individuals have a major responsibility."

He told them that every American bore a personal responsibility for the Vietnam War. "You cannot point to others and say, 'This is their choice; this is not my responsibility,' For when elected or appointed government officials act . . . they act in your name. When they conduct a war . . . they do so for your future and really in the name of the American people."

He connected their responsibility to specific events in Vietnam, mentioning the American officer who said it had been necessary to destroy the town of Ban Tre in order to save it, and telling them, "Now he wasn't saying that for himself; he was saying it also for you. And he was saying it for the American people. . . . These are moral problems, they're security problems. They're problems for all of you, for all of us as American citizens."

Then, concerned he still had not reached them, he spoke about Mississippi. "Here in America there are children so underfed and so undernourished that many of them are crippled for life in mind and body before the age of three . . . children who are starving to death—not malnutrition—actually starving to death. . . . I've seen them with extended stomachs, with faces covered with sores of starvation."

After describing "families in ghettoes [who] huddle ten to a room fighting off the night terrors of cold and rats" and "young men on Indian reservations so filled with despair and the bitter prospects ahead that the leading cause of death among teenagers in many tribal areas in the United States is suicide," he returned to Mississippi. "I have seen these children. . . . We don't speak of statistics, numbers. We speak of *human beings*," he implored. "We speak of a child who will never walk properly; who will never work and learn and raise a family because of *our* indifference."

The psychologist Robert Coles once observed that Kennedy had a tentative way of moving and speaking. He thought it indicated "a man who has a lot to say, but isn't quite sure how to say it; who has a lot stirring in him but doesn't know how to put it into words; who has a lot of emotional things happening to him."

Kennedy's Ball State speech was full of repetitions, pauses, and "ums" and "ahs." He appeared to be thinking out loud, asking the audience to help him find a solution. "Only three out of ten students graduate from ghetto high schools. No jobs. No employment. So what would you do? What should they do?" he demanded. "Seventeen thousand people bitten by rats every year. What would you do? Only forty percent of men who live in the ghetto have jobs paying more than $65 a week. How can you support a family on that?"

After speaking for thirty-four minutes he spent almost as long answering the students' questions.

The first came from a student who accused him of "telling jokes" and "double talking," but not offering any specific solutions. When the gymnasium erupted in boos, Kennedy said, "He's perfectly entitled to disagree with me and that's the only way we're going to make progress in this country—if people stand up and speak their minds."

Asked about the draft, he said he wanted a professional army, believed the draft was "inequitable and unfair," supported a lottery system that would treat everyone equally, and was opposed to student deferments because they favored the wealthy who could afford a college education. He reminded them that "it's the poor that have to carry the burden of the war," and asked, "Can you really defend draft deferments for students on a moral basis?"

A stocky young man, one of only twenty black students in the Ball State audience, stood up in the balcony and said, "Mr. Kennedy, I agree with the programs and proposals you are making. But in order for them to work, you're placing a great deal of faith in white America. My question: Is this faith justified?"

"Yes!" Kennedy said, in a loud and confident voice. "I'm also placing faith in black America." He pointed out that there were extremists on both sides and insisted that only a small minority of whites opposed treating blacks equally, that "the vast majority of [the] American people want to do the decent and right thing here within our country."

As he was responding to these questions, Dr. Martin Luther King Jr. stepped onto the second-story balcony of the Lorraine Motel in Memphis and was shot by an assassin firing a high-powered rifle from the bathroom of a nearby flophouse. Three of King's associates rushed onto the balcony and pointed toward the flophouse. As Justice Department official James Laue knelt down and pressed a towel against the wound in King's right cheek, trying to stanch the bleeding, he thought, "Kennedy . . . Kennedy . . . Kennedy," the Kennedy in question being John F. Kennedy.

AS ROBERT KENNEDY was preparing to board his plane at the Muncie airport, a teenage boy asked if he had heard about Dr. King.

"Was he shot?" Kennedy asked quickly, proving that the danger of an assassination was never far from his mind.

"He's in critical condition."

Marshall Hanley, the Muncie attorney who had introduced Kennedy at Ball State, heard the news on a police radio and gave Kennedy more details as he was boarding the plane.

Kennedy stared at the ground and asked, "Is he dead?"

"Wounded," Hanley said.

After takeoff, Kennedy moved seats so he could sit next to John Lindsay of *Newsweek*. Lindsay had also been sitting alongside him when they landed in Manchester, New Hampshire, in 1966 and learned that Ethel Kennedy's brother, George Skakel, had been killed in a plane crash. Kennedy told Lindsay he was upset at having just told the black student at Ball State to have faith in white Americans, "then I walk out and find that some white man has shot their spiritual leader." (An early NBC radio news bulletin from Memphis, presumably relayed to Kennedy by Hanley, reported that people were searching for a white man who had fled the scene.) He knew what Mrs. King and her children were going through, he said, confirming Lindsay's suspicion that King's assassination was forcing Bobby to relive his brother's.

While Kennedy's plane was en route to Indianapolis, physicians at St. Joseph's Hospital in Memphis pronounced King dead. Jim Tolan was awaiting Kennedy's arrival at Weir-Cook Airport in Indianapolis when Pierre Salinger called on his mobile phone with the news. Tolan telephoned John Nolan in Washington, who reported that Burke Marshall and Joe Dolan were recommending that Kennedy issue a statement at the airport and cancel his appearances. Disturbances were already breaking out in Memphis, and they feared someone might shoot him in revenge.

Tolan called Walter Sheridan, who was at the rally site at Seventeenth Street and Broadway with two black Kennedy staffers, John Lewis and Earl Graves Jr. Lewis and Graves had just circulated through the crowd and believed that most people were unaware of the assassination. Lewis argued that Kennedy had to attend, saying, "You can't have a crowd like this come, and something like this happen, and send them home without anything at all. Kennedy has to speak, for his own sake and for the sake of these people."

Richard Harwood boarded Kennedy's plane after it landed and gave him the news. Kennedy's face went blank and he jerked his head backward, as if the bullet had struck him, too. Then he covered his face with his hands and murmured, "Oh God, when is this violence going to stop."

Chicago Sun-Times reporter Dave Murray, who witnessed this, said later, "It was unbearable to watch him [and] to know that he was thinking about his brother."

Tolan boarded the plane to find Kennedy "shook, really shook," more disturbed than he had ever seen him.

Kennedy asked Tolan about his schedule.

"You have two stops. One is to open your headquarters, and the second is at Seventeenth and Broadway in the middle of the worst part of the black ghetto." He presented Kennedy with three options: canceling both events and driving directly to the Marott Hotel, sending someone in his place to the rally to read a statement, or going himself.

"I'm going to Seventeenth and Broadway," Kennedy said. "I'm going there and that's it, and I don't want any police going in with me."

Once the others had disembarked, Kennedy asked Frank Mankiewicz what he should say.

"You should give a very short speech," Mankiewicz replied. "It should be almost a prayer."

Kennedy sat alone in the plane for several minutes. When he emerged he was wearing his dead brother's topcoat and his eyes were moist. He stood on the tarmac and, in a voice close to breaking, said, "Dr. King dedicated himself to justice and love between fellow human beings. He gave his life for that principle and I think it's up to those of us who are here to end the divisions which exist so deeply in our country, and to remove the stain of bloodshed from our land."

Indianapolis police chief Winston Churchill urged Kennedy to cancel the rally. He warned that riots were certain to erupt in the city, adding, "It's not safe for you to go there."

"I could take my wife and family and we could sleep in the middle of the street at Seventeenth and Broadway and there would be no problem," Kennedy replied. "If you can't do that, it's your problem."

Before leaving the airport, Kennedy walked his wife to a waiting car, put her in the backseat, and told Bill Gigerich, a young campaign volunteer, "Stay with her until I get to the hotel." Gigerich would often escort Ethel around the state in the coming weeks, and remembers her being a lively and talkative companion, except on April 4. "She did not say more than five words during the drive," he recalls. "I think she was praying."

As Kennedy was being driven to the rally he stared out the window and scribbled some notes on a sheet of yellow legal paper. He spoke only once, asking Dutton, "What do you think I should say?"

FIVE

A PRAYER FOR OUR COUNTRY

APRIL 4–5, 1968

Two groups of people, numbering around three thousand in all, awaited Robert Kennedy at the small neighborhood park at Seventeenth and Broadway. The first was comprised of those who had arrived early and were gathered close to the flatbed truck that would serve as his dais, and contained most of the small number of whites in the audience. Many in this group were already supporters and wore Kennedy buttons and carried Kennedy signs. Because he was running late, they had arrived before King was shot and had not heard the news. The second group consisted of people who had poured into the streets after learning of King's death. They had surrounded those standing near the truck and were growing more numerous by the minute. Some wanted to share their grief with their neighbors, but others, like the Ten Percenters, an organization of young black militants, hoped to incite a riot. Among those in this second crowd were people like nineteen-year-old Darlene Howard, who had been trying to flee the neighborhood before violence erupted, but found herself swept up by the crowds heading to the rally. She saw guns and knives, heard chains clanging, smelled fumes from gasoline hurriedly poured into bottles and cans, and became convinced, she says, that, "the black people in this neighborhood were going to burn the city down."

There was tension along the border between those in the black crowd who knew about the assassination and the whites who did not, and some heard shouts of "What are you doing here, Whitey?" and "Get out of here you white son-of-a-bitch!" A black woman grabbed a white pastor by the arm and cried, "Dr. King is dead and a white man did it, why does he [Kennedy] have to come here?"

The rally's organizers became increasingly nervous that Kennedy would be attacked. They decided against announcing King's death over a loudspeaker, instructed the band to keep playing, and told some men to climb trees and watch the surrounding buildings for snipers. A contingent of black plainclothes police officers had also infiltrated the crowd, and two police marksmen were stationed on the roof of the nearby Broadway Christian Center.

Had Kennedy known that some in the crowd were armed, he would have been even more determined to address the rally. After Dallas, he had embraced risk. He copied Emerson's "always do what you are afraid to do" into his daybook, and dove into piranha-infested waters in Brazil, faced a rhinoceros at twenty feet in Africa, and rafted through treacherous rapids. Like JFK, he considered moral courage more difficult to demonstrate than physical courage. In 1966, he had told students in South Africa that moral courage was "a rarer commodity than bravery in battle or great intelligence," and extolled it as "the one essential, vital quality of those who seek to change a world which yields most painfully to change," saying, "Each time a man stands up for an ideal, or acts to improve the lot of others, or strikes out against injustice he sends forth a tiny ripple of hope, and crossing each other from a million different centers of energy and daring those ripples build a current which can sweep down the mightiest walls of oppression and resistance." Now, in Indianapolis, he could demonstrate both kinds of courage: the physical courage to address a predominantly black audience two hours after a white man had murdered the most beloved black leader in U.S. history, and the moral courage to announce his death and deliver a speech offering comfort and hope.

JOHN MARTIN, JEFF Greenfield, and Adam Walinsky had all flown to Indianapolis directly from South Bend. They learned of King's death while dining in the Marott Hotel with the television personality Jack Paar, who was scheduled to interview Kennedy later that evening. They discussed whether Kennedy should attend the rally, and Martin later asked a police inspector who was sitting in a squad car in the hotel driveway what he thought. "I sure hope he goes," the policeman said, "If he doesn't, there'll be hell to pay. He's the only one who can do it." Walinsky had jotted down some ideas for a speech, and persuaded the inspector to drive him to the rally. They stopped on the way at Kennedy campaign headquarters and picked up Joan Braden, an Honorary Kennedy from California who had assisted in organizing the event.

Braden and Walinsky arrived moments before Kennedy. As Walinsky headed for the platform, Braden climbed onto the hood of a car parked at the edge of the crowd. Those surrounding her knew about the assassination and spoke in low voices. She looked up and saw people leaning from tenement windows, watching silently as Kennedy's car arrived. Kennedy motioned for her to join him on the platform. "No, there's no room up there. Just go," she shouted. As he climbed onto the flatbed truck, those surrounding it cheered and waved his signs.

Mankiewicz gave Kennedy a sheet of paper containing ideas for his speech. Kennedy put it in his pocket without looking at it. When Walinsky approached the dais with his notes, Kennedy waved him off. After asking the dignitaries on the platform not to introduce him, he stood alone at the microphone, looking drawn and shaken.

The night was cool, in the upper thirties, and a light rain fell. A single spotlight swept the leaden sky, and two floodlights mounted on poles waved in a gusty wind, leaving most of the crowd in the shadows. It was so dark that *Life* photographer Bill Eppridge, who disliked using a strobe light, was unable to shoot.

As Kennedy began speaking, a man jumped onto the hood of the car where Braden was standing and grabbed her hand. She looked down to see that the hand gripping her own was black. "Fear was palpable. . . . It hung in the air, a warning of an event about to happen," she said later. "The man who had his hand over mine knew it and I knew it and Bobby knew it as he spoke."

Before starting, Kennedy asked one of the dignitaries on the platform, "Do they know about Martin Luther King?"

"To some extent," someone replied, adding, "We've left that up to you."

Kennedy began by saying, "I'm only going to talk to you for a minute or so this evening because I have some very sad news for all of you."

Some of those standing near the truck, ignoring or misconstruing his somber words, continued to cheer and wave signs.

He asked them to lower their signs, then said in a trembling voice, "I have some very sad news for all of you and I think some sad news for all of our fellow citizens and people who love peace all over the world. And that is that Martin Luther King was shot and was killed tonight in Memphis, Tennessee."

The next moment reminded one witness of the instant before a lightning bolt strikes, or after an artillery shell bursts, when the air seems to have been sucked out of a place. The crowd gave up a huge moan, an "Oooh" so loud that a woman driving two blocks away wondered what Kennedy had said to produce such a reaction. Then men cursed and women screamed and fell to their knees, praying and weeping. There were shouts of "Oh, Jesus!" and "No!" Some young men on the fringes of the crowd stormed away; others pumped their fists in the air and chanted "Black Power!"

Kennedy had promised to talk "for a minute or so." He could have easily done that, following his announcement of King's death with a brief eulogy, and asking everyone to return home and pray. Delivering a longer speech was a gamble. If he offended this audience he could damage his reputation with his most loyal constituency. But even if his speech was pitch-perfect, if there were riots in Indianapolis that evening, he would be blamed for inciting them.

The speech he had prepared for this occasion contained lines such as, "The gulf between the races seems to be widening," and "We face rising crime, assassination of leaders, riots, looting and burning." He could easily have adapted them to the occasion. Instead, he spoke extemporaneously for almost seven minutes.

On June 11, 1963, when JFK had suddenly decided to deliver a televised address to the nation on civil rights after ordering the Alabama National Guard to protect two black students who were attempting to enroll at the University of Alabama, he had only a few hours to prepare his speech. Bobby had urged him to speak extemporaneously, arguing that an impromptu speech would be more effective than a prepared one. JFK had compromised, scribbling some thoughts on the back of an envelope and glancing briefly at a speech that Ted Sorensen had handed him minutes before air time. He told Americans they were "confronted by a moral issue . . . as old as the Scripture and as clear as the American Constitution," and the speech is considered one of the finest of his presidency (although on reflection Bobby thought that if it had been purely extemporaneous, it would have been as good or better). Now Bobby was about to do what he had urged on his brother, although with much less preparation, and under far more trying circumstances.

At first, he spoke haltingly and deliberately, repeating phrases and words, as if groping for the most fitting, pausing after one sentence to compose the next. His voice was hollow, close to breaking, and tears welled in his eyes. The wind tangled his hair and the spotlights made him look pallid and haunted. The crowd, noisy and fretful at first, quieted and drew closer to the platform as he said:

> Martin Luther King dedicated his life to love and to justice between fellow human beings. He died in the cause of that effort. In this difficult day, in this difficult time for the United States, it's perhaps well to ask what kind of a nation we are and what direction we want to move in. For those of you who are black—considering the evidence evidently is that there were white people who were responsible—you can be filled with bitterness, and with hatred, and a desire for revenge.
>
> We can move in that direction as a country, in greater polarization—black people amongst blacks, and white people amongst whites, filled with hatred toward one another. Or we can make an effort, as Martin Luther King did, to understand, and to comprehend, and replace that violence, that stain of bloodshed that has spread across our land, with an effort to understand, compassion and love.

For those of you who are black and are tempted to be filled with hatred and mistrust of the injustice of such an act, against all white people, I would only say that I can also feel in my own heart the same kind of feeling. I had a member of my family killed, but he was killed by a white man. But we have to make an effort in the United States, we have to make an effort to understand, to get beyond, or go beyond these rather difficult times.

My favorite poem, my favorite poet was Aeschylus. And he once wrote: "Even in our sleep, pain which cannot forget / falls drop by drop upon the heart, / until, in our own despair, / against our will, / comes wisdom / through the awful grace of God."

What we need in the United States is not division; what we need in the United States is not hatred; what we need in the United States is not violence and lawlessness, but is love and wisdom, and compassion toward one another, and a feeling of justice toward those who suffer within our country, whether they be white or whether they be black.

So I ask you tonight to return home, to say a prayer for the family of Martin Luther King—yeah, it's true—but more importantly to say a prayer for our own country, which all of us love—a prayer for understanding and that compassion of which I spoke.

We can do well in this country. We will have difficult times. We've had difficult times in the past. And we will have difficult times in the future. It is not the end of violence; it is not the end of lawlessness; and it's not the end of disorder.

But the vast majority of white people and the vast majority of black people in this country want to live together, want to improve the quality of our life, and want justice for all human beings that abide in our land.

Let us dedicate ourselves to what the Greeks wrote so many years ago: to tame the savageness of man and make gentle the life of this world. Let us dedicate ourselves to that, and say a prayer for our country and for our people.

Most so-called extemporaneous campaign oratory is a patchwork of a candidate's favorite anecdotes and quotations, woven into passages from earlier prepared speeches, and delivered so often that it quickly loses any spontaneity. Kennedy had several such stump speeches in his repertoire, and employed them at airport arrival ceremonies and street-corner rallies. But Indianapolis was different, a speech composed from scratch as he was delivering it.

His statement that "the vast majority of white people and the vast majority of black people want to live together" echoed his reply to the black student at Ball State. His request that the audience "say a prayer for our country" may have stemmed from Mankiewicz's advice to offer "almost a prayer." The speech was what Fred Dutton would call "pure Bob Kennedy," an unalloyed expression of the content of his character, and proof that although he had not drafted some of his most stirring speeches, he could have easily done so.

The speech flows so naturally that it is hard to believe that he composed it on the fly. After praising King for dedicating his life "to love and to justice between fellow human beings," he presented the audience with two possible responses to his death: greater division and hatred, or compassion and understanding. To persuade them to choose the latter, he reminded them of his brother's assassination and quoted Aeschylus. Then he offered the hope that most Americans were "people of good will who want justice," and summoned them to a noble cause, "to make gentle the life of this world."

In his first inaugural address, Lincoln had expressed the hope that Americans would "yet swell the chorus of the Union, when again touched, as surely they will be, by the better angels of our nature." At Indianapolis, Kennedy tried to summon forth Lincoln's "better angels" by insisting that "the vast majority of white people and the vast majority of black people in this country want to live together . . . and want justice for all human beings that abide in our land."

Anyone who knew Robert Kennedy knew that King's assassination had to have reminded him of his brother's. But no one had imagined him mentioning it, and all were stunned when he did.

During his Senate campaign, he had refused to say "November 22" or "Dallas," and even in private would refer only to "the events of November 1963." He had declined to read the report of the Warren Commission, asking aides to brief him on its contents. He could not even bear to utter Oswald's name, saying on one occasion, "I agree with the conclusions of the report that the man they identified was the man, that he acted on his own." But in Indianapolis he had suddenly, without being prompted, mentioned his brother's assassination. John Lewis considered it "an incredibly powerful and connective and emotionally honest gesture," and believes it forged an immediate bond with the audience.

After sharing his brother's death with this grieving crowd, Kennedy offered them the words that had comforted him. Several months after Dallas, Jackie Kennedy gave him a copy of *The Greek Way*, Edith Hamilton's study of ancient Greece. He read it that spring, underlining passages, reciting them to friends, and inserting them into his speeches. Hamilton depicted Aeschylus as living in an age similar to the early sixties—"one of those periods of hope and endeavor which now and again light up the dark passages of history." When she called Aeschylus a "born fighter" who had "perceived the mystery of suffering," she could have been describing Robert Kennedy. When she wrote that Aeschylus had gained "a piercing insight into the awful truth of human anguish," she could have been describing the insight that Kennedy shared with this audience.

WHEN KENNEDY FINISHED, some in the crowd behaved as if he had just delivered a campaign speech. They rushed the platform, cheering and reaching for him. (Jim Tolan thought they were trying to tell him, "You're our last hope.") But most stood still, weeping and stunned into silence. They dispersed quietly and within minutes the park had emptied. A month later, one of the militant Ten Percenters told researchers Karl Anatol and John Bittner of Purdue University, "We went there for trouble, after he [Kennedy] spoke we couldn't get nowhere." Another militant told them, "After he spoke we realized the sensible way was not to kill him the way [they] killed his brother." Another claimed that Kennedy's speech had saved Indianapolis from violence, saying, "The black power guys didn't get no place after the man speak."

Had Kennedy skipped the rally, or delivered a less successful speech, there would have been a riot at Seventeenth and Broadway that evening. Anatol and Bittner speculated that "a racially mixed, congested crowd would have erupted into physical conflict between black and white with lives being lost and women and children caught in the melee. Furthermore, if a riot had taken place, a national television audience would have been witness to its commencement. The prospect of chain reactions in other areas cannot be over-ruled."

During the next twenty-four hours, riots broke out in 119 American cities, leaving forty-six dead, twenty-five hundred injured, and destruction unmatched since the Civil War. But in Indianapolis, where race relations were notoriously tense, no guns were fired or Molotov cocktails thrown, and it was the only major American city to escape the violence. Three decades later, former mayor (and now U.S. Senator) Richard Lugar would call Kennedy's appearance at the rally "a turning point" for his city.

Kennedy was driven from the rally to the Marott Hotel, a structure that bore an eerie similarity to the Texas School Book Depository, the building that Lee Harvey Oswald used as a sniper's perch. The buildings are roughly the same height and stand alone, facing open ground and overlooking wide boulevards. When Bobby pulled into the hotel's circular driveway he noticed police officers standing on its roof. They were also stationed in the marble lobby, and on every corridor for the same reason that security around a vice president is increased following an attempted presidential assassination. If King's murder was part of a conspiracy to eliminate anyone advancing the cause of civil rights, then Bobby Kennedy was obviously next.

John Lewis recalls that soon after arriving at the Marott, "Kennedy broke down on a bed, lay there on his stomach, and cried," adding that "a lot of people were crying." Later that evening, Kennedy cried again in front of Joan Braden. He stood in the doorway of her room, staring at her silently for several seconds before saying, "It could have been me." (When Martin Luther King Jr. heard that JFK had been assassinated, he told his wife, "This is what is going to happen to me. This is such a sick society.") Then he put his arms around her and pulled her onto a bed where they lay together weeping.

Despite his tough guy image, Kennedy cried easily. In 1964, he had shed tears for his brother. But after then, he began crying for others, breaking down after walking through slums in northeastern Brazil and migrant labor camps in upstate New York, seeing starving children in Mississippi, and learning that an Indian child had died of hunger while he was touring her reservation.

But for whom was Kennedy crying on April 4? For King? For Coretta Scott King and her children—whom he could imagine suffering as Jackie, Caroline, and John Kennedy Jr. had? For America? For his murdered brother? Or for himself?—*"Joanie, it could have been me."*

Those who encountered Kennedy that evening use similar words to describe his state of mind. Tolan remembers him being "shook, really shook." Pierre Salinger, who called him from Washington, thought King's assassination had made "a very, very deep impression" on him, and left him "very, very shaken." Walinsky describes him as *"really, really* I mean . . . *terribly* upset," and believes that although "an enormous mixed bag of things" upset him that evening, he felt little remorse for King, "except as a symbol and leader."

He shocked Walinsky and Jeff Greenfield saying, "You know, the death of Martin Luther King Jr. isn't the worst thing that's ever happened in the world." Greenfield was appalled by the callousness of the remark but, like Walinsky, decided that Kennedy was simply comparing King's assassination to his brother's, and judging it the lesser tragedy.

In an oral history interview conducted several months after Dallas by *New York Times* journalist Anthony Lewis, Kennedy admitted that neither he nor JFK had given much thought to civil rights during the 1960 election. When Lewis asked if he had been aware of the "special horror of life for Negroes in the South," he replied, "No."

At the beginning of the Kennedy administration, Robert Kennedy and King had been natural opponents: Kennedy was attorney general, the nation's chief law enforcement officer, while King was leading a movement relying on civil disobedience to achieve its goals. At first, Kennedy had viewed the civil rights movement as his brother did, through a Cold War lens, and attempted to prevent or defuse the kind of confrontations between Southern law enforcement agencies and civil rights demonstrators that might hand the Soviets a propaganda victory. On one occasion, when he attempted to persuade King to concentrate on working through the courts instead of going into the streets, King rebuffed him, saying, "Help us where you can and if you cannot, we're willing to bear the burden and pay the price," a pointed reiteration of John Kennedy's inaugural address pledge to "pay any price, bear any burden." In the spring of 1961, King had further irritated Kennedy by refusing to call off the Freedom Riders, whose attempts to integrate interstate bus transportation were resulting in bloody confrontations with Southern mobs and damaging America's image abroad. When a white mob surrounded King and a group of Freedom Riders at a church in Montgomery, King and Kennedy had a testy telephone conversation that left Kennedy believing that King was a coward, and King believing that Kennedy was callous and unsympathetic to black aspirations.

JFK disappointed black leaders in the same way, and for many of the same reasons, that President Franklin D. Roosevelt had. Both had raised the hopes of black Americans at the start of their administrations only to disappoint them because they needed the electoral votes of Southern states to win the presidency, and Southern Democrats in Congress to pass their legislative programs. But by 1963 the intransigence of white Southern officials and the violence directed against peaceful black demonstrators by the Birmingham police department had prompted JFK to send Congress a civil rights bill. Meanwhile, the vigorous enforcement of court-ordered desegregation by the Justice Department had made Bobby Kennedy a hero to many black Americans. Nevertheless, the personal relationship between Robert Kennedy and Dr. King remained stiff and distant, and was complicated by FBI director J. Edgar Hoover's anti-King crusade. Kennedy, mistakenly believing that two of King's associates were active Communists, had approved Hoover's request to tap King's telephones. The taps, however, were only a small part of a campaign of vilification and harassment that Hoover launched against King in December 1963, while Kennedy was distracted by grief.

Although Kennedy and King had had little personal contact in the years following JFK's assassination, their relationship slowly evolved into one of respect—"a distant camaraderie which needed no formal tie or physical link," according to King lieutenant Andrew Young. By 1967, the two men found themselves running on parallel tracks, focusing on poverty, economic inequality, and the plight of inner cities.* King moved his family into a Chicago ghetto, and Kennedy launched his Bedford-Stuyvesant project, an attempt to revitalize a disadvantaged Brooklyn neighborhood through a partnership of private enterprise and the government. Kennedy and King both spoke about the connection between race and poverty and the Vietnam War and racial injustice, both protested that black Americans were doing a disproportionate share of the fighting and dying in Vietnam, and both believed that America was undergoing a spiritual crisis and needed a moral awakening. During a speech delivered at New York's Riverside Church in April 1967, King called Vietnam "an enemy of the poor" and advocated "a radical revolution of values" that would remake America into a "people-oriented" instead of "thing-oriented" society. In 1967, Kennedy began criticizing the "thing-oriented" GNP for measuring everything "except that which makes life worthwhile." In the fall of 1967, he suggested to King through mutual friends that King lead an interracial coalition of poor people in a march on Washington. King embraced the idea and began planning the Poor People's Campaign. Soon after King's funeral, columns of impoverished Americans began marching on Washington.

THE PHONE IN Kennedy's hotel suite rang all evening with calls from civic leaders and mayors asking him to fly to their cities and speak. His television delivered bulletins of new outbreaks of arson and looting, and rebroadcast a tape of King's last speech in Memphis, so that as he and his advisers debated whether to suspend his campaign until after the funeral, they heard King saying, "We've got some difficult days ahead. But it really doesn't matter with me now. Because I've been to the mountaintop. And I don't mind. Like anybody, I would

---

*If anything, Kennedy probably made the connection between civil rights and poverty sooner than King, telling Anthony Lewis in 1964, "The problems of the North are not easily susceptible to passage of legislation for solution. You could pass a law to permit a Negro to eat at a Howard Johnson's restaurant or stay at the Hilton Hotel. But you can't pass a law that gives him enough money to permit him to eat at the restaurant or stay at the hotel. I think that's basically the problem of the Negro in the North, and that's why I think it's more difficult to be dealt with."

like to live a long life. Longevity has its place. But I'm not concerned about that now." By 11 p.m. riots had broken out in over thirty cities, and there were reports of snipers firing on police and black mobs dragging whites from their cars. Americans would learn later that many of the reports were exaggerated or imaginary, and not the precursors to a revolution or all-out race war. But on the evening of April 4 no one, including Robert Kennedy, knew this.

King's death upset Kennedy's youngest aides the most. Walinsky and Greenfield thought it might rip America apart. Dutton disagreed, saying, "People forget, life goes on. Let's not get excited and cancel everything." Kennedy said, "There are a lot of people who just don't care." John Bartlow Martin was the oldest man in the room, and admittedly the least affected by King's death. (He wrote that he had already done his weeping for JFK.) But when even he recommended suspending the campaign Kennedy decided to cancel everything except a scheduled address the following day at the City Club of Cleveland.

Kennedy called Coretta Scott King. While the call was being placed, he asked the room, "What should I say to her?" When no one else answered, Martin said, "Just tell her how you feel. It has to come from you."

Kennedy offered his condolences and, unsure of what to say next, fell back on the usual question one asks anyone who has experienced a terrible loss. "Is there anything I can do?" She said she needed her husband's body brought back to Atlanta. He promised to arrange it and, perhaps recalling the calls jamming the White House switchboard following JFK's assassination, volunteered to have more phone lines installed in her home. His opponents later portrayed his assistance to Mrs. King as a cynical attempt to pander to black voters, but no one else had made a similar offer, including Lyndon Johnson, who could have dispatched Air Force One to Memphis to collect King's remains.

Tolan had arranged for fourteen leaders of the Indianapolis black community to meet Kennedy at the Marott after the rally. Other aides had criticized the plan on the grounds that many of the leaders had police records, but Tolan held his ground, saying that there was scarcely a worthwhile black leader in Indianapolis without a record.

Kennedy decided to hold the meeting despite the assassination, and so gathered in Tolan's hotel room that evening, dressed in dashikis, skull caps, clerical collars, and Black Panther black, some itching to lash out at the nearest white man, was a typical sixties aviary of ghetto leaders: a street-corner firebrand named Ben Bell, two preachers, the Reverends Mozell Sanders and Melvin Gritten, and Snooky Hendricks, the local spokesman for militant H. Rap Brown, who had become famous for once calling violence "as American as cherry pie."

While Kennedy was deciding if he should suspend his campaign, the black leaders had been debating whether they should meet with him. Hendricks said talking was pointless: the only way to cure America was to burn it down. Another said, "Let's talk to him; let's see what he's going to do." Witnessing the discussion was Gerard Doherty, a Massachusetts political operative close to Ted Kennedy, who had drawn the assignment of entertaining the black leaders.

Kennedy finally arrived and settled into an easy chair. He puffed on a huge cigar as the leaders vented their anger and grief. One man said, "Our leader is dead tonight, and when we need you, we can't find you." Another accused him of being no better than other white politicians who bought black votes with empty promises.

Kennedy was in no mood to humor them. "You think I like sitting here in this hotel?" he asked. "Wouldn't I rather be at home with my family? I happen to believe that I have something to offer to you and your people. Yes, you lost a friend. I lost a brother. I know how you feel."

When one of the leaders accused him of belonging to "the white establishment," he said, "You talk about the establishment. I have to laugh. Big business is trying to defeat me because they think I am a friend of the Negro. You are down on me because you say I am part of the establishment." This morning he had been trying to raise money for his campaign only to be told that he was too close to black Americans. "Now I'm sitting in a room with blacks who tell me I'm too close to the others." He finally lost his temper and said, "I don't need all this aggravation. I could sit next to my swimming pool. You know, God's been good to me and I really don't need anything. But I just feel that if He's been that good, I should try to put something back in. And you all call yourself leaders and you've been moaning and groaning about personal problems. You haven't once talked about your own people."

By the time the meeting ended the leaders were pledging to support him and discussing how to get their followers to the polls. As he rose to leave, one man lashed out, complaining that he would fly away tomorrow and forget them. "You're absolutely right!" he said. He could not worry about the specific problems of Indianapolis any more than he could about Oakland, or any other city. But he would appoint someone as his liaison. Gesturing to Doherty, he said, "The reason that Gerry Doherty is with me is that he's my brother Edward's closest political intimate. When you're talking to him, you're talking to me." Afterward, he told Doherty, "Well, I've assured that your next five weeks around here will be really interesting."

Larry O'Brien, another Massachusetts Honorary Kennedy, once remarked that "the pendulum just swings wider [for Robert Kennedy] than it does for most people." It had rarely swung as wide as on April 4. The Dallas echoes, the emotional rally at Seventeenth and Broadway, and the necessity to change his campaign for the second time in four days had wound up a man who was already so tightly wound that his gears were ready to explode through the housing. Fred Dutton remembered a "very, very eerie" evening when "some very funny things happened."

As the night wore on, Kennedy was by turns talkative, irascible, and tender. He wandered the corridors, knocking on doors, waking aides, and wandering in and out of rooms.

He exploded upon learning that Earl Graves and John Lewis, who had the assignment of bringing King's body to Atlanta, planned to spend $800 to charter a plane to fly to Memphis because they could not find a convenient scheduled flight. "Don't you realize that people work for a year to make $800," he thundered, "and you're going and spending it like that?"

He strolled into a room where Tolan, Mankiewicz, and Doherty sat talking and leaned against a bureau, swigging beer from a bottle while discussing King's death. He told them that if he lost the nomination he would support Humphrey, because unlike McCarthy, he was an honest and compassionate man who cared about the poor. When asked if

King's death had brought back memories of Dallas, he said, "Well, that. But it makes me wonder what they might do to me, too."

He walked into Walinsky and Greenfield's room as they were writing a new speech for him to deliver in Cleveland the next day. It was the only time that Greenfield or Walinsky could remember him ever visiting their hotel room. Kennedy said, "You know, that fellow Harvey Lee Oswald—whatever his name is—set something loose in this country." Greenfield had never heard him mention Oswald before, and realized he had switched the assassin's first and middle names because that was how Oswald had been identified in early news flashes from Dallas.

Kennedy returned at 2:30 a.m. to find Walinsky asleep over his typewriter and Greenfield passed out on his bed. Greenfield woke to find Kennedy pulling the covers over him. "You aren't so ruthless after all," he said. "Shhhh," Kennedy whispered. "Don't tell anybody."

KENNEDY SAT DOWN for an interview with Jack Paar the next morning. He was in no mood for light repartee, so when Paar asked, "Do you think the White House is big enough for ten children?" he replied, "Do you think that is going to be my biggest problem?"

"What do you say when they say, 'Why doesn't he get his hair cut?'" Paar asked.

"I think I'll get it cut again."

He responded to Paar's serious questions. Asked if jobs were the solution to the despair in black neighborhoods, he said that jobs were important, but needed to be accompanied by "compassion for one's fellow human beings."

"What did you think when you heard Dr. King had been assassinated?" Paar asked.

"That more and more people are turning to violence. And in the last analysis it's going to destroy our country."

On April 5, this already appeared to be happening. The arson and looting had come within two blocks of the White House, and there had been riots in small cities with no history of racial violence. Blacks were anguished and furious; whites were panicky and furious. Some blacks believed that King's death proved that nonviolence was futile; some whites believed the riots proved that blacks were "ungrateful" for all progress in civil rights. Some of the blacks predicting a race war were militants, but even Whitney Young, head of the moderate National Urban League, warned of possible guerrilla warfare, and later that summer Norman Mailer, capturing the unease of white liberals, would write of himself, "The reporter became aware after a while of a curious emotion in himself . . . it was a simple emotion and very unpleasant to him—he was getting tired of Negroes and their rights. It was a miserable recognition, and on many a count, for if he felt even a hint this way, then what immeasurable tides of rage must be loose in America itself?"

As Kennedy was driving into Cleveland in a white convertible on the morning of April 5, an aide in the mobile phone car waved him down to report that police believed a sniper might be hiding in a steeple overlooking the hotel where he was to address the City Club. Bill Barry, Kennedy's unarmed bodyguard, suggested he wait by the side of the road while he drove ahead to investigate. "No. We'll never stop for that kind of threat," Kennedy said, angry that Barry would even suggest it. He continued into town with the top down. The last time he had driven from the airport to downtown Cleveland, in August 1964, it had been to open an exhibit honoring his slain brother.

He spoke for just ten minutes to a well-dressed audience of twenty-two hundred civic leaders. He was solemn and muted, like a mourner struggling to maintain his composure while delivering a eulogy, but his words were some of the most radical uttered by a major party candidate for president.

He began by uncoupling violence and race: "The victims of the violence are young, are black and white, rich and poor, young and old, famous and unknown. They are, most important of all, human beings whom other human beings loved and needed."

He equated King's assassin with the rioters: "A sniper is only a coward, not a hero, and the uncontrolled, uncontrollable mob is only the voice of madness, not the voice of reason."

Then, on a day when rioters were still exchanging gunfire with police and soldiers, and Mayor Daley—whose support was crucial to

Kennedy's nomination—had instructed Chicago police to kill arsonists and wound looters, he placed the violence of the rioters on an equal moral footing with the unchecked violence of law enforcement agencies: "Whenever any American's life is taken by another American unnecessarily—whether it is done in the name of the law, or in the defiance of the law, by one man or a gang, in cold blood or in passion, in an attack of violence or in response to violence . . . the whole nation is degraded."

He told City Club members that American culture and foreign policy could not escape responsibility for the riots: "We calmly accept newspaper reports of civilian slaughter in far-off lands. We glorify killing on movie and television screens and call it entertainment. We make it easy for men of all shades of sanity to acquire what weapons and ammunition they desire. Too often we honor swagger and bluster and the wielders of force; too often we excuse those who are willing to build their own lives on the shattered dreams of others."

He declared that white Americans, including those in this audience, bore responsibility for the riots, saying, "Some who accuse others of inciting riots have by their own conduct invited them" and "violence breeds violence, repression brings retaliation, and only a cleansing of our whole society can remove this sickness from our soul."

Finally, in a speech that was supposed to establish his interest in business problems, he told these pillars of the Cleveland establishment that their public and private institutions were also at fault. "For there is another kind of violence, slower but just as deadly and destructive as the shot or the bomb in the night," he said. "This is the violence of institutions; indifference and inaction and slow decay. This is the violence that afflicts the poor. . . . This is the slow destruction of a child by hunger, and schools without books and homes without heat in winter. This is the breaking of a man's spirit by denying him the chance to stand as a father and as a man among other men."

These were profoundly radical words, even for 1968. Walinsky and Greenfield had written them in consultation with Ted Sorensen, and they reflected their emotions during the turbulent hours following King's assassination. But they also expressed positions that

Kennedy had taken during his Senate years.* Kennedy had not only read and approved the City Club speech, he had edited it during the flight to Cleveland, and it was ultimately his decision to equate the violence perpetrated on the poor by America's institutions with a rioter's bullet or a Molotov cocktail. It was the kind of speech that had prompted Alice Roosevelt Longworth, daughter of President Theodore Roosevelt, to observe that "Bobby could have been a revolutionary priest," and that had led *Look* photographer Stanley Tetrick to tell Kennedy, "What you really are is a revolutionary. You should be in the hills with Castro and Che," and Kennedy to respond, "I know it." (Kennedy once asked his aide Richard Goodwin to describe his impressions of Che. When Goodwin finished, he told him, "You know, sometimes I envy the bastard. At least he was able to go out and fight for what he believed. All I ever do is go to chicken dinners.")

The "violence of institutions" passage flew under the political radar of Kennedy's opponents, perhaps because the nation was preoccupied with King's death and the riots. But Nixon would surely have used it against him in the general election, probably to great effect. In a second passage that escaped notice, at least until June 5, Kennedy said, "No one, no matter where he lives or what he does, can be certain who next will suffer from such a senseless act of bloodshed."

The social ills that Kennedy described to the City Clubbers called for a revolution. But instead of a revolution in the streets, he concluded by calling for a revolution of the heart. Reconciling white and black Americans was not a matter of new programs, he said, but of "whether we can find in our own hearts that leadership of humane purpose that will recognize the terrible truths of our existence." What was required was an understanding that "our own children's future cannot be built on the misfortune of others" and "that those who live with us

---

*During the Watts riots of 1965, when politicians of both parties were delivering tough law-and-order speeches, Kennedy told a convention of the Independent Order of Odd Fellows, "Just saying obey the law is not going to work. The law to us is a friend, which preserves our property and our personal safety. But for the Negro, law means something different." In the South, he said, it had meant "beatings and degradation," while in the North it did not fully protect black lives and dignity.

are our brothers, that they share with us the same short moment of life; that they seek, as we do, nothing but the chance to live out their lives in purpose and in happiness, winning what satisfaction and fulfillment they can."

It was reported that many women in the audience had been in tears as Kennedy spoke. When he finished, the civic and business elite of Cleveland gave him a standing ovation. Jeff Greenfield later called the City Club address "the best-written speech of the campaign." It was also the clearest expression of Kennedy's conviction that the nation's wounds could only be healed when Americans participated in a moral revival that removed the "sickness" of violence from the national soul.

As Kennedy's chartered plane took off for Washington, he noticed that *Life* reporter Sylvia Wright was staring out a window and weeping. Knowing that she had become close to King while covering the civil rights movement, and that his death had hit her hard, he changed seats with the photographer sitting next to her and, although famously reluctant to talk about his feelings, distracted her with a monologue about the campaign. "People think I'm wasting my time because I'm a bright man," he said, "and someone in my position shouldn't have to be arriving at airports and saying things like, 'It's nice to see you all here!' and 'How nice of you to come out.' But . . . for every two or three days that you waste time making speeches at rallies full of noise and balloons, there's usually a chance in every two or three days . . . where you get a chance to teach people something; and to tell them something that they don't know because they don't have the chance to get around like I do, to take them some place vicariously that they haven't been, to show them a ghetto, or an Indian reservation." And it was moments like these, he said, that made a political campaign, despite all its banalities and indignities, "worth it."

After riots had devastated Newark and Detroit during the summer of 1967, Kennedy had told Frank Mankiewicz that if he ever became president he would persuade the networks to cooperate in producing a documentary depicting the life of poor black Americans. "Let them [the television networks] show the sound, the feel, the hopelessness, and what it's like to think you'll never get out," he said. "Show a black teenager, told by some radio jingle to stay in school, looking at his older brother, who stayed in school and who's out of a job. Show the Mafia pushing narcotics; put a *Candid Camera* team in a ghetto school and watch what a rotten system of education it really is. Film a mother staying up all night to keep threats from her baby. . . . Then I'd ask people to watch it and experience what it means to live in the most affluent society in history—without hope." He believed that after viewing this documentary Americans would demand a change. But now King's assassination had made this change of heart too urgent to await his presidency. So instead of awakening the consciences of Americans with a documentary, he would attempt to do it with his campaign.

SIX

"GUNS BETWEEN ME
AND THE WHITE HOUSE"

APRIL 5–7, 1968

The sixties was an incendiary decade. Carpets of napalm fell on Vietnam, American soldiers set fire to hooches, and Buddhist monks burned themselves alive. Americans torched flags, draft cards, and recruiting stations. Militants shouted, "Burn, Baby, Burn!" and in the summer of 1967, blacks burned Newark and Detroit. Later, studies and commissions would decide that greed and anger more than revolutionary fervor had motivated the looting and fires that followed King's assassination, but no one in the chartered plane bringing Robert Kennedy back to Washington from Cleveland knew that, and they returned to a city besieged by its own citizens, occupied by the military, and apparently facing an insurrection.

The passengers fell silent as the pilot circled Washington. Below, they saw smoke blanketing the Mall, and artillery pieces and army trucks ringing the White House—evidence of the greatest civil calamity to strike America since the Civil War. Jim Tolan thought, "My God! What's happening to us?" John Bartlow Martin believed they were witnessing the civil rights movement turning into the black revolution, and Adam Walinsky, remembering the previous summer's riots in Newark and Detroit, thought, "Well, it's finally Washington's turn."

Kennedy asked the pilot to circle the city again. After landing he said, "I think I can do something with these people." He proposed driving into the riot zone, and attempting to calm the mobs of looters and arsonists. His aides were appalled. Dutton, stalling for time, pointed out that as a courtesy Kennedy should first inform the mayor of the District of Columbia, Walter Washington. Martin told him that he could not accomplish much while people were still rioting, and warned that he would appear to be grandstanding. Kennedy reluctantly agreed to go home.

Two days later, he and Ethel visited the riot zone to attend 8 a.m. Palm Sunday services at the New Bethel Baptist Church. Its pastor, the Reverend Walter Fauntroy, was the local representative of Dr. King's Southern Christian Leadership Council (SCLC), and he and Kennedy had become friends while coordinating King's 1963 March on Washington. Fauntroy's sermon compared the final weeks of Jesus Christ and Martin Luther King Jr., and he told the congregation that during their last conversation King had said, "I'm afraid this country just isn't ready for nonviolence."

Stokely Carmichael, the militant widely blamed for inciting the riots in Washington by delivering an incendiary speech to a street-corner mob, was also in the congregation. On April 4, he had waved a revolver in the air while shouting, "When the white man comes he is going to kill you . . . go home and get you a gun and then come back because I got me a gun." He was probably carrying that gun this morning.

Kennedy took communion with the congregation. Within hours, the Bishop of Washington had learned that a member of America's most illustrious Catholic family had received the sacrament in a Protestant church. When a Catholic cleric called Frank Mankiewicz to protest, he dismissed the story as an improbable rumor. Later that afternoon, a sheepish Kennedy admitted it was true, explaining that everyone else had been drinking the grape juice so he had simply joined in. John Kennedy, who had been scrupulous about observing church ritual, but was less devout than Bobby, would never have made such an error, but Bobby's politics were devoid of religious calculation.

After the service, Fauntroy and Kennedy stood together at the church door shaking hands with the congregation. When Kennedy asked about destruction in the surrounding neighborhood, Fauntroy said, "Let me show you." They began walking toward Fourteenth Street, which had suffered some of the worst destruction. Ethel Kennedy, Peter Edelman, and a small group of reporters and parishioners followed behind. They passed workmen using wrecking cranes to demolish gutted buildings and firemen playing hoses on embers. They heard burglar alarms clanging and sound trucks announcing a 4 p.m. curfew, stepped on shards of glass, and gagged on smoke and tear gas. They saw firebombed white-owned stores and black ones saved by their SOUL BROTHER signs. They may have noticed that rioters had spared the office of the local voting precinct while torching the adjoining offices, not because someone had scrawled SOUL BROTHER across its plate glass window, but because someone had hung Robert Kennedy's photograph in it.

As Kennedy picked his way through this postwar Berlin landscape of smoldering rubble, coughing and wiping his eyes, he muttered, "It's bad. It's terrible. We've got to do something."

The crowd surrounding him grew with every block, becoming so large and boisterous that a squad of National Guard troopers mistook it for a mob of looters and put on gas masks and fixed bayonets. Policemen who had been following in a squad car accelerated and swerved into their line of fire, and soon Kennedy and the soldiers were shaking hands.

Ethel pointed to some apartments over a row of burned-out stores and asked, "Who lived there, white people?"

"No! Black people," the crowd shouted.

Women leaning from windows yelled, "Is that Kennedy?" then waved and cheered when they saw it was.

He stopped at one of the only grocery stores remaining open. A man waiting in line grabbed his hand and said, "I have ten children, too, and I want a better life for them." A woman stared at him in disbelief. "Is that *you*?" she asked. "I knew you'd be the first to come here, darling."

After reaching a rise in the road Kennedy and Fauntroy stopped, momentarily stunned by a panorama of destruction reaching almost to the White House.

Fauntroy asked Kennedy how his campaign was going. Kennedy replied that it was going well, and that if he won Indiana and Nebraska, he thought he could win Oregon and California, and if he won California, he thought he could win the nomination. He paused for a moment, as if carefully considering his next words before saying, "But there's one problem."

"What's that, Bobby?"

"I'm afraid there are guns between me and the White House."

Fauntroy froze, stunned that Kennedy had suddenly voiced the silent fear of everyone who knew him, walked through a crowd with him, stood with him on a street corner surrounded by tall buildings, or rode with him in an open car.

Had this been the only time that Kennedy had made a comment like this, it might be dismissed as an aberration, perhaps prompted by King's death, and by the troops whose guns were at this moment surrounding the White House. But on the night of King's assassination he had told Joan Braden, "It could have been me," and a month from now he would tell author Romain Gary, "There is no way to protect a candidate during the campaign. You must give yourself to the crowd, and from then on you must take your chances. . . . I know that there will be an attempt on my life sooner or later. Not so much for political reasons, but through contagion, through emulation."

It was not just the campaign that made him nervous. Several months after Dallas, he had told Ken O'Donnell, "I knew they would get one of us, but I always thought it would be me." In 1965, at a surprise fortieth birthday party that Ethel had organized for him while he was traveling through Brazil—a trip scheduled so he would be away on the second anniversary of his brother's death—some guests pulled on some party crackers, and at the sound of the bangs he had dropped his head into his hands and cried, "Oh, no . . . please don't." Four days later, on the anniversary of his brother's assassination, he was sitting with an American woman at an outdoor café in Rio de Janeiro when several loud bangs sent him leaping out of his chair. When he realized they came from a backfiring car he told her, "Sooner or later. Sooner or later."

On March 10, 1968, six days before announcing his candidacy, he had imagined seeing an assassin mingling with a crowd of farmworkers at an outdoor rally in Delano, California, that he was attending with

Cesar Chavez. The man had brown hair and gray eyes, and wore blue jeans and a blue jean jacket. Kennedy pointed him out to Dolores Huerta, one of Chavez's deputies. She questioned him in Spanish and became suspicious when he did not respond. Afterward, she asked some union members to stand behind Kennedy and cover his back. Kennedy noticed the man again while being escorted to his car by union official Mack Lyons. "Watch that guy," he told Lyons. "He has a gun." Lyons saw a middle-aged man with a smooth complexion and yellowish skin. He went over and stood next to the man until he disappeared into the crowd. As Lyons helped Kennedy into the car he could feel his body shaking.

Every public appearance that Kennedy made that spring was an act of courage; every motorcade in an open car an act of defiance. Before King's assassination, an attempt on his life had seemed likely; afterward it seemed inevitable.

Some farmworkers told Chavez they would not vote for Kennedy because they were afraid that if he won the nomination someone would shoot him. Jerry Bruno recalls going into small towns to advance Kennedy rallies and being told, "I like Kennedy, but they won't let him live to be president." An underground newspaper in San Francisco published an imaginary interview with the ghost of President William McKinley in which he said, "Don't waste your vote on Kennedy. They're going to kill him." A city official in Logansport, Indiana, told reporters he had stationed policemen on roofs because "we just want to make sure he [Kennedy] leaves town the same way he came in."

The possibility of an assassination "was on our minds all spring," John Bartlow Martin said, and whenever he and Kennedy rode together in a motorcade or walked through a crowd, Martin watched windows and studied faces. When a man whose face was twisted in anger asked Kennedy a hostile question during a whistle-stop, Martin's eyes never left him, and if the man had reached into his pocket, he was prepared to push Kennedy out of the line of fire.

Life's Loudon Wainwright described the Kennedy press corps as "a partisan band, obsessed with the future of the candidate, sensitive to his moods and . . . concerned to the point of anxiety about his safety and his success." As reporters became more fond of Kennedy, they became more protective, unsettled by firecrackers and backfiring cars, and encircling him in crowds whenever there were rumors of death threats. Some were prepared to take the bullet for him, like the female reporter who told him, "If anything happens, I'll save you. I'll throw myself in front of you."

Photographers and reporters who had covered JFK found it difficult to cover Bobby. One of Bill Eppridge's colleagues at *Life* told him, "Look, you'll notice that there are not a lot of guys who worked with his brother. Why? Because they're all looking over their shoulders at the crowd instead of at the candidate."

Some newsmen were concerned they might miss the assassination of a second Kennedy. One network ordered its film crews never to leave his side. AP reporter Joe Mohbat remembers that "if there was a handshaking reception at 11:30 on a Saturday night with fifteen people—you couldn't make a newspaper or a TV spot at that hour—somebody would say, 'I'm going back to the hotel and get a drink. I'm bushed.' And everybody would sort of look at him and say, 'Really? Where are you going to be when it happens?' Or 'Where are you going to be when the shots ring out?'" One evening, Mohbat skipped a rally and remained on the chartered plane. When Bobby and Ethel returned, she tugged on his jacket and said, "Joe, where were you? I almost got killed." He almost went into shock before realizing that she was joking.

The more a reporter admired Kennedy, the more painful it was to cover him. Hays Gorey thought that by campaigning "virtually unprotected," and by letting anyone who wanted to get close to him touch him or pull him from a moving convertible, Kennedy had turned his campaign into a form of slow-motion suicide.

John Lindsay believed that everyone in the press bus viewed an attempted assassination as inevitable. "All they could do was protect him from personal injury like rock-throwing," he said, "but it was not possible to protect him from what ultimately happened. There wasn't a single person in this outfit who didn't know that."

Six months after his assassination, Sylvia Wright engaged in a stream-of-consciousness unburdening, telling an interviewer, "I used to get very cross with Chuck [Charles Quinn]. . . . I would say, 'Look, I don't want to hear all your pessimistic, sadistic talk. I think it's sick.'

Because that's just what they talked about. Every time I would say, 'I have to get stuff on an 8:30 flight, otherwise I won't be able to get it on until 1:30. . . . Then I can change clothes and be ready, and you won't have to wait for me to go to dinner. And Chuck would say, 'then you won't be there if he gets shot.'" Wright herself was not immune to the death-watch atmosphere. When Bobby's sister Pat Lawford had suggested waiting on the press bus during a chilly evening rally, Wright had said, "I really can't, Pat. It's outdoors and anything can happen outdoors because you can't control who's around."

Few politicians have been loved and hated as passionately as Bobby Kennedy, or made enemies as dangerous as Jimmy Hoffa and J. Edgar Hoover. An FBI informer reported that Teamsters boss Jimmy Hoffa had said, "I've got to do something about the sonofabitch Bobby Kennedy. . . . He doesn't even have any guards on his house. What do you know about plastic bombs?"

The threats spiked after Kennedy began running for president. Many originated in California. Ethel received a copy of a political cartoon depicting him as a little boy dragging a sack of his father's money into Indiana. "This is a perfect likeness of your 'groovy' husband," someone had typed across its top, "Why don't you all get out of Indiana before it is too late!" An FBI informant reported that the Mob had put out a contract of several hundred thousand if Kennedy appeared poised to win the nomination, and every week FBI agents provided Frank Mankiewicz with photographs of potential assassins. Mankiewicz scanned faces at airports and rallies, searching for a match.

Kennedy appeared to face the threats with an insouciant fatalism. If someone raised the subject of a possible assassination he would say, "What happens, happens," or "If anyone wants to kill me, it won't be difficult," or he would quote Camus: "Knowing that you are going to die is nothing." When Warren Rogers of *Look* asked if he ever feared that his unruly fans or his enemies might injure him, he said, "Oh hell, you can't worry about that. Look at their faces. These people don't want to hurt me. They just want to see me and touch me," but then he added, "Well, doing anything in public life today is Russian roulette."

He would tolerate small detachments of plainclothes men, but only if they remained at a distance and were inconspicuous. He resisted surrounding himself with uniformed police officers in the belief that they excited a crowd and made it more aggressive, and made it appear that he was afraid of the public.

Former FBI agent Bill Barry, who served as his one-man unarmed security detail, was as vigilant as possible under the circumstances. He and other aides covered Kennedy from the front and rear when he moved through crowds, hid his motorcade cars overnight to prevent them from being wired with explosives, and had plainclothes police officers watch his room while he slept. But Barry could not prevent him from taking his cocker spaniel Freckles out for a walk, or wandering alone through hotel lobbies. Nor could Barry turn off the television lights at nighttime rallies that made Kennedy an easy target. He urged him to hire a second bodyguard, and complained to Jimmy Breslin, "I get mixed up with crowds and I can't see. And I get tired. Maybe I won't be able to react quickly enough. I wish someone would talk with him."

Kennedy felt safest when surrounded by a crowd, and most at risk if he left an auditorium, ballroom, or building through a back exit, kitchen, or underground garage. After Adam Walinsky and Jerry Bruno tricked him into leaving a hall in Montana through a rear exit, he became furious, telling them, "You must *never* do anything like that again. . . . I don't care what you've heard or what the cops say. I want it to stop. If someone wants to kill me, they're going to kill me. I do not want to live from day to day with this constant threat."

During the tour, Barry and Tolan had incurred his wrath by bringing him to the ballroom of Seattle's Olympic Hotel through its kitchen and scullery. When they tried steering him out the same way, he jumped from the dais into the crowd and headed toward the main door. A few days later in Salt Lake City, police received a tip that a bomb was set to explode in the Terrace Ballroom of the Hotel Utah while he was speaking. Bruno told him about it, adding that to avoid a panic the police had decided not to inform the audience. A police official intercepted Kennedy in the lobby of his hotel and ordered him to stay away from the event. Kennedy refused. The official blocked his car with police cruisers. Kennedy stuffed his hands in his pockets, put his head down, and walked. He told the audience about the bomb and said, "If you want to leave you should leave in an orderly fashion. Be careful of the children. Anyone who wants to stay, I'll stay with you." After no one left, he said, "This is what I call opening the campaign with a bang. But let me tell you, if I have to go, I can't think of anybody I would rather go with than you people here tonight."

LIKE OTHERS WHO loved Robert Kennedy, Walter Fauntroy had wanted to believe that he was oblivious to the dangers of an assassination. Knowing that whenever Kennedy rode through a city in an open car he also imagined, like many of those traveling with him, Jackie in her pink suit and the Texas Book Depository, was too painful. Fauntroy was so upset by Kennedy's remark about guns that he continued walking with him and missed the start of his 11 o'clock service. Finally, unable to contain himself any longer, and wondering if there had been some specific threat, he asked Kennedy what he had meant about guns separating him and the White House.

Kennedy fixed Fauntroy with a piercing stare and said, "Nothing."

But in a way, he had said everything. He had said that, like Jackie, he feared that what had happened to Jack could happen to him. He had explained why Fred Dutton noticed his adoring crowds transporting him "out of whatever morbid state he was in at the time"; why Jim Stevenson detected "a resident, melancholy bleakness" in his face; and why, after traveling with him in Indiana, AP reporter Saul Pett noticed moments when, "almost alone at last, quiet at last," he would stare straight ahead, "beyond all other things in sight." At that moment, Pett wrote, "there comes then into those blue eyes, like a shadow over a turquoise sea, a look of such infinite sadness, or such terrible hurt, one feels compelled to look away."

It was assumed that during these moments of infinite sadness Kennedy was thinking about his late brother. But his comment to Fauntroy, like those to Joan Braden, Romain Gary, Dolores Huerta, Mack Lyons, and others, suggests that the fear that guns lay between him and the White House was always with him. It was these guns that led his press corps and staff to treat him with a tenderness customarily extended to the terminally ill, and that explain why he campaigned so passionately, as if this campaign might have to serve as legacy, and epitaph.

Four days after walking through Washington with Fauntroy, Kennedy was in Lansing, Michigan, when Fred Dutton suddenly burst into his hotel room and began drawing down the shades. He explained that police had spotted a man with a rifle on the roof of a neighboring building. Kennedy, angrier than Dutton had ever seen him, said, "Don't close them. If they're going to shoot, they'll shoot." Meanwhile, Bill Barry had persuaded a delegation of local politicians to meet Kennedy in an underground garage instead of the hotel lobby. After discovering what Barry had done, Kennedy told Dutton, "Don't ever do that. We always get into the car in public. We're not going to start ducking now." (He later told Dick Tuck, "I do not go out back doors; I do not go through basements.") He ordered his driver to stop in the street outside the hotel and jumped out, making himself an easy target. But two weeks later, when teenagers attending a rally in Scottsburg, Indiana, set off a string of poppers that made a loud bang and shot streamers into the air, he flinched and scanned the crowd, looking for the source of the explosions. Shirley Amick, a local supporter sitting next to him on the platform, has never forgotten the look in his eyes, and says, "I saw real fear there."

SEVEN

"PROPHETS GET SHOT"

APRIL 9, 1968

While fires were still smoldering, stores being looted, and Molotov cocktails thrown in some American cities, private planes bringing mourners to Martin Luther King Jr.'s funeral converged on Atlanta in such numbers that some circled for forty-five minutes before landing. They brought Nelson Rockefeller, George Romney, Eugene Mc-Carthy, Hubert Humphrey, and Robert Kennedy—"the greatest gathering of presidential candidates ever assembled in one place at one time," according to the *Atlanta Constitution*. They brought Sammy Davis Jr., Sidney Poitier, Eartha Kitt, Marlon Brando, Jackie Robinson, Floyd Patterson, Paul Newman, Aretha Franklin, Diana Ross and her Supremes, and Little Stevie Wonder. They brought Jackie Kennedy and Betty Shabazz, already widowed by assassins, and Governor Otto Kerner of Illinois, whose bleak conclusions about race relations had obviously not been bleak enough, and former vice president Richard Nixon, whose response to Kerner's report had been a call for "swift and sure retaliation" against rioters.

Exploding flashbulbs and screaming fans greeted the celebrity mourners. The entertainers smiled and waved, but the politicians were more tentative, less certain of the etiquette. America's racial nerves had never been so exposed and sensitive, and they knew that an awkward gesture or ill-chosen remark could outrage grieving blacks, while any appearance of pandering to blacks might infuriate the backlash whites.

Governor Ronald Reagan of California, who also nursed presidential ambitions, skipped the funeral and issued a statement blaming King's assassination on his philosophy of nonviolent disobedience, calling his death a "great tragedy that began when we began compromising with law and order, and people [i.e., King] started choosing which laws they'd break." At first, Senator Eugene McCarthy had said he would not attend the rites and predicted in private that they would be "a vulgar public spectacle." But he eventually bowed to pleas from his wife and campaign manager and flew to Atlanta. King's funeral promised to be particularly tricky for Nixon, whose Southern Strategy called for placating GOP moderates by paying lip service to civil rights while using code words like *law and order* to let segregationists know that he was on their side. This meant he would have to attend King's funeral, yet convince Southerners that he was a reluctant mourner. The task of communicating this fell to the director of his Southern campaign, Brad Hayes, who informed prominent Southern politicians that Hayes was as "concerned" as they were about Nixon's presence in Atlanta, excusing it as "something the candidate felt he had to do."

The only scheming that preceded Kennedy's arrival in Atlanta concerned the make of car he would drive. His staff rejected the Thunderbird that the city had offered as too flashy, requested a Plymouth, and compromised on a Ford Galaxie.

King's funeral also promised to be tricky for Kennedy. The riots had complicated his strategy of turning out blacks in record numbers while winning back many of the working-class whites who had defected to former Alabama governor George Wallace in 1964. These backlash voters already viewed Kennedy as the champion of black voters. Film of him speaking to blacks in Indianapolis and walking through Washington at the head of a black crowd had reinforced this impression, and his attendance at King's funeral was certain to further it. In the days following the riots, members of both parties had delivered tough law-and-order speeches. Kennedy, too, had called violence "unacceptable," but had always coupled this statement with an equally strong denunciation of racial injustice. He was also a reluctant mourner and, after watching him arrive, Remer Tyson of the *Atlanta Constitution* wrote that his twitching hands and sad eyes showed "how close the thought of his brother's assassination must have been with him when he stepped off that plane."

There was scarcely a moment during the next twenty-four hours when Kennedy would not be reminded of his late brother.

He was driven from the airport to Coretta Scott King's home, where one of her friends told him that of the twelve thousand telegrams Mrs. King had received, the one touching her most had come from Lee Harvey Oswald's mother. It said, "My heart bled when I heard the news. We had two assassinations in our life with our dear son [killed by Jack Ruby] and our dear President," implying that JFK's murder and Oswald's had been similar tragedies.

After hearing this, he and Ethel were ushered into Mrs. King's bedroom for a private audience during which King's widow begged him to persuade Jackie to attend the funeral. He replied this would be "very hard" for her "because of her own experiences," a comment suggesting that the ceremony might not be easy for him, either. Mrs. King was adamant, saying, "It would mean a great deal to me if she did come," leaving him no choice but to call Jackie and persuade her to fly to Atlanta.

The only photograph of this meeting shows a middle-class bedroom at mid-century: a department store bedroom set, a clock radio on a nightstand, and a La-Z-Boy. Coretta Scott King is perched on the edge of a double bed, Ethel sits in a straight-backed wooden chair, and Bobby is in the La-Z-Boy, King's favorite chair and where he read, napped, and wrote his sermons. It was the most comfortable seat in the room and it is unlikely he would have chosen it unless Mrs. King had insisted.

Minutes after sitting in King's favorite chair, Kennedy stood in the dimly lit sanctuary of Ebenezer Baptist Church, gazing down at King's corpse, dressed in a black suit and white shirt with a black tie and a handkerchief in the breast pocket. A witness described Kennedy's face as solemn, and "perhaps lined with the memory of another casket."

On the night of his brother's assassination, he had had to decide whether the casket should remain closed or be opened for the viewing and funeral. The bodies of deceased presidents were customarily considered the property of the American people, and Lincoln, Garfield, McKinley, and Harding had been displayed in open coffins. Jackie had wanted her husband's coffin to remain closed, but his aides, more sensitive to protocol, argued for having it open. Bobby agreed with them at first, but after hearing Jackie's vehement protests, he cleared the East Room of everyone except a few close friends, opened the coffin, and changed his mind. Minutes later, he was heard weeping for the first time that night.

Kennedy went from the church to his suite at the Hyatt Regency, where he hosted three meetings with groups of black politicians, entertainers, and civil rights leaders. He opened each by saying that he was there to listen and learn what he could do to carry on Dr. King's work.

The first meeting, with regional black political leaders, was uneventful. But the second one included entertainers such as Bill Cosby, Peter Lawford, Sammy Davis Jr., Alan King, and Harry Belafonte, and quickly turned acrimonious. After someone accused white Americans of being unable to communicate with poor blacks, the white comedian Alan King shot back, "You Uncle Toms can't identify with your own people in the streets. The minute you get in government you become . . . middle class." Another man, referring to Kennedy's popularity with young blacks, shouted, "Bobby Kennedy can lie to you and he can lie to me. But the only guys that Bobby can't lie to are the guys in the street. They *really* believe him." Some of the entertainers boasted about their charities, and after one expounded at length about her work with juvenile delinquents, Bill Cosby called the meeting "a lot of shit" and stormed out. "I bet you've been to a lot of meetings like this before," Kennedy told Georgia legislator Julian Bond afterward, "[and] I bet you don't want to go to any more, do you?"

The last meeting brought Kennedy together with a group of Dr. King's friends and aides from the Southern Christian Leadership Conference (SCLC), who were at this moment perhaps the most heartbroken and traumatized men in America. They cursed Kennedy, questioned his motives, and implied that he had come to Atlanta to court black voters. One preacher shouted, "Who are you, white man, to ask for our help?" The Reverend James Bevel, a King aide who had organized many of the SCLC's nonviolent protests, said, "Whoever is the next President of the United States has got to have an economic program to bring poor people into the economy and society," and asked Kennedy, "Do you have a program?" Kennedy said he did, but refused to discuss it on the eve of King's funeral.

Reverend Hosea Williams, who had led the SCLC's first Selma-to-Montgomery march in 1965, said that many of the men in this room, like many in the black community, had lost any hope in the future. After warning that "a hopeless man is a very desperate, dangerous man—almost a dead man," he concluded, "You have a chance to be a prophet. But prophets get shot."

Reverend Ralph Abernathy had been Dr. King's closest friend, and the following day he would be elected to succeed King as president of the SCLC. He had been fasting since King's assassination and was weak from hunger and grief. Finally, he struggled to his feet and hugged Kennedy, signaling that the meeting was over. His embrace was also symbolic, affirming that for the moment Kennedy was Dr. King's real successor, and that for the first time since the presidency of Abraham Lincoln, black Americans were placing their hopes in a white man. Hosea Williams later acknowledged this, saying, "The thing that kept us going was that maybe Bobby Kennedy would come up with some answers for this country . . . [and] after Dr. King was killed, there was just about nobody left but Bobby Kennedy." John Lewis also felt himself transferring his loyalty from King to Kennedy, and thinking, "Dr. King may be gone but we still have Bobby Kennedy, so we have hope."

King's death had come at a difficult time for the civil rights movement. The black leadership was divided between advocates of nonviolent protest like King, and the growing Black Power movement. King had also been such a towering figure that there was no black leader of similar stature. Robert Kennedy's position as his de facto successor would never have been more than a temporary one, but at the time he was the only politician in America who had the trust of blacks and could absorb and defuse their rage. According to a poll taken shortly after King's death, 94 percent of the black community believed that he possessed "many of the same outstanding qualities of his brother," while only 39 percent of the general population shared this sentiment. Soon after King's funeral, Kennedy began receiving the kind of communications that had previously gone to Dr. King. Among them were a telegram from a group of black women in New Haven, Connecticut, asking him to protect them from "white gangs," and a letter from black soldiers serving in Vietnam who complained of fighting for freedoms unavailable in their home states of Mississippi and Tennessee.

Several times that evening, Ethel had emerged from the bedroom to beg her husband to finish his meetings and get some sleep. But after the SCLC leaders left at around 2:30 a.m., he insisted on returning to the Ebenezer Baptist Church to view King's remains again. He and Ethel arrived around 3 a.m. to find the building empty except for an honor guard, and illuminated only by some flickering candles. They knelt together before King's coffin and prayed for several minutes.*

Perhaps Kennedy had returned here because he had been moved by his conversations with King's friends, by Abernathy's embrace, and by being called the next prophet to black America. Perhaps he felt guilty for having ordered King's phones tapped, or for having failed to know him better. (The night before coming to Atlanta, he had discussed King with the political activist Allard Lowenstein, and had been surprised to learn that King had possessed excellent political instincts and a sharp sense of humor.) Or perhaps because now that King had suffered the same fate as John Kennedy, he felt a bond that had not existed while King was alive.

If it did not occur to Kennedy as he knelt before King's coffin, perhaps it had struck him as he was sitting in King's favorite chair, or being hugged by his best friend, that by assuming the hopes that black Americans had placed in King, he had also assumed the hatred of those who wanted to frustrate those hopes, and that by adding King's mantle to his brother's, he had, at a stroke, doubled his enemies. And it may have also struck him that although King had lived with the expectation

---

*On the night of his brother's funeral, Bobby had impulsively decided to revisit his grave. After the other mourners had left the White House he had turned to Jackie and said, "Should we go visit our friend?" They drove to Arlington where, watched only by two military policemen and the cemetery superintendent, they knelt under a flickering torch by his grave and bowed their heads in prayer.

that an assassin's bullet could end his life at any moment, he had refused to surround himself with armed guards, and that for Kennedy to
do any less would make him appear less courageous than King.

KING'S FUNERAL UNFOLDED in an atmosphere of grief, hysteria,
and menace typical of the spring of 1968, and unlike that surrounding
President Kennedy's service. By the time Kennedy was buried, his
assassin had been apprehended and murdered but King's killer remained at large. The grief following Kennedy's death had united
Americans, while the riots following King's had divided them.
Kennedy's assassination had seemed an anomaly, a crime against nature, but after King's assassination, Americans assumed there were
more to come.

Although the Ebenezer Baptist Church seated 750 people, almost
half its pews had been reserved for white politicians. Roger Wilkins,
who directed the community relations service in the Justice Department, was bitter that President Johnson, after declining to attend himself, had sent a planeload of white politicians "who took seats that
could have gone to people who risked their lives on lonely roads with
Martin."

The thirty senators, fifty U.S. congressmen, the vice president, cabinet members, and assorted governors, wives, Secret Service agents,
presidential candidates, and bodyguards who made it into the church
that morning had to pass through a gauntlet of sixty thousand praying,
weeping, and singing mourners who filled the surrounding streets.
The dignitaries entered the church to shouts of, "Crocodile tears!"
"Why are the whites going in?" and "This is our man! This is our funeral!" Prominent senators like Charles Percy, Ed Muskie, and Clai-
borne Pell never made it inside and spent the funeral in the street,
perspiring, neglected, and watching as basketball star Wilt Chamber-
lain entered to shouts of "Make way for Wilt."

Cries of "Politicking!" greeted former vice president Richard
Nixon. Vice President Hubert Humphrey, who had once posed arm in
arm with Lester Maddox, Georgia's racist governor, heard boos. As
Senator McCarthy's wife, Abigail, walked through the crowd, women

grabbed her arm, telling her they belonged to the congregation and begging her to take them inside. When Jackie Kennedy climbed from her car someone shouted, "What's *she* doing here? She does her marching with Lord Harlech." After ushers briefly detained Stokely Carmichael and his six bodyguards, people cried, "Let him in!" and, "He's a black man!" Robert Kennedy was the only white politician to hear only cheers and applause.

As the King family made its way through this crowd, America's white political establishment sat thigh to thigh and nose to neck, perspiring, whispering pleasantries, exchanging nods and forced smiles, or ignoring one another, like Jackie Kennedy, who rewarded Nixon's attempt to engage her in conversation with an icy stare.

Jammed into these pews and standing along the walls was almost every black American who had played an important role in the civil rights movement, or risen to the top of the two fields, sports and entertainment, where black accomplishment was rewarded. As this uneasy congregation awaited King's family, it was hard not to notice that none of these white governors and congressmen came from the South, or that many had avoided meeting with King in the early days of the civil rights movement, or to ignore the stir that Stokely Carmichael and his bodyguards created as they marched down the aisle in mirrored sunglasses, zippered boots, and dark blue Mao shirts, or the woman who yelled, "Oh, what is the matter with us all? Why, what is the matter? Martin's dead, Martin's dead," or the commotion that Vice President Humphrey caused by arriving with so many Secret Service agents that Governor Rockefeller, Mayor Lindsay, and others had to surrender their seats and stand along the wall with their backs to the open windows, prompting someone to shout, "Cover Rockefeller. Cover Rockefeller there. That's dangerous against the windows."

King's funeral would be seen by 120 million people, making it the most widely viewed televised spectacle since the Kennedy funeral. It may have lacked that event's pomp and pageantry, but Americans could not help but see King's open coffin, and recall Kennedy's closed one, or see Coretta Scott King dressed in black and holding the hands of her children, and recall Jackie, dressed in black and gripping the hands of hers. And when the camera behind the altar panned across the congregation, they saw many of the same people who had filled the pews at Washington's St. Matthew's Cathedral on November 26, 1963, some of whom were coming face-to-face for the first time since then.

The funeral's first great heartbreaking moment, when tears mixed with perspiration, voices in the choir quivered, women sobbed, and men dropped their heads into their hands, came when the congregation reached the refrain of "Softly and Tenderly," and sang, in the same building where King had been baptized, confirmed, and preached his first sermon, "Come home, come home. You who are weary, come home."

The second came when mourners heard a tape of King delivering a sermon three months earlier in the same church. At President Kennedy's funeral, Archbishop Hannan had brought mourners to tears by reading passages from JFK's inaugural address; at King's, they cried upon hearing King say, "If any of you are around when I have to meet my day, I don't want a long funeral. . . . I'd like someone to mention that day that Martin Luther King Jr. tried to give his life serving others. I'd like for somebody to say that day . . . that I did try to feed the hungry. And I want you to be able to say that day that I did try in my life to clothe the naked. . . . And I want you to say that I tried to love and serve humanity."

Mourners at a funeral often recall earlier ones and grieve for other deceased loved ones, particularly if they died at a similar age or under similar circumstances. In the church that morning were four men whose brothers had been assassinated by white Southern men lying in wait: Dr. King's brother, A. D. King, who sat with Coretta Scott King and her children in a front pew; Edward and Robert Kennedy, who were several rows behind the King family; and Charles Evers, whose brother, civil rights leader Medgar Evers, had been gunned down in front of his home in Jackson, Mississippi, in June 1963. Robert Kennedy had also attended Medgar Evers's funeral, and had comforted Charles Evers when he broke down. They spoke and corresponded afterward, and Dallas strengthened their bond. That day Kennedy sat near Evers because he knew that the King funeral would be difficult for him, and when Evers began sobbing, he again took him in his arms.

Kennedy left the church flanked by Evers and Earl Graves Jr. Evers urged him to ignore the outstretched hands so he would not appear to be campaigning. Kennedy told him, "If they want to shake my hand, I want to shake their hands."

As he moved through the crowd, he kept his head down, to avoid being scratched, and his suit jacket buttoned up, to avoid having it ripped off his back. A man who grabbed his hand reported it "shaking like a leaf."

Pallbearers loaded King's coffin onto the mule-drawn farm cart that would carry it four miles to his alma mater, Morehouse College, a method of transportation that the *Atlanta Constitution* said was "bound to evoke memories of the Washington scene in November 1963 when the body of President John Kennedy traveled through Washington on a horse-drawn caisson."

So many joined and left the procession that determining its size was difficult, but most estimates numbered the marchers and spectators at between 150,000 and 200,000. Kennedy marched with elderly men in shiny suits and elderly women carrying umbrellas against the hazy sun, with African diplomats in crisp business suits, militants in dashikis and Mao shirts, and sharecroppers in overalls, with white clergymen and nuns in sensible black shoes, and with many of the Northern whites and Southern blacks who had marched with King in Birmingham, Selma, Montgomery, and Washington.

He marched with singer Ray Charles, who held on to the arms of his companions, with Aretha Franklin, who led the marchers in "We Shall Overcome," with Dizzy Gillespie, who belted out "Oh Freedom!" and with Sammy Davis Jr., who wore a pair of oversized orange sunglasses to hide his tears and told *Life* magazine, "No one relates to the black man like Bobby . . . [he] can talk to the Uncle Toms and the militants."

He marched a few yards behind Ralph Abernathy, who believed that by succeeding King as president of the Southern Christian Leadership Council he had become the "number one target of racist assassins." When Abernathy had marched with striking black garbage workers in Memphis three days earlier, he had been haunted by vivid imagining of his own assassination, wondering "if the next person I passed wouldn't pull out a gun or start blasting away or if a bullet fired from some distant window wouldn't suddenly tear into my head, even before I heard the sound of the shot."

The mourners headed down Auburn Avenue, the "richest Negro street in the world" according to a 1956 article in *Fortune*, but already becoming a seedy strip of small groceries and taverns. They passed the gold-domed Georgia Capitol, where Governor Maddox had surrounded himself with hundreds of state troopers, vowing that if anyone stormed the building, he would "stack them up."

They marched through a downtown of white-owned stores such as Rich's department store that had been shuttered more out of fear than respect, since their suburban branches remained open. (It had been at Rich's that a young Martin Luther King Jr. had accidentally stepped on a white woman's foot, causing her to spit in his face and call him a "nigger," an insult he never forgot.) They crossed the railway yards on a bridge and entered a middle-class black neighborhood, following a boulevard that would be renamed to honor King, past bungalows where spectators rushed from their porches into the street with ice water and cold Cokes.

They walked sixteen, twenty, and thirty abreast, over cobblestones, asphalt, and concrete, for more than two hours during the hottest part of this sultry day. The men kept removing their jackets, so that by the time the vanguard of the procession began climbing the last hill to Morehouse, what had started as a mass of black funeral suits had become a checkerboard of black and white. Kennedy removed his jacket despite Evers's protest that it was in poor taste for a white man to attend a black funeral in his shirtsleeves. Within minutes a white girl darted from the crowd and ripped it from his hands.

Thousands dropped out, fainted, and collapsed. Nelson and Happy Rockefeller gave up and drove to Morehouse. Nixon and Humphrey skipped the procession and went to the airport. McCarthy refused to march on principle, telling his wife that it was not the kind of thing he would "enter into any competition about." But he later changed his mind and joined the procession as it neared Morehouse because, his wife explained, he "began to feel the simple emotion of the situation."

Kennedy walked the entire way, and his emotions must have been anything but simple. After monitoring civil rights marches from his office in the Justice Department since 1961, coordinating the 1963 March on Washington with King's aides, watching on television as police in Birmingham attacked black marchers with dogs and fire hoses, and police in Selma beat Ralph Abernathy, John Lewis, Hosea Williams, and other men who were now walking a few paces ahead of him—after watching all this from a distance, a man who relied on his experiences to shape his convictions and emotions was finally marching through a Southern city with thousands of singing and weeping black Americans.

King's funeral procession had all the trappings of a traditional civil rights march. Black and white walked arm in arm, singing "We Shall Overcome," "This Little Light of Mine," and "Keep Your Eyes on the Prize." There was an atmosphere of racial solidarity and intimacy that was still so uncommon in the South that reporters considered it noteworthy that "white and black women stood quietly in line to drink from a common hose," "black and white drank out of the same cup Tuesday at Morehouse College—and were grateful to do so," and "paper cups and empty soft drink bottles were filled and passed around from hand to hand and shared by black and white alike."

The next day, the editor of the *Atlanta Constitution*, Eugene Patterson, argued that television was incapable of closing the distance between black and white, writing, "You've got to sit between the mourners and touch shoulders with them in the crowd and feel the heat come up through your shoes from the hot pavement as you march with them. . . . You do not know them until you join them, and look them in the face, and white Americans have not done that yet." At King's funeral, Robert Kennedy had done just that.

Unlike the other white dignitaries, he was continuously applauded and cheered. One headline reported that "Kennedy Stirred Crowd the Most," and John Maguire, a white former freedom rider who marched near him, was struck by the fact that of all the white and black celebrities in the procession, the crowd only accorded constant and spontaneous applause to two men: Robert Kennedy and Sammy Davis Jr.

Harris Wofford, who had worked in JFK's presidential campaign and served in his administration as a special assistant on civil rights, marched behind Kennedy. He reminded Wofford of a lightning rod in an electric storm. All along the route black arms kept reaching for him and black leaders and children clustered around him. Wofford walked with a group of black civil rights veterans who had once been angry at Bobby and JFK for not moving fast enough on integration and voting rights, or offering enough federal protection to civil rights workers. But time had softened their complaints, and Wofford decided that "for almost all of them Robert Kennedy had emerged as the one point, the central person, around whom black and white, young and old civil rights workers were ready to rally."

Kennedy walked alongside Jimmy Breslin and Charles Evers. Breslin was surprised at seeing so few white spectators and asked Kennedy if he believed King's assassination would change anything. It would not, Kennedy said. Then, turning to Evers, he asked, "*You* think this will change anything?" Evers said, "This won't change nothing. It meant nothing when my brother was killed," a comment that may have prompted Kennedy to reflect on what his own brother's death had changed or accomplished.

By the time Kennedy reached the handsome campus of Morehouse College with its brick buildings, white columns, and cupolas, hundreds of marchers lay prostrate on its lawns, felled by heat and dehydration. Thousands more filled the quadrangle and pushed against a platform erected opposite Harkness Hall. Kennedy's arrival compounded the chaos, sending spectators climbing into the flowering dogwoods and leaping into the air to see him.

After the Morehouse Glee Club finished a medley of spirituals, Ralph Abernathy took the microphone and said, "I see Senator Robert F. Kennedy out there. Will you please make way for him to come to the platform? Let's give him a hand." The crowd cheered as Kennedy joined Coretta Scott King, Rosa Parks, Hosea Williams, Andrew Young, and other black dignitaries, becoming the only white on the platform.

During the singing of "O God, Our Help in Ages Past," the Reverend Wyatt Walker and other representatives of the white politicians in the audience rushed to the stage and were seen arguing furiously with Abernathy. Walker had formerly been King's secretary and was now an adviser to Governor Nelson Rockefeller. When the hymn ended, Abernathy announced, "As I said, Senator Robert Kennedy will come to the stage as well as the many distinguished visitors who are here today." He then named Rockefeller, Nixon, McCarthy, Humphrey, and others, although some had already left town. As Rockefeller and others struggled through the crowd, aides to politicians that he had failed to mention shouted, "Senator Morse is here!" "Senator Gruening is here!" and so on. Upon hearing this, Rosa Parks pulled out a large white handkerchief and wept.

Almost half the congregation at the church had been white, but the Morehouse audience was overwhelmingly black, and speakers were more candid about who or what they blamed for King's death. King's father stood up and shouted, "We wanted him to live, but *they* killed him."

During a eulogy one white witness described as "surprisingly bitter," Dr. Benjamin Mays, King's former mentor and president emeritus of Morehouse, said, "But, make no mistake, the American people are in part responsible for Martin Luther King's death. The assassin heard enough condemnation of King and of Negroes to feel that he had public support. He knew that millions hated King."

Mays's eulogy contained a passage similar to what Robert Kennedy would tell black and white audiences in coming weeks: "Let us see to it that we do not dishonor his [King's] name by trying to solve our problems by rioting in the streets. . . . But let us see to it that the conditions that cause riots are promptly removed." He concluded by braiding together the King and Kennedy assassinations, saying, "I close by saying to you what Martin Luther King Jr. believed: If physical death was the price he had to pay to rid America of prejudice and injustice, nothing could be more redemptive. And, to paraphrase the words of the immortal John Fitzgerald Kennedy, permit me to say that Martin Luther King's unfinished work on earth must truly be our own." (JFK had concluded his inaugural address with "Let us go forth to lead the land we love, asking His blessing and His help, but knowing that here on earth God's work must truly be our own.")

When Mays finished, Kennedy and the other dignitaries joined hands and, swaying back and forth, sang "We Shall Overcome." They looked down from the platform and saw ten thousand weeping and distraught people joining them. It was the largest crowd to sing this civil rights anthem since Dr. King's March on Washington.

Afterward, Walter Fauntroy noticed Kennedy sitting alone on a windowsill near the platform. He walked over and told him that he remained haunted by their conversation in Washington. "Bobby," he implored, "can't you tell me *why* you think there are guns between you and the White House?"

Kennedy stared at him blankly for several seconds. Then, slowly and without speaking, he shook his head and looked away.

PART III

✦

RED STATE PRIMARIES

EIGHT

LIKE FRANK SINATRA
RUNNING FOR PRESIDENT

APRIL 10–15, 1968

Kennedy realized that the tour's high-spirited campaigning and hysterical audiences had frightened older white voters, and he knew that the riots following King's assassination had left whites ready to embrace a candidate who appeared capable of calming the nation's cities. On April 7, the night before flying to Atlanta for King's funeral, he had discussed all this during a six-hour meeting at Hickory Hill with his political and media advisers, among them filmmakers Charles Guggenheim and John Frankenheimer, and Ted Sorensen, Fred Dutton, Dick Goodwin, and John Bartlow Martin, who later singled out the evening as an example of how Kennedy "ran a meeting hard."

When one of the advertising men boasted about having his "people" in Indiana, Kennedy became so exasperated that he interrupted to say that he did not want his "people" there, he wanted *him* there. Then he sent the media people out of the room and told the others that he wanted to deliver more serious speeches when he returned to Indiana on April 10, and that he thought the frenzied crowds of the previous weeks had made him look "like Frank Sinatra running for President." Martin warned that he risked being seen by many Hoosiers as the candidate of students and blacks. He agreed, saying that he wanted to do something in the Polish backlash suburbs of Gary.

The so-called backlash voters were typically blue-collar whites, mostly Catholics and Eastern European ethnics who had become upset by the sexual revolution, the lack of respect accorded to the older generation by young people, disturbances on college campuses, and black inner-city crime. Because many lived in Northern cities and nearby suburbs in close physical and economic proximity to blacks, they felt threatened by black political and economic gains. The term *law and order* appealed to them because it was both a call for draconian law enforcement in ghetto neighborhoods and a code for keeping black Americans confined in these neighborhoods.

In 1964, George Wallace of Alabama, the populist, segregationist governor who had stood in the door of a building at the University of Alabama to prevent the enrollment of black students, had profited from the backlash vote and polled over 30 percent in Democratic presidential primaries in Wisconsin, Maryland, and Indiana, where he won 38 percent of the vote, his best showing in the nation. Wallace had announced in February that he would run for president in 1968 as a third-party candidate. But during the next three months he suspended his campaign while his wife battled cancer. The post-King riots had been a godsend for him, energizing his supporters, reinvigorating his campaign, and ensuring that he would remain a presence throughout the spring, haunting the candidates and the Democratic bosses, who believed that to beat Nixon they needed a nominee who could recapture the backlash voters.

Robert Kennedy's more optimistic supporters believed that the riots might increase his appeal to backlash voters who viewed him as a tough former attorney general, and the only white politician whom black Americans respected, and who could therefore control them. Most, however, believed that because Kennedy had become the champion of black Americans the riots had damaged him, making it even harder for him to win over backlash voters in Indiana.

The April 7 meeting at Hickory Hill would be among the first of many similar ones, stretching from 1968 to the present, that have wrestled with the question of how Democrats could reassemble the New Deal coalition of blue-collar workers, ethnics, Catholics, farmers, Southerners, Northern liberals, and blacks that had elected Franklin

Roosevelt, Harry Truman, and John F. Kennedy to the White House before being shattered by the Vietnam War and the civil rights movement.

Because Kennedy was the first Democratic presidential candidate to attempt to reunite the New Deal coalition, and because Indiana would be the first place he would attempt to do it, the 1968 Indiana primary is sometimes compared to the 1960 West Virginia primary, where JFK demonstrated that a Catholic could defeat Protestant Hubert Humphrey in a heavily Protestant state. After Robert Kennedy entered the Indiana primary in March, the columnists Evans and Novak wrote that the move "typifies the audacity with which the Kennedys have always played politics and exactly duplicates the gamble taken by John Kennedy in West Virginia in 1960." During the Hickory Hill meeting, Kennedy had himself said, "Indiana is the ball game. This is my West Virginia." Martin objected to the comparison on the grounds that it placed too much importance on a state Kennedy might lose. Sorensen suggested saying that Indiana could pick a president. Kennedy took his advice and in the coming weeks he would frequently say, "Indiana can help choose a president."

It was agreed at the Hickory Hill meeting that when Kennedy resumed campaigning in Indiana he would emphasize his former role as the nation's top law enforcement officer, reassure white audiences that he would not tolerate violence and riots, reassure black audiences that he would not tolerate injustice, and deliver the same message to both. He would also stress several positions that he had taken in the Senate that would appeal to the state's conservative Democrats, including welfare reform, incentivizing private enterprise to provide jobs and housing in poor urban neighborhoods, and giving local government and organizations more control over the administration of federal programs. His positions on these issues had led some commentators to compare him to Barry Goldwater and charge him with being a conservative politician with a large liberal constituency. But in question-and-answer sessions following his prepared speeches he made it clear that although he advocated tax credits to encourage private enterprise to invest in ghetto neighborhoods, he thought that the government should be the employer of last resort;

that although he wanted to end the bias in the welfare system that penalized poor families if a father remained at home, he opposed cutbacks in welfare spending in order to fund the space program or the Vietnam War; and that although he believed that a huge federal bureaucracy had stifled local initiative, he also believed that the federal government had a responsibility to help the disadvantaged, and supported closing tax loopholes that favored the wealthiest Americans.

Before returning to Indiana on April 10, Kennedy received two memoranda that could only have reinforced the decisions that he and his advisers had made at Hickory Hill. The first, from Arthur Schlesinger, described Indiana as a "middle-class, small-town, suburban state, fearful of challenge," whose Democrats did not want to be "summoned to the barricades and told they have to do great things to meet great crises." Schlesinger recommended that Kennedy mount a low-key campaign in the state, stating his views "with sobriety and precision." The second memorandum, from his Washington headquarters, offered a gloomy assessment of his prospects, calling Branigin the clear front-runner, and warning that Hoosiers were suffering a "high level of anxiety" following the riots and yearned for "a return to normalcy." It cautioned him that "motion, action, change, New Frontierism are not the order of the day for the short run," suggested that "calls for action should be limited to trying to get the business community involved in direct efforts to employ the poor, and local governments and civic-minded groups involved in helping their neighbors at the local level," and recommended that he stress "the restoration of law and order."

The first indication that Kennedy was ambivalent about this strategy came during his first appearance in Indiana after King's funeral, a speech at Fort Wayne's Scottish Rite Temple on the morning of April 10. The audience, largely white and middle class, was precisely the kind that he was supposed to court by stressing law and order, emphasizing his more conservative positions, and avoiding New Frontier–style calls for action and sacrifice. Because he often edited his prepared speeches as he delivered them, eliminating whole passages or using them as the framework for lengthy extemporaneous remarks, the only accurate record of what he said at the Scottish Rite Temple, and

at similar events, is the sound track recorded by Charles Guggenheim's film crew. A transcript shows Kennedy beginning inauspi-
ciously by telling the Temple audience that he did not intend "just to
talk about matters that deal with Indiana." Then he observed, "I look
out in this audience and . . . I see very few black faces, and there is only
a small population that is black in this community, and in the state. So
that someone might argue that a speech of this kind is perhaps more
appropriate in some other part of the United States." So much for
courting Hoosier voters.

After this combative opening, he raised rather than lowered the
anxiety in the hall by warning that Americans were facing "what is rap-
idly becoming the most terrible and urgent domestic crisis to face this
nation since the Civil War," an accurate description of the situation,
but one sounding shrill and alarmist. He called King's death "one of
those huge events that signals a turning point in our country's history,"
and said it could be an opportunity to ensure that America became
"one nation of all our people, equal in justice and equal in opportunity," or the beginning of a prolonged period of civil strife that would
turn America's cities into "armed camps" and its streets into "passage-
ways for violence and fear."

Instead of stressing law and order, he said white Americans bore responsibility for black frustration and violence. Dr. King had persuaded
black Americans that nonviolence and democracy would bring justice
and opportunity, but some blacks were now "losing faith in the good will
of this nation" and in the "possibility for change through peaceful
means." This was a dangerous situation, he said, because "frustrated
hope and loss of faith breeds desperation, and desperate men finally take
to violence, and they take to the streets." Repression would fail "because
there is no sure way to suppress men filled with anger, who feel they
have nothing to lose." Instead, white Americans should fulfill the "simple claims" of black Americans for decent jobs, and give them a sense
"that they are part of this country," or expect more riots that would
threaten their safety and comfort, and "diminish the idea of America."

He concluded by telling an audience that undoubtedly cared about
homes and salaries, that it was not "income and homes" that made
a nation great, but "shared ideals and purposes." He followed this by a

New Frontierish summons to the barricades, saying that laws and government programs could not guarantee racial peace and that instead, every American had a responsibility to "make one nation out of two."

He next flew to Terre Haute, where two thirds of residents polled by a local television station viewed him as an "opportunist." As he drove into town, white spectators chanted "coon-catcher, coon-catcher."

The driver of the press bus told newsmen that he would not vote for Kennedy because his hair was too long, adding, "It's like having a beatnik running for President." (Although Kennedy understood that in towns like Terre Haute, long hair on a man was interpreted as an indication of free love, drugs, revolution, anarchy, homosexuality, hippies, and substandard personal hygiene, he did not appreciate being told to cut it, once saying, "If everyone would stop telling me to get a haircut, I'd get one.") After receiving tepid applause at the outdoor rally, he remarked that one of the signs at the airport had said BEAUTIFY AMERICA—GET A HAIRCUT, adding, "I'm so interested in winning . . . in Indiana that I'm having my hair cut," a comment that, if you think about it, was not very flattering to the Hoosier electorate. In fact, during the early weeks of the campaign his six-inch forelock had been gradually retreating, and an AP story from Terre Haute concluded, "Thus Kennedy follows the footsteps of his late brother in yet another way. Shortly after John F. Kennedy announced his presidential candidacy in January 1960 he, too, shortened what had been an exceptionally long hair style."

The next morning, Kennedy had breakfast with 150 Terre Haute housewives. He sped through his prepared speech, becoming more animated as he answered questions. Stunned by the apparent complacency of the audience, he began lecturing them about the poor, saying, "They are hidden in our society. No one sees them any more. They are invisible. A small minority in a rich country. Yet I am stunned by the lack of awareness of the rest of us toward them and their problems . . . and every year their lives are more helpless than ever and yet we wonder what's wrong with them after all we've done for them."

After warning that Americans must choose between "violence and discord" or "compassion and love and understanding," he lost himself in a lengthy stream-of-consciousness riff about the lives of the hidden poor. At Ball State, he had insisted that white Americans wanted "to do the right thing." In Indianapolis, he had said that most white and black people wanted "justice for all human beings that abide in our land." Now he wanted to persuade these Terre Haute housewives to justify his optimism. He said:

> I traveled in the Delta area of Mississippi . . . where they, these children never had more than two meals a day which consisted basically of bread and gravy and occasionally they had beans but very, very rarely did they ever have meat. . . .
>
> [T]he poor are so hidden—you know, as Camus said, there is no one who is really going to speak for them—I mean, it's a small minority now . . . and so to focus attention on them or have them focus attention on themselves, is very, very difficult. . . . Well, if you live in a city in Mississippi and you were doing relatively well, why would you ever be up in the Delta area of Mississippi to see children starving? The chances are that you would not. You don't come in contact with the poor if you live in those kind of conditions. How many people go into an Indian reservation or see those children and talk with them? . . . there is much less awareness of what exists in the rest of the country amongst the poor, amongst the deprived and the ones who are so filled with hopelessness. So it is much much more difficult for us to understand—we think, we pay these taxes, we pass all these programs, why are they unhappy? Why aren't they pleased with what we've done? But for them the conditions aren't better. . . .
>
> But we had doctors who went down to the Delta area of Mississippi and said those children were destroyed. They will never be the same—they can never have their full mental faculties for the rest of their lives because they've been starved by the time they're three years old—so I mean those are the conditions that exist in the United States—not in Southeast Asia, not in Africa, but—it's unacceptable that in our own country that children are bitten by rats—there are more rats in New York City than there are people. . . . We're going to discuss these issues—we're going to discuss what we have to do about it. And I think we need to do something about it.

When he finished, an employee of the Terre Haute post office presented him with a pair of zip code cuff links. He put them on to laughter and said, "Thank you very much. This is something I have always wanted." One wonders if, at this moment and at ones like it, he recalled his conversation with Sylvia Wright as they flew to Washington, and decided that these cuff links were the price for having the chance "to teach people something."

During a flight to Ann Arbor afterward he discussed the breakfast with reporter David Halberstam, telling him, "So far in Indiana they seem to want to see me as a member of the black race—I don't think I can win if that happens. . . . That breakfast was very good and you could feel them coming around, but how many people in Indiana will get that much exposure, how many chances will you have to talk at that length?" A moment later, reflecting on the gap between what he wanted to tell these audiences and what they wanted to hear, he said, "These people never ask me, 'What are you going to do about the Negro problem, or what can we do for the Negro?' They always ask: 'what are you going to do about the violence?'"

In Ann Arbor, he told University of Michigan students that white and black Americans "live in different worlds and gaze out over a different landscape," and seen through the eyes of a young and disadvantaged black, the world was "a dark and hopeless place indeed." He asked them to imagine the inner lives of the young black men who had burned and looted their own neighborhoods, saying, "Every day, as the years pass, and he becomes aware that there is nothing at the end of the road, he watches the rest of us go from peak to new peak of comfort. A few blocks away or in his television set . . . [he] sees the multiplying marvels of white America: more cars and more summer vacations, more air-conditioned homes and neatly kept lawns. But he cannot buy them. He is told that Negroes are making progress. But what can that mean to him? He cannot experience the progress of others, nor should we seriously expect him to feel grateful; because he is no longer a slave, or because he can vote, or eat at some lunch counter. He sees only the misery of his present and the darkening years ahead."

Yet again, what Kennedy was saying bore little resemblance to the strategy mapped out at Hickory Hill. Perhaps the reason was that the meeting had preceded King's funeral, and after being embraced by Abernathy and hailed by black crowds as he marched to Morehouse, he was less willing to take his black supporters for granted, and "do something" in the backlash suburbs.

Kennedy made his first foray into the heart of Indiana backlash territory on April 15. A crowd at a rally in South Bend stared silently as he walked onto a platform on the steps of the St. Joseph County Courthouse. An aide clapped into the microphone, trying to encourage some applause; his solitary claps echoed off the walls of surrounding buildings. Finally someone shouted, "Let's hear it for Ethel Kennedy!" and there was scattered applause.

Since the 1967 riots, Kennedy had coupled any statement condemning violence with an equally strong one condemning racial injustice. Martin noticed that whites in Kennedy's audiences tended to applaud the law-and-order part of his statement while tuning out the rest, while blacks did the reverse. This is what happened in South Bend. After Kennedy said, "I don't think violence or lawlessness or disorder or riots have any role or any place in either white or black societies in the United States of America," the mostly white crowd applauded loudly. When he followed this with, "But I also don't think that a man, because of the color of his skin, or his religion, or the place that he lives, who is unable to get a decent job for his family, who is unable to get a decent education for his children, who is unable to get decent housing; I don't think that has any place in America in the year 1968," they applauded again, although less enthusiastically.

Several hours later, Kennedy delivered the same message to a friendlier crowd at the LaPorte County Building in Michigan City, Indiana. When he said, "I don't think that we can expect and should expect to have riots and lawlessness" they shouted, "Yeah, Yeah." When he followed this with, "nor are we going to have injustice, a man having a difficult time getting . . . decent employment because of the color of his skin, that's unacceptable," they shouted "Yeah, Yeah" just as loudly. But when he spoke about using tax credits to encourage the private sector to invest in ghetto neighborhoods, no one responded and he interrupted himself to say, "Clap!" adding that it might look good if the newspapers reported that spontaneous applause had broken out.

From Michigan City he traveled by motorcade into neighboring

Lake County, a place of steel mills, refineries, factories, rail yards, junkyards, polluted waterways, and grimy cities notorious for bad air, racial tension, and corrupt public officials. The largest city, Gary, was 60 percent black. In 1967, its voters had elected Richard Hatcher to City Hall, making it the first large city in the nation headed by a black politician, and accelerating white flight into the suburbs. Lake County's other cities were dominated by first- and second-generation working-class Catholics from Eastern Europe, and Protestants who had migrated north from Appalachia. Hammond was a sprawling immigrant melting pot bisected by dozens of level crossings. Whiting was an enclave of Slovaks and former hillbillies next to the Illinois line where blacks were discouraged from lingering after their refinery shifts ended, and rough-and-tumble East Chicago was known for taverns and a sizable Hispanic population.

Kennedy had the strong support of black voters in Lake County and the affection that many of its blue-collar whites still felt for John F. Kennedy. Otherwise, no county in Indiana promised to be more hostile to his candidacy and less amenable to his goal of reconciling urban blacks and backlash whites. Not only had Lake County given Wallace his largest Indiana plurality in the 1964 Democratic primary, but the Branigin machine was so powerful that supporters of Kennedy holding state jobs had been afraid to collect signatures to put him on the ballot and volunteers had to be bused in from Chicago. The county clerk was a Branigin and Johnson loyalist who had to be compelled by a court order to accept the Kennedy petitions. Lake County's machine Democrats had not forgotten that Kennedy's Justice Department had indicted George Cacharis, a popular Gary mayor, while union members had not forgotten his rough handling of union officials during the McClellan Committee hearings. Gary was considered such a racial minefield that some in Kennedy's campaign had urged him to skip it on April 15, or take a circuitous route through its white precincts, avoiding its black downtown. Had it not been for Richard Wade's strenuous protests, this might have happened.

Wade was a distinguished urban historian and an Honorary Kennedy of long standing who had met John Kennedy after inviting him to address his students at Harvard in 1946. He had worked in

Attorney General Robert F. Kennedy and his brother, President John F. Kennedy, conferring at the White House. During the Kennedy administration, Bobby's agenda was indistinguishable from his brother's. But when he ran for the presidency, he told British journalist David Frost, "We're living in a different time," adding that he was concerned about "what *can* happen in 1969, not what happened in 1963." *(John F. Kennedy Library)*

BELOW: When Robert Kennedy announced his candidacy in March 1968, he and Ethel had ten children. A month later Ethel learned that she was pregnant with their eleventh. She would give birth to this child, Rory Kennedy, on December 12, 1968, six months after her husband's assassination. Robert Kennedy was famously fond of children. The wife of Burt Glinn, who took this photograph, has said that she was struck by how he refused to kiss them as other politicians did. Instead, he would brush a child's face with his fingers, or touch them gently on their head, as if trying to feel their thoughts. *(Burt Glinn, Magnum)*

Kennedy discussing the assassination of Martin Luther King Jr. with press secretary Frank Mankiewicz shortly after arriving in Indianapolis on the evening of April 4. Moments earlier, a reporter had told Kennedy that King had just died of his wounds. Less than an hour later he brought the news of King's death to several thousand black Americans at a political rally in a tough Indianapolis neighborhood. When he finished the crowd dispersed peacefully and Indianapolis was the only major American city not to experience riots that evening. *(John F. Kennedy Library, photographer unknown)*

The Kennedys pay their respects to Coretta Scott King on the eve of her husband's funeral in Atlanta. Robert Kennedy is sitting in Dr. King's favorite chair, where he read, napped, and composed his sermons and speeches. In the coming weeks many black Americans would view Kennedy as Dr. King's de facto successor, and on the eve of King's funeral, one of King's lieutenants, the Reverend Hosea Williams, would tell him, "You have a chance to be a prophet. But prophets get shot." *(Flip Schulke/CORBIS)*

After attending Palm Sunday services, Kennedy walked through neighborhoods in Washington, D.C., devastated by the riots following King's assassination. One woman who met him there said, "I knew you'd be the first to come here, darling." At one point he turned to his companion, the Reverend William Fauntroy, and said, "I'm afraid there are guns between me and the White House." *(Burt Glinn, Magnum)*

ABOVE RIGHT: The way crowds swarmed over Kennedy reminded one witness of the relationship between the famed Spanish matador Manolete and his voracious fans. *(Bettman/CORBIS)*

ABOVE LEFT: During a 1967 visit to the Mississippi Delta, Kennedy found children starving in windowless shacks reeking of mildew and urine. That evening he returned home to Virginia and told his children, "Do you *know* how *lucky* you are? Do something for your country." *(JFK Library, photographer unknown)*

Kennedy liked slow-moving motorcades because they permitted tens of thousands of people to see him. But the motorcades made some aides nervous, calling to mind JFK riding through Dallas in an open limousine. When a friend told Kennedy that by making himself so accessible, he was giving his enemies a chance to hurt him, Kennedy replied, "Well, so many people hate me that I've got to give the people who love me a chance to get at me." *(Bettman/CORBIS)*

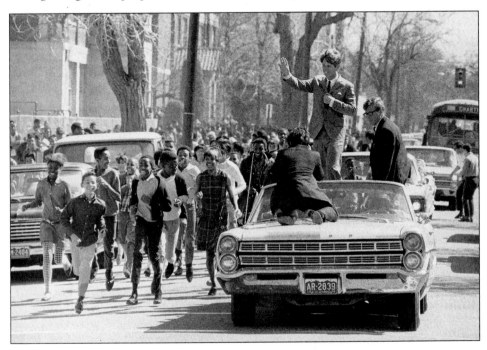

ABOVE LEFT: During Kennedy's visit to the Pine Ridge reservation he met Christopher Pretty Boy, a recently orphaned Indian. Kennedy kept Pretty Boy at his side throughout the day and invited him to spend the summer at the Kennedy compound on Cape Cod. *(Courtesy of Red Cloud Indian School, Pine Ridge, South Dakota)*

ABOVE RIGHT: Kennedy surprised many by winning large percentages of rural voters in Indiana and Nebraska. One of his friends believed he did so well with rural voters because his down-to-earth self-deprecating humor made him appear to be a kind of "Midwestern New Englander." *(Courtesy of Dan Lykins)*

Kennedy surrounded by youths in Vincennes, Indiana. His opponents discounted his crowds, saying they were dominated by hysterical teenagers, and Kennedy himself sometimes asked, "Is there anyone here old enough to vote?" *(Burton Berinsky)*

During a flight from Portland, Oregon, to Los Angeles on May 24 Ethel arranged a birthday party for bodyguard Bill Barry. During the celebration one of the balloons burst and Kennedy, fearing it was a gunshot, instinctively threw his hands over his face. *(Burton Berinsky)*

After losing the Oregon primary, Kennedy called Los Angeles his "resurrection city" because of the enthusiasm of his black and Hispanic supporters. The most frenzied reception of the entire campaign came when Kennedy rode through the streets of minority neighborhoods in Los Angeles on May 29. As crowds cheered and people swirled around his open car he pumped his fist in the air and shouted, "These are my people! These are my people!" *(John F. Kennedy Library)*

After declaring victory to supporters in the Ambassador Hotel, Kennedy uttered his last public words, "So my thanks to all of you, and on to Chicago and let's win there." *(Bettman/CORBIS)*

Throughout June 5, 1968, well-wishers held a vigil outside Good Samaritan Hospital in Los Angeles, where Kennedy clung to life for a day. Early the next morning, press secretary Frank Mankiewicz told reporters gathered there, "Senator Robert Francis Kennedy died at 1:44 a.m. today, June 6, 1968. . . . He was forty-two years old." Mankiewicz says he remembers Kennedy whenever he hears "The trumpet shall sound" aria in the *Messiah*, "because Bob Kennedy was the trumpet, and he's still sounding for me." *(Bettman/CORBIS)*

Mourners watch the funeral train carrying Kennedy's body from New York to Washington, D.C. No one had imagined that on a steamy Saturday afternoon two million people would spontaneously head for 226 miles of tracks: wading through marshes, hiking across meadows, filling tenement balconies, clambering onto factory roofs, standing in junkyards and cemeteries, looking down from bridges, viaducts, bluffs, and waving hand-lettered GOODBYE BOBBY signs. *(Burton Berinsky)*

JFK's Senate and presidential campaigns, and in Bobby's Senate campaign. In 1968, he was teaching at the University of Chicago and had became a close confidant to Mayor Richard Daley, who had made him Chicago's Commissioner of Housing, an influential position putting him in charge of sixty thousand apartments.

The first meeting between Wade and Daley concerning Kennedy's presidential bid occurred on March 6, ten days before Kennedy made his public announcement. Wade, as usual, was ushered into Daley's office past lieutenants who had been waiting hours in his anteroom. Daley, a mountainous man resembling Brando in his *Godfather* years, faced him across a gleaming desk whose surface was always preternaturally clear of papers. Because Daley always kept his office door open, he spoke in a low voice to avoid being overheard and communicated as much with gestures and expressions as with words, like a Mafia don.

Wade explained that he had agreed to head a Kennedy for President committee in Illinois, partly to keep the nascent organization from being controlled by operatives that Daley might find less palatable. He assured Daley that Kennedy would not embarrass him by entering the Illinois primary (an easy concession since Illinois was a preferential primary that did not bind delegates to vote for the winner), and that the Kennedy organization would be in "responsible hands," that is, Wade's. He then offered to spare Daley any embarrassment by resigning from his position on the Chicago city planning commission. Daley waved a pudgy hand in the air and told him to stay on.

Although Daley believed that the Democratic nominee should be chosen by a dozen powerful party leaders such as himself, considered it heresy for a Democrat to challenge a sitting president of his own party, and would publicly condemn Kennedy's candidacy, comparing him to Judas Iscariot, when he spoke about Robert Kennedy with Wade he winked, and Wade left their meeting convinced that he was pleased Bobby was running. Wade knew that Daley had loved JFK, wanted to see another Irishman in the White House, and had become increasingly disillusioned by the Vietnam War. During their meeting, Daley mentioned the recent battle for Hamburger Hill, a futile and bloody engagement costing many American lives. "Professor, you tell me this," he said to Wade. "You're a smart man. All they've got is a piece of real estate." Then, grabbing Wade by the arm, he asked, "What's all this about? Just fighting over real estate?"

Wade met with Daley again after Kennedy's March 16 announcement to tell him he was opening a Kennedy for President headquarters in Chicago. They agreed to meet on the Wednesday following every primary to discuss the results. As they parted, Daley stared at Wade and said in a deliberate voice, "The primaries count. . . . The primaries count. . . . The primaries count."

Wade was close to Gary's black mayor, Richard Hatcher, and could also walk into his office unannounced. He had urged Hatcher to run for mayor, encouraged Robert Kennedy to provide him with financial and organizational support, worked for his campaign, bused in volunteers from Chicago, and had given him informal tutorials on urban affairs. Although Hatcher had not endorsed Kennedy, he permitted Wade to run the Lake County campaign from his office, using his private phone lines and his silver telephone, a gift from Hubert Humphrey.

Some Kennedy advisers, including Ted Kennedy, who had sent a large contingent of his own political operatives into Indiana, were wary of Wade and believed that he overemphasized the importance of black voters. They urged Bobby to skip Gary, keep Hatcher at arm's length, and concentrate on winning over Lake County's backlash whites. Wade countered that Kennedy could only win Indiana if he inspired blacks to vote in record numbers, and that anything dampening their enthusiasm would be fatal. He also knew that if Kennedy appeared to be soft-pedaling his position on racial justice, he would find it difficult to recruit white liberals and black activists from Chicago to work for the campaign in Lake County.

When Wade heard that some aides were proposing that Kennedy fly into Gary on April 15 instead of arriving by motorcade in order to avoid meeting Hatcher at City Hall and driving through black neighborhoods, he called Kennedy to complain. He reached him at Hickory Hill on the evening of April 9, soon after he had returned from King's funeral. "Make sure you don't ever make a trip *around* Gary, going to just the white areas," he told him. "We can never risk people thinking you're running a racially calculated campaign." He suggested that

Kennedy meet Hatcher at the Gary line so he could ride into the city with him, and recommended having a rally in downtown Gary to reassure Hatcher that he was not taking the black vote for granted.

Kennedy agreed, and on the afternoon of April 15 he met Hatcher and Mayors John Nicosia of East Chicago, Joseph Klen of Hammond, and Frank Harangody of Whiting, at the Gary exit of the Indiana Toll Road. They claimed to be offering him "an official courtesy" and denied that their presence represented an endorsement, yet all four of them packed themselves into the backseat of his convertible and rode with him into downtown Gary, waving at crowds that were sparser than expected because the route had been changed at the last minute after an anonymous caller warned police that a man who had been seen carrying a gun into the high-rise Gary Hotel had also been overheard threatening to shoot Kennedy.

Kennedy entered the Gary Memorial Auditorium to chants of "RFK! RFK!" A largely black audience of five thousand shouted "We Want Bobby!" as Mrs. Odi Williams, head of Gary Volunteers for Kennedy, presented Ethel with a bouquet of roses. After an introduction from Hatcher that bordered on an endorsement, Kennedy took the podium and opened a black loose-leaf notebook containing a prepared speech that stressed economic issues and avoided civil rights.

He looked out at the audience and saw thousands of black faces, hungry for hope, and looked down at a speech about health care, tax credits, and welfare reform that had been organized into a seven-point program with paragraphs beginning "First . . . Second . . ." that would make good reading downstate. He put the speech aside and said, "May I say just before I talk in a more formal way . . ." For fifteen minutes he delivered the speech that this audience wanted to hear, and that after a week during which he had been told he could be a prophet to black Americans and had marched behind King's coffin, he must have felt he owed them.

He said, "It is time to end the violence and time to begin reconciliation. It is time to end injustice, and it is time to begin equality for every American citizen," and the auditorium shook with cheers. He said, "The violent youth of the ghetto is not simply protesting his tradition, but making a destructive and self-defeating attempt to assert his own worth and dignity as a human being," and there was more thunderous applause.

Then he raced through his prepared speech, delivering it so quickly that some had difficulty understanding it. Reporters comparing it with the advance text discovered that he had cut over half.

As he was leaving, he told Wade, "Well, I guess that didn't go over very well."

"The speech didn't," Wade replied," but you did."

Crowds of children ran alongside his open car as he was leaving Gary. He noticed that a black boy who had his arm in a cast was dragging his sister behind him. He told his driver to stop and invited them into his car. When they were seated, the boy took his sister's face in his hands, turned it toward Kennedy, and said, "Look! Here's Senator Kennedy." They rode together for several minutes before Kennedy diverted his motorcade to take them home. He presented their mother with Ethel's bouquet of roses and praised her children. The woman cried, and he sat with her on the front porch of her small wood-framed house, chatting and drinking iced tea while his motorcade waited. Then he continued to Chicago's Midway Airport and flew to Fargo, North Dakota. The next morning he flew on to the Pine Ridge Indian reservation in South Dakota. Within sixteen hours he had traveled from one of America's poorest cities to its poorest Indian reservation, from a city where the poor seldom voted in large numbers, to a rural county where people who were even poorer were even less likely to vote.

NINE

BRAVE HEART AND
CHRISTOPHER PRETTY BOY

April 16 and May 11, 1968

A photograph hanging in the office of Father Peter Klink, president of the Red Cloud Indian School in Pine Ridge, South Dakota, shows Robert Kennedy sitting on the edge of a bed with Christopher Pretty Boy, a ten-year-old Lakota Sioux with silky hair and large ears whose parents had died the week before in an automobile accident. The cabin where they are sitting belongs to Mrs. Veronica James, who has adopted Pretty Boy and his three siblings after the accident, meaning that nine people are living in this single room. Kennedy's hands are jammed into his trouser pockets and he is smiling, as if there was nowhere he would rather be than sitting on a worn blanket with a heartbroken orphan in a shack in Calico, one of the poorest communities on the poorest Indian reservation in North America.

A Jesuit Father from the Red Cloud Mission took the photograph, and because Kennedy had asked aides and reporters to remain outside, it is the only record of this meeting. In 1997, the Red Cloud School basketball team played in a tournament in Washington, D.C., and Klink invited Robert Kennedy's daughter Kerry to join the boys for lunch. He presented her with a framed copy of the photograph lacking only the note penciled onto the back of the original: "Taken at Calico Village Pine Ridge Reservation, April 16, 1968. Christopher

Pretty Boy and Senator Robert F. Kennedy were both dead a year after this picture was taken."

Klink remembers that he and Kerry Kennedy, who had been nine in 1968, struggled to make sense of the photograph. Since then, he has decided that it demonstrates that "what Kennedy wanted for America was often at odds with what was politically expedient."

The reporters and aides standing outside Mrs. James's home that morning were also trying to make sense of Kennedy's meeting with Pretty Boy, and of his obsession with Native Americans. It had started when he was attorney general and discovered that the Justice Department routinely litigated Indian land claims. He immediately reversed this policy and became such a vigorous advocate for Indian rights that at the 1963 convention of the National Congress of Indians in Bismarck he was adopted into the tribes and given the name Brave Heart. He told representatives of ninety tribes that they were being held in bondage by social and economic oppression, a situation he called "a national disgrace," and said that although the Kennedy administration was trying to provide them with better housing, education, medical care, and job opportunities, these only amounted to "spiritual first aid," and they deserved much more.

After being elected to the Senate in 1965, he visited reservations in upstate New York, called Indians "victims of racial discrimination in their own land," collected so many tomahawks, arrows, and belts that his office resembled a teepee, and was heard to remark, "I wish I'd been born an Indian."

He was interested the most in Indian education. While campaigning for Democratic congressional candidates in 1966, he had visited a reservation school in North Dakota and asked its principal to show him the books about Indian history and culture in the school library. The only one contained an illustration of Cherokees scalping white settlers. The principal told Kennedy that Indians lacked any history or culture, so why should there be books on those subjects? Kennedy's aide Dick Tuck, who witnessed the exchange, remembered that "Bob was incensed—not incensed; he was upset—not upset: he was mad."

Kennedy also came away mad from an Indian orphanage in New

Mexico whose director joked that if Ethel Kennedy really thought the kids were so cute he could sell her one, and madder still after touring an Indian boarding school where students could not go home for Christmas because funds had not been allocated for their transportation. While visiting a reservation near Pocatello, Idaho, he became so furious after seeing a library book with an illustration of an Indian scalping a blond girl that NBC correspondent Sander Vanocur decided he was someone who functioned "in a near constant state of outrage."

In 1967, Kennedy persuaded his fellow senators to create a subcommittee on Indian education and make him chairman. During a trip to Los Angeles he persuaded Nicole Salinger, the wife of JFK's former press secretary, Pierre Salinger, to accompany him to a reservation school outside the city. She remembered three boys who had been painfully shy. But they opened up to Kennedy after he asked them questions such as "Did they smoke?" and "Did they have brothers and sisters?" that indicated, according to Salinger, an ability to put himself in the place of these children.

No issue outraged Kennedy more than the high suicide rate among Indian teenagers. When he announced that he was running for president he condemned what he called "the inexcusable and ugly deprivation which causes . . . young Indians to commit suicide on their reservations because they've lacked all hope and they feel they have no future." He kept talking about Indians throughout his campaign, telling Indiana steelworkers and Nebraska farmers that the reservations were a national disgrace, and that after discovering that an Indian child had died of starvation on the same day that he visited her reservation, "a little bit of me died, too."

Of approximately seventy events that Kennedy attended during the first month of his campaign, ten were on Indian reservations or at Indian schools. His aides believed he was wasting his time and tried to remove these appearances from his schedule. He called them "callous sons of bitches" and reinstated them. Fred Dutton begged him to cut back, arguing that Indians only amounted to a couple of hundred thousand voters in an electorate of sixty million, while the ones who actually voted numbered "pretty near zero."

During the final three days of the tour, four of his nine events in

Arizona and New Mexico involved Indians. On March 29 in Albuquerque, he told the superintendent of an Indian school who reported spending twenty-two cents a day to feed each pupil, "When I was Attorney General, we spent more than that on the prisoners in Alcatraz."

In Tucson, he boarded a small propeller plane for a two-hour flight to the Navajo capital at Window Rock, Arizona. As it bumped through choppy weather, heading for an unpaved strip illuminated by the headlights of two rows of automobiles, Dutton snapped, telling him, "We're in a campaign and you should knock off the Injuns." Kennedy was suffering from laryngitis and scribbled his reply on a yellow legal pad. He wrote, "Those of you who think you're running my campaign don't love Indians the way I do, you're a bunch of bastards."

His speech at Window Rock was the most passionate of the tour. It was largely ad-libbed, and concerned three topics that moved him—Indians, children, and education. He asked the Bureau of Indian Affairs (BIA) bureaucrats sitting in the front row, "Is it not barbaric to take children as young as five and send them a thousand miles from their families to a boarding school?" After reminding them that two boys had recently frozen to death after fleeing a reservation school, he said, "When the United States can spend $130 million a year on Indian education but does not have enough money to send a child home for Christmas then something is pretty bad." Cheers and war whoops rang through the hall. As he was leaving an elderly man grabbed his hand and said, "I've waited all my life for a white man to say that."

Before deciding to run, Kennedy had scheduled hearings of his subcommittee on Indian education at the Pine Ridge reservation on April 16. He could have easily postponed them until after the June 4 South Dakota primary, a contest that had assumed greater importance after Johnson's withdrawal. The state promised to be a difficult one for him. Senator Eugene McCarthy represented neighboring Minnesota and was considered an honorary South Dakotan. Minnesota's other U.S. senator, Vice President Hubert Humphrey, had been born and raised in the state. Aside from Kennedy and McCarthy, the ballot also listed a slate of Johnson-Humphrey delegates who were publicly backing Humphrey. The South Dakota and California primaries both fell on June 4, and Kennedy victories in urbanized and diverse California and rural and conservative South Dakota would impress Daley and the other bosses and hurt Humphrey because, as one South Dakota newspaper pointed out, "It would be quite a lever at the national Convention if he [Kennedy] could say that Hubert couldn't even carry his home state." Because more delegates were at stake in California, Kennedy could only spend two days in South Dakota, making his decision to spend most of one of them on a sparsely populated Indian reservation even more remarkable, or foolhardy. Father Jim Fitzgerald of the Holy Rosary Mission, who helped to arrange Kennedy's visit, had believed until the last minute that he would cancel the trip because, as Fitzgerald puts it, "I mean, how many votes could he get?" Later, Fitzgerald decided that Kennedy had come so his press corps could see the reservation's desperate poverty—part of what Fitzgerald calls Kennedy's "educational agenda."

The nearest airport to Pine Ridge was at Chandron, Nebraska. When Kennedy landed there on April 16, the sons and daughters of the region's conservative ranchers and farmers, who had been given a school holiday in his honor, pushed down a steel fence and mobbed his plane. His official welcoming party included Judi Cornelius, an Indian college student who had arranged the Pine Ridge visit, and Sam Deloria, a Yale-educated Indian who ran the reservation planning office. Deloria rode on the press bus so he could brief reporters. During the ninety-minute journey they asked two questions: "How long until we arrive?" and "How long until we leave?" When the bus stopped near Pretty Boy's cabin at Calico, most remained on board, like students boycotting a boring field trip.

Kennedy had dragged them to a Connecticut-sized reservation with sixty miles of paved roads, no public transportation, and not a single supermarket, bank, motel, library, or movie theater. In cities, poverty hides behind doors. In Appalachia, forests and hollows camouflage it. But Pine Ridge's prairies made it impossible to ignore the junked cars and tumbledown shacks. Half its inhabitants were classified as "destitute," and two thirds of its buildings as "dilapidated." It had a 75 percent unemployment rate and the lowest per capita income in the nation. Only half of its households had electricity, and even fewer had running water. The average life expectancy was forty-eight for men and fifty-two for women, twenty years below the national average, and the lowest in the Western Hemisphere except for Haiti. Its youth suicide rate was three times the national average and, according to former Pine Ridge chief Johnson Holy Rock, it was not uncommon for a young woman to go out to collect firewood and be found hanging from a tree, or a young man to drive into a utility pole on purpose.

Since his brother's assassination, Robert Kennedy had not only sought out extreme physical challenges, but also extremes of poverty and suffering. On April 16, sitting in Mrs. James's ramshackle cabin in Calico with the orphaned Pretty Boy, he had finally reached the ground zero of human suffering on the North American continent.

Among those waiting for him to emerge from the cabin was David Harrison, an Honorary Kennedy from Massachusetts whom Ted Kennedy had recruited to organize North and South Dakota. Harrison had arranged for key North Dakota Democrats to meet Kennedy at his Fargo hotel on the evening of April 15. But after a predawn flight from Washington, two motorcades in Indiana, a television taping, and a rally at Fargo's civic auditorium at which Kennedy was supposed to have spoken about the farm crisis but had ignored his prepared speech and spoke instead about the racial crisis, he had told Harrison he was too exhausted to meet the delegates. Harrison pleaded with him, saying, "If you're going to win over these guys, you've got to at least *see* them." Kennedy relented and gave the delegates a few minutes. Now, twelve hours later, Harrison was astonished that he would spend so much time with Christopher Pretty Boy. "And it was not some quickie drive-by, either," Harrison remembers. "I mean he really spent *time* with that kid."

When Kennedy emerged from the cabin he was holding Pretty Boy by the hand. As they walked through Calico, he frequently leaned down to talk to the boy. "I mean, if you didn't fall in love with Kennedy then," Judi Cornelius says, "you didn't have a heart."

He stopped to speak with an elderly woman who was making bread in an outdoor oven next to her home, a rusty delivery van, and told her, "It makes me sad to see how your people live. You were the first people on this continent. But mark my word—in years to come there will be brand-new houses here."

He woke a sick boy who was sleeping in an abandoned car and stroked his feverish head. After questioning his mother and discovering that doctors at the hospital had claimed to be too busy to examine him, he told an aide to return the boy to the hospital.

Pretty Boy and Kennedy remained together all day. One news clip shows a solemn little boy in a light blue shirt gripping Kennedy's left hand as they walk through a crowd of Indians.

At the Red Cloud Indian School, Kennedy climbed onto the hood of a car and shouted to students in the parking lot, "You are the most important and significant Americans!" During a speech in its gymnasium, he told them, "Your tremendous culture has been unequaled by any other group in the United States!" Pine Ridge was poor, he said, "because the white man has not kept his word." His words were reported across South Dakota and may have unsettled voters whose land would have belonged to the Sioux had the white man kept his word.

Kennedy's Indian education subcommittee convened in Billy Mills Hall, a low brick building named for a Pine Ridge track star who had medaled at the 1964 Olympics. It was the largest space on the reservation, but even with its bleachers pulled out and folding chairs covering the basketball court, it could not comfortably accommodate an audience of over a thousand. When Kennedy noticed tribal elders standing along a wall, he stopped the proceedings and insisted that chairs be found so they could sit in the front, a gesture that is still remembered on the reservation.

Fred Dutton thought Indians liked Kennedy because they were thrilled someone was finally paying attention to them. John Nolan believed Kennedy liked Indians because they were like him: quiet and soft-spoken, but if you riled them up, they raised hell. Senator George McGovern of South Dakota, who accompanied Kennedy to Pine Ridge, was impressed by how quickly Indians warmed to him. He called it "a special response" that had eluded other politicians, including Hubert Humphrey, who had never been popular because Indians distrusted white men who spoke too fast. Kennedy, however, spoke like they did: softly and in halting sentences broken by "ahs" and "ums."

The psychologist Robert Coles believed Kennedy appealed to poor people like Native Americans because he seemed to be, as they were, unsure of himself. His body had "a tentative quality," Coles said, and he moved and spoke like someone who had a lot to say but was not quite sure how to say it—"who has a lot stirring in him but doesn't know how to put it into words."

A month of campaigning outdoors had also given Kennedy an Indian-like face, darkly tanned and deeply lined. The Indian activist Vine Deloria Jr. later wrote, "Spiritually, he was an Indian!" and believed Kennedy became a hero to native peoples because, like their most famous chiefs, he had a reputation for ruthlessness.

Kennedy's ruthlessness was not in evidence at Billy Mills Hall, perhaps because he was interrogating the powerless instead of the powerful. He persuaded Leona Winters, a nervous tribal councilwoman from remote Wanblee, to answer questions rather than read her prepared statement, frequently interrupting to say, "Now, you're doing very well."

Their exchange was as stark and discouraging as Pine Ridge. When Kennedy asked about the unemployment rate in Wanblee, Winters said that in her community of 350 people "there is no employment." When she told him that the Wanblee medical clinic was only open on Thursdays, he asked how far people had to go if they made the mistake of getting sick on one of the other six days. A hundred miles, she answered, and there was no ambulance. "What do people eat in Wanblee?" he asked. "Cornmeal," she replied. When she finished, Kennedy said that considering that America was spending $30 billion a year in Vietnam, "it seems it could spend some in the United States to alleviate the great poverty here."

During the hearings, McGovern mentioned that the most important site for Great Plains Indians was nearby at Wounded Knee, where a monument commemorated the 1890 massacre of 249 Sioux, many of them women and children, by soldiers of the 7th Cavalry. When Kennedy insisted on going McGovern protested that they were already running late and had an important rally that evening in Rapid City. Kennedy cut the hearings short and asked the remaining witnesses to place their statements on the record.

As the sun was setting, he and Pretty Boy arrived at Wounded Knee and climbed hand in hand to a hilltop monument overlooking miles of bleak prairie.

After Chief Big Foot left his reservation without permission from federal authorities, four hundred soldiers had surrounded his party at Wounded Knee and demanded that they surrender their weapons. Before they could respond, someone fired a shot and the cavalry opened fire. Photographs show soldiers standing over mass graves, guns pointed downward like big game hunters with their kill. A year later, the victims' relatives erected a granite plinth topped by an urn and faced with tablets that said, "Many innocent women and children who knew no wrong died here." After reading it, Kennedy said, "I should have brought flowers."

He added Pine Ridge's desperate poverty to his litany of injustices, mentioning it in his stump speeches and in conversations with friends. While relaxing in a hotel room in Omaha a few weeks later with folk singer John Stewart, he spoke about five-year-old Indian children being sent to schools a thousand miles from their homes. "Who are the people who are doing this?" Stewart asked. Kennedy stared at him and said, "You"—the same answer he would have given if Stewart had asked who was responsible for the dead civilians in South Vietnam. As Stewart rose to leave, Kennedy said he had just ordered eggs for them from room service. Stewart said he felt embarrassed to be eating after hearing about Pine Ridge. "Yeah, I know exactly what you mean," Kennedy said.

Since Robert Kennedy, no presidential candidate has visited Pine Ridge. President Clinton stopped there in 1999 during a whirlwind five-state "Poverty Tour" organized to promote his New Markets Initiative—a plan for increasing jobs and economic activities in impoverished communities with tax incentives that resembled what Robert Kennedy was proposing in 1968. A reporter who returned to Pine Ridge on the fifth anniversary of Clinton's visit found that the hopes he had raised had amounted to little. In fact, statistically, Pine Ridge has scarcely changed since 1968. Its inhabitants remain the poorest in the nation, and live twenty years less than the average American. Its teen suicide rate is still three times the national average, its unemployment rate hovers around 75 percent, only 39 percent of its households have electricity (1 percent less than in 1968), and its people still live in abandoned cars, trailers, and one-room cabins like the one where Kennedy met Pretty Boy.

While Kennedy was flying to Rapid City, he instructed an aide to call the Holy Rosary Mission and tell the Fathers that he had invited Pretty Boy and his sister to spend the summer with his family in Hyannisport. The invitation, the predictable result of Kennedy imagining himself, or his children, orphaned and living in Calico, would not have surprised his children. Kathleen Kennedy can remember driving with her father through a poor neighborhood in Washington and hearing him say, "Look, there are no playgrounds. There's no place for these kids to play. They're just like you; they have the same wants and needs." Then he raised funds to build a playground and brought his children to the opening ceremony.

Pretty Boy never went to Hyannisport. Like Kennedy, he was dead within the year. Some at Pine Ridge believe that he died in an automobile accident. Others say he killed himself, although he would have been younger than most Indian suicides. A third theory has him accepting a ride from a despondent older boy who then drove his car off the road on purpose, killing them both.

One of Kennedy's favorite quotations was Camus's observation that "perhaps we cannot prevent this world from being a world in which children are tortured. But we can reduce the number of tortured children. And if believers don't help us, who in the world can help us do this?" (When he repeated it in a speech he usually changed "tortured" to "suffering.") He had used it as the epigram to his 1967 book *To Seek a Newer World,* and it expressed two pillars of his faith: that everyone has a duty to alleviate suffering, and that no one can live a fully happy life while surrounded by the unaddressed misery of others.

When the British television personality David Frost asked Kennedy how he would like to be remembered, he had replied, "That I'd made some contribution to my country; to those who were less well off. I think back again to what Camus wrote about the fact that perhaps this world is a world in which children suffer, but we can lessen the number of suffering children, and if you do not do this, then who will do this? I'd like to feel that I'd done something to lessen that suffering." His invitation to Pretty Boy to spend the summer in Hyannisport was more evidence that Kennedy meant what he said, and would not ask Americans to do anything that he was unwilling to do himself.

A reporter meeting Kennedy's plane in Rapid City described him as "a man who had put in a strenuous day." As a delegation of Indians presented him with a peace pipe and moccasins, he shivered uncontrollably.

He rode into town with Bill Daugherty, a rancher and cattle trader whom he had met in 1959 while canvassing the state for JFK. Daugherty had started a Kennedy for President organization in the fall of 1967. He had been undeterred by a call from a Kennedy staffer who had told him, "A fellow usually likes to decide for himself if he's going to undertake the effort of running for the presidency of the United States." When McGovern, acting at Ted Kennedy's behest, had asked Daugherty to stop circulating petitions to put Kennedy on the ballot (a candidate could be entered in the South Dakota primary without his signature or permission), he had shot back, "The hell with it, he's going in." But even Daugherty's boundless confidence wavered as he and Kennedy drove through dark, deserted, and heavily Republican Rapid City in the pelting rain to a rally scheduled to begin two hours earlier. Just as Daugherty said, "Bob, I don't think this is going to be a good hit," they turned a corner and four thousand people gathered in a downtown square let loose a tremendous cheer.

Kennedy tried to rise to the occasion, joking that when he flew over Mount Rushmore on the way to Rapid City, he had noticed that "there's still lots of room." But he was exhausted and gave a second-rate stump speech.

McGovern delivered the evening's most memorable lines. Kennedy's candidacy had placed him in a difficult position. Not only were Humphrey and McCarthy personal friends and popular in South Dakota, but he also needed their support in his own difficult reelection campaign that fall. He had told friends that he planned to remain officially neutral, helping Kennedy "in a discreet way." But after spending the day with Kennedy at Pine Ridge, he told the crowd at Rapid City that Kennedy possessed "the absolute personal honesty of a Woodrow Wilson, the stirring passion for leadership of Andrew Jackson, and the profound acquaintance with personal tragedy of Abraham Lincoln." Then, unwilling or unable to hide his true feelings any longer, he added, "You people know the affection and esteem I held for President

Kennedy, but it is my carefully measured conviction that Senator Robert Kennedy, even more than our late beloved President, would now bring to the Presidency a deeper measure of experience and a more profound capacity to lead our troubled land into the light of a new day. . . . If he is elected President of the United States, he will, in my judgment, become one of the three or four greatest Presidents in our national history."

What could this be *but* an endorsement? None of Kennedy's opponents would have dared suggest that *they* might be better presidents than JFK. After McGovern finished, Kennedy grabbed his hand and squeezed it. During his own speech he did not dispute McGovern's introduction, perhaps because he had reached the same conclusion.

Kennedy returned to South Dakota for a second and final day of campaigning on May 10. He ended that day with a speech at the Corn Palace in Mitchell, McGovern's hometown. This time, McGovern introduced him with a quotation from "The Impossible Dream," a song from *The Man of La Mancha*, the 1966 musical about Don Quixote that Robert Kennedy listened to as obsessively as JFK had to the *Camelot* sound track. Kennedy repaid McGovern for his Rapid City introduction by saying that of all the U.S. senators, he was "the person who has the most feeling and does things in the most genuine way."

McGovern had not seen Kennedy for almost a month and was shocked by his lifeless eyes and deeply lined face. Kennedy delivered a rambling speech, slurring his words and repeating his favorite George Bernard Shaw quotation three times. At dinner afterward he scarcely spoke. After one painful silence he said, as if talking to himself, "I know there are times when I am not as capable or as forceful as Jack was. There are times like today, when I realize I just don't perform very well. Jack was the one. I just am not Jack. I can't do what he did. I am not Jack."

McGovern and the others at the table were shocked into silence.

In a low voice, Kennedy asked, "George, going back to what you said earlier, do you really think the dream is impossible?"

McGovern replied that winning the nomination was not impossible, just tough. Johnson would back Humphrey, and so would the party regulars. "But the point is you're willing to make the fight and I think you're doing well," he said, "and I wanted the audience to understand that it's worth making the effort—whether you win or lose."

"Well, that's what I think," he said.

The next morning, McGovern drove Kennedy to the airport, watching as he walked through the mist to a small chartered plane. McGovern had found that at different times and in different places, Robert Kennedy appeared to be a man of different sizes, sometimes large, but at other times slight and frail. (He was actually five feet nine and weighed between 150 and 160 pounds.) This morning he struck McGovern as being very small. As he crossed the tarmac, alone and stoop-shouldered, head down, his jacket slung over his shoulder, he looked so vulnerable that McGovern claims to have been seized by "a deep and profound feeling of sadness."

It would be the last time he would see Kennedy alive, so perhaps that colored his memory of this moment. But others made similar observations during the campaign. NBC took some still photographs of Kennedy during his Indiana whistle-stop. The one he liked best showed him sitting alone in the Pullman car. David Brinkley called it "a terribly poignant little picture, just a picture of Bobby, looking sort of lonesome, kind of small . . . in the middle of that big political entourage." After traveling with him for weeks in Indiana, John Bartlow Martin observed, "More than most candidates, despite his big staff, he seemed alone. What he did and said was largely his own. . . . He also looked so alone, too, standing up by himself on the lid of his convertible—so alone, so vulnerable, so fragile, you feared he might break."

TEN

"HOW DOES IT LOOK
FOR ME HERE?"

APRIL 22–24, 1968

After leaving Rapid City, Kennedy spent several days campaigning in Oregon, California, and Nebraska before returning to Hickory Hill for the weekend. While he was on the West Coast, John Bartlow Martin flew back to Washington and urged Ted Kennedy, Joe Dolan, and Ted Sorensen to persuade Kennedy to change the tone and direction of his campaign in Indiana.

Despite Kennedy's insistence that he did not want to resemble Frank Sinatra, Martin felt that his rallies had still been too frenzied. (Following Kennedy's appearance in Grand Rapids on April 11, newspaper headlines had read, "Fans Mob Kennedy on Brief Visit Here" and "Hysteria Keynotes RFK Visit.") He suggested that Kennedy cut down on inter-city motorcades and campus visits, and visit historical sites and rural county seats instead. He proposed that when Kennedy went to Vincennes on Monday he tour the memorial to Revolutionary War hero George Rogers Clark and visit the home of former president William Henry Harrison, then spend the afternoon on the Lincoln Trail, the route followed by Abraham Lincoln's family while traveling across southern Indiana to their new homestead. He also recommended that Kennedy make a whistle-stop tour along the route of the famous Wabash Cannonball, visiting Kokomo and Marion, small industrial cities with large populations of recent migrants from Appalachia who were as antagonistic to blacks as the Eastern Europeans of Lake County, then return to southern Indiana, a Republican stronghold where Democratic leaders remained hawkish on the Vietnam War and were supporting Branigin.

The drawback to Martin's plan was that Kennedy might trade frenzied crowds for sullen ones, razzle-dazzle for hostility. Vincennes was the seat of conservative Knox County, "log cabin and corn-liquor country," and in Scottsburg, Protestant churches had held services on the eve of the 1960 election so parishioners could pray that JFK would lose. The Klan remained active in Kokomo, whose Democratic mayor strongly supported the Vietnam War and Branigin. Bedford had been another Klan stronghold, although its black population was so minuscule that the Klan had terrorized Catholics instead, staging torchlight parades past churches.

When Kennedy reviewed Martin's schedule at Hickory Hill, he asked if courting Kokomo's rednecks and Klansmen was really worth the effort. Martin countered that he *had* to go into cities like Kokomo because they were heavily Democratic, and if he condemned the violence of the rioters and racial injustice as equally intolerable, he might win them. He also recommended that Kennedy praise private enterprise when he spoke at businessmen's lunches like the one scheduled in Vincennes the next day. Kennedy replied that he could do that in good conscience since the mission of his Bedford-Stuyvesant Corporation was to encourage corporations to invest in distressed ghetto neighborhoods. But he poked fun at Martin's briefing papers, criticized the speech he had written for him to deliver at the Vincennes luncheon, called his proposed historical tour "a waste of time," and dismissed his suggestion that he bring along some of his children.

Nevertheless, he appeared at National Airport the next morning with three of his children—David, Courtney, and Michael. And upon landing in Vincennes he said, "I have come because I believe that the seeds of national greatness lie in the greatness of the past. To meet our responsibilities we will need the courage of George Rogers Clark, the resourcefulness of William Henry Harrison, and the humility and wisdom and sheer humanity of Abraham Lincoln."

Greeting Kennedy at the airport was Jim Osborne, a twenty-three-year-old high school teacher and political neophyte who cochaired the local Kennedy for President Committee. He had opened a headquarters in a former motorcycle repair shop, recruited town historian Gus Stevens to guide Kennedy around the historic sites, invited leading businessmen to a lunch at the Ramada Inn, and prepared himself for a catastrophe. The Knox County Democratic establishment was solidly behind Branigin, and Osborne had failed to persuade a single elected official to meet Kennedy. His cousin Frank Myer had agreed to loan his convertible to the campaign for the day, but balked at driving Kennedy himself because he was a Branigin man. The first indication that things might turn out well came when Myer arrived at the airport driving the Oldsmobile.

The Clark Memorial, the largest memorial to a military battle outside of Washington, D.C., is a classical granite structure with sixteen columns, a rotunda, a bronze statue of Revolutionary War hero George Rogers Clark, and murals illustrating the opening of the American West. Kennedy lingered longer than other dignitaries that Stevens had brought to the memorial. He studied the murals, murmuring "magnificent," and reading the inscriptions aloud, such as Clark's declaration, "Great things have been effected by a few men well conducted."

Osborne feared that no one would attend a noon ribbon-cutting ceremony at Kennedy headquarters. But at eleven the front doors of his storefront burst open and a mob of local politicians, among them the city's Republican mayor, rushed into the room, jockeying for positions and forming a receiving line. Kennedy shook their hands and asked, "How does it look for me here?" Even the Republicans told him it looked "great."

At Grouseland, the ancestral home of President William Henry Harrison, twelve hundred Vincennes University students besieged his car, shouting questions and making him an hour late for a "Business and Professional Men's Luncheon" at the Ramada Inn being sponsored by the Vincennes Civitan Club.

The kitchen could only serve sixty lunches, but so many Civitan, Kiwanis, and Rotary Club members wanted to attend that Osborne had invited an additional eighty people on condition that they stand along the walls and go hungry. Half were Kennedy supporters and the rest were interested in his candidacy enough to attend. When it was announced that Kennedy would be late the men began to eat. He arrived to find a banquet room filled with middle-aged white businessmen devouring Salisbury steaks.

The speech Martin had written for the occasion, "The Role of Private Enterprise," was a compendium of positions that Kennedy had taken as a senator, and would presumably appeal to an audience of businessmen. Kennedy delivered it in a perfunctory manner. John Nolan, who had scheduled many of his appearances in Indiana, had often witnessed him struggling to relate to groups like this one. He remembered the Vincennes luncheon as "grim." Not only did Kennedy dislike appearing before bar associations and Kiwanis Clubs, he knew he came off poorly. When Martin criticized him for spending too much time with the poor and minorities who already supported him, he had replied plaintively, "But those are the audiences I *like* to talk to. I feel at home with them." Martin agreed, later writing that, "It was true. He had no feel for the petite bourgeoisie, the suburbanites."

Kennedy prefaced his response to the first question in Vincennes with, "I know most of you are Republicans." In fact, they were not, but it was a reasonable assumption given a survey of the nation's 160 top businessmen that showed that 91 favored Richard Nixon while 3 listed Kennedy as their first choice for president.

The Vincennes audience asked Kennedy about gun control, the federal imposition of daylight savings time on Indiana, and congressional legislation funding rat-control programs in inner-city neighborhoods, on the supposition that he would number it among the wasteful federal programs he had criticized in his prepared speech. Instead, his voice turned hard and he said, "Do you know there are more rats in New York than people, and there are nine million people there?"

This was met with nervous laughter. Jim Osborne believes that no one in the room had been to New York, and most assumed Kennedy was joking.

Kennedy's face tightened and the veins on his neck bulged. Speaking slowly and deliberately, and perhaps remembering the girl in Brooklyn whose face had been scarred by rat bites, he said, "DON'T LAUGH!"

Tom Congdon Jr. of the *Saturday Evening Post* witnessed the exchange, and wrote that Kennedy "gave up all notion of speaking to the audience on the matters that concerned it most—such as law and order—and instead tried to stir it with the matters that most concerned him. To the club members—big, heavy men, most of them well-fleshed and still occupied in shoveling in their lunch—the Senator from New York spoke of children starving, of '*American* children, starving in *America.*' It was reverse demagoguery—he was telling them precisely the opposite of what they wanted to hear." He added that after the exchange about the rats, "The room hushed and the program soon broke up, with audience still ruffled and confused."

Vincennes proved to some that Kennedy could only flatter an audience so much, and that forced to choose between Rotarians and rat-bitten children, he would choose the children. But Osborne considers the exchange a misunderstanding and a minor blemish on an otherwise successful visit that persuaded many of the Democratic bigwigs to abandon Branigin. His cousin Frank Myer experienced a similar conversion, talking nonstop about Kennedy afterward and convincing his mother, who had never voted for a Catholic, to support him.

Kennedy asked Osborne and Stevens to tag along for the rest of the day, and they drove with him through rural counties where Republicans ruled and Democrats were conservative. Still, a large and enthusiastic crowd of German-American Democrats greeted him in Jasper, despite Martin's prediction that they were "remote from the world's troubles" and wanted to be left alone.

In Daviess County, where Senator Homer Capeheart, a right-wing Republican icon, owned a farm and Nixon had crushed JFK in 1960, the schools released students early so they could attend Kennedy's rally, and the newspaper reported "a welcome usually reserved for matinee idols." Instead of delivering a law-and-order speech Kennedy told them that Americans had a moral responsibility for the war being waged in their name. "All of us are, to some degree, responsible for this," he said. "And it is going to take the best efforts of all of us to get our country out of it."

Kennedy's jazzy, slap-happy style captivated Gus Osborne. He liked how Kennedy played word games with his children and made him and

Myer and Stevens feel like Honorary Kennedys. But at dusk, as they were driving to their last stop in Evansville, a barrage of eggs hit the side of the convertible. Myer swerved onto the shoulder. Kennedy was suddenly nervous and wary. He walked back to check on Ethel, who had recently learned that she was pregnant with their eleventh child, and Osborne realized how traumatic it must be for a Kennedy to be hit by anything, even an egg, while riding in an open car.

Two days later, Kennedy delivered the most important foreign policy address of his campaign to four thousand students at the University of Indiana in Bloomington. Johnson's peace initiative and decision not to seek reelection had temporarily sidelined the Vietnam War as an issue. Kennedy reintroduced it with this speech and explained why he opposed Johnson's policies, and how a similar catastrophe might be avoided in the future.

He began, "Long ago it was said, 'The time for taking a lesson from history is ever at hand for those who are wise,'" and what follows makes for painful reading. Substitute "Iraq" for "Vietnam" and "terrorist" for "Communist" and the speech becomes one that four decades later a presidential candidate could deliver verbatim. For example:

"We should give no more assistance to a government against any internal threat than that government is capable of using itself, through its agencies and instruments. We can help them but we cannot try to do their jobs for them. . . .

"For one thing, Vietnam has proven that all the might and power of America cannot provide or create a substitute for another government, or for the will of another people. . . .

"Their [American troops'] presence can transform a factional struggle within a country into a nationalist struggle against foreign domination. Their introduction commits our prestige to the outcome of diverse struggles we may barely understand. It may lead the government and the people to refuse essential sacrifices. Most ironic of all, ill-considered military intervention may well increase the very Communist influence they are aimed to prevent."

Kennedy identified four genuine threats that America faced. The first two were the challenges posed by the Soviet Union and China. The third was an "overcommitment in rhetoric and action" and an "automatic use of military force." The fourth, he said, "is here at home. It is the danger that absorption in the problems of others will cause us to neglect the health and quality of our own society. We cannot continue to deny and postpone the demands of our own people while spending billions in the name of the freedom of others."

He concluded by saying that although the United States had become a great military power, and although Americans could not renounce that power, "neither can we forget that the real constructive force in the world comes not from bombs but from imaginative ideas, warm sympathies, and a generous spirit. These are qualities that cannot be manufactured by specialists in public relations. They are the natural qualities of a people pursuing decency and human dignity in its own undertakings without arrogance of hostility or delusions of superiority toward others; a people whose ideals are firmly rooted in the realities of the society we have built for ourselves."

Bloomington was the most liberal campus in Indiana, and its students interrupted him sixteen times with applause. The question period turned into a revival meeting, with Kennedy asking them to wipe away the stain of Vietnam by making a personal commitment to end poverty, prejudice, and illiteracy.

It was the kind of serious and substantive speech that he had told Martin he wanted to deliver. Adam Walinsky had drafted it, and Peter Edelman had spent three days showing it to foreign policy specialists in Washington. Its tough but humane foreign policy sprang from Kennedy's experience as a foreign policy adviser to his brother.

During the 1962 Cuban Missile Crisis, he had argued that a surprise attack on Soviet missile sites there would be the moral equivalent of the Japanese sneak attack on Pearl Harbor. In *Thirteen Days*, his account of that crisis, he wrote, "The strongest argument against the all-out military attack, and one no one could answer to his [President Kennedy's] satisfaction, was that a surprise attack would erode if not destroy the moral position of the United States throughout the world." He claimed to have pointed this out during the deliberations, adding that President Kennedy's advisers had "spent more time on this moral question during the first five days than on any single matter." Secretary of the Treasury Douglas Dillon, who attended these meetings, remembered Bobby saying, "I can't help remembering Pearl Harbor, and we cannot have a Pearl Harbor that was created by the United States." Dillon observed, "Everyone in the room . . . felt this was absolutely right and the whole shift of the thinking changed and we proceeded then on the course that turned out to be successful."*

Kennedy had come to view Vietnam through a similar moral lens, opposing Johnson's escalation not only because it was failing, but because it was inflicting unnecessary suffering on the Vietnamese people and wounding the American soul. He had explained his opposition to a sneak attack on Cuba in *Thirteen Days*, by writing, "Our struggle against Communism throughout the world was far more than physical survival—it had as its essence our heritage and our ideals, and these we must not destroy."

Condemning the Vietnam War on moral grounds at a liberal American campus in 1968 was like throwing a match onto kindling. Some students took Kennedy's words as encouragement to resist an immoral war. When students asked what he would do if he were facing the draft, he said he would serve rather than go to Canada or to jail, a reply somewhat at odds with his moral fervor. His position was further complicated by an executive order that President Johnson had signed in February ending draft deferments for anyone attending graduate schools or becoming a teacher. Male students in the class of 1968 now had to choose between wheedling their way into a National Guard unit, fleeing to Canada, submitting to the draft, or going to jail.

This was the moral dilemma faced by Jerry Abramson, president of Students for Kennedy at the University of Indiana. He had introduced Kennedy at Bloomington and had told him afterward that he was considering fleeing to Canada or going to jail instead of submitting to the draft. When he accompanied Kennedy to other Indiana campuses, they often discussed his predicament. Kennedy urged him to choose the draft over jail, arguing that if he were someone famous like David Eisenhower (President Eisenhower's grandson) and went to jail rather

---

*Kennedy obviously did not consider the clandestine attempts to eliminate Fidel Castro, undertaken by the CIA at his urging, to be as morally reprehensible as a surprise military attack, and there is no evidence that he regretted his involvement in these schemes.

than serve, then his decision would make the front pages and his protest would accomplish something. Instead, his refusal to serve was unlikely even to merit much mention in local newspapers, and it would make it more difficult for him to reach a position of influence where his protest could be effective. Once he had become influential, Kennedy said, then he would have a moral responsibility to make a difference, and draw attention to issues like Vietnam and poverty. Abramson was drafted, served in the armed forces, attended law school, gave his son "Robert" as a middle name, entered public service, and later became mayor of Louisville, Kentucky. He believes that when Kennedy told him to work within the system, play the game, wait until you reach a position of influence, then use your visibility to make a difference, he was explaining why he had decided to run for president.

AFTER BLOOMINGTON, KENNEDY headed south and stopped at more of the rural county seats where Martin had imagined him lowering the temperature of his campaign and impressing Hoosiers with his sobriety. As his motorcade arrived at Oolitic High School, a reporter noticed him reading the signs before leaving his car, as if he would have driven on if they had not said ALL THE WAY, BOBBY BABY and WE'RE BEHIND BOBBY. A crowd of a thousand representing almost the entire population of Oolitic cheered him as he walked into an outdoor playground. The captain of Oolitic High School's championship basketball team presented him with a basketball and they shot baskets together. A reporter for the Bedford *Daily Times-Mail* wrote, "For the brief five to ten minutes that he was in Oolitic, and especially as he stood on the sidewalk leading to the high school playground, he [Kennedy] looked almost like he belonged," and concluded that "Kennedy may have just about won the hearts of everybody there."

Oolitic bills itself as the Limestone Capital of the World, and its quarries have provided the stone for the Empire State Building and the Pentagon. During a ceremony in the playground, Lawrence County Democratic chairman Al Walker presented Kennedy with an Indianashaped granite paperweight. Martin's briefing paper had identified Walker as a Branigin man who would probably not attend the courthouse rally in Bedford. Instead, he had driven to Oolitic so he could arrive in Bedford with Kennedy and have the honor of walking him onto the platform. Walker says that not doing this would have been "a slap in the face," although it was obviously a slap at Branigin that he did.

As they drove to Bedford, the county seat and former Klan stronghold, Kennedy asked Walker his customary "How am I doing" question. Walker was more honest than the Democratic leaders in Vincennes. "You don't have a prayer of winning this county," he said. But when they arrived, Walker was stunned to see Circuit Court Judge Charles Davis on the courthouse platform. Davis, who liked to boast of never having supported a Democrat in his life, insisted that he should have the honor of introducing Kennedy because the rally was being held on the grounds of "his" courthouse.

A high school teacher who belonged to the right-wing John Birch Society had persuaded her students to bring some anti-Kennedy signs to the rally. Kennedy read them out loud, adding his own comments. "'HANOI LOVES YOU BOBBY' That's nice to know," he said. "'INDIANER IS NOT FOR SALE' I know." "'GO HOME MOPTOP' Is Moptop here?" The audience howled and the students lowered the signs. When Kennedy finished speaking, everyone stormed the flatbed truck and Dutton had to jump onto the hood of a car and point out his location to policemen who rescued him from the crowd.

Kennedy was concerned that after he left towns like this the enthusiasm would evaporate. He told Jim Tolan, "I don't know if whatever I say makes any difference. They're not even listening to me."

"It doesn't really make any difference right now that they're not listening," Tolan said. "The important thing is that you were here. . . . They've fallen in love with you, and they'll listen to what you have to say afterwards."

Although the prepared speeches that Kennedy may or may not have delivered made less of an impression on audiences like the one in Bedford than his physical presence, they disturbed liberal circles. Arthur Schlesinger called Martin to complain that Kennedy's Indiana speeches were making for "very curious reading in the East." The *New York Times* accused him of "moving to the right" with speeches that sounded "like Republican paeans to free enterprise." A *New Republic* writer charged that "Kennedy has taken an unbelievably 'conservative' stance on the stump" and that "his standard stump speech includes all the euphemisms of the backlash," pointing to his appeals for "law and order" and pitches for getting Americans off welfare and into jobs. In a column titled "RFK Keeper of the Flame No Longer," columnist Mary McGrory, once a Kennedy fan but now a fervent McCarthy supporter, attacked him for going the law-and-order route and "inveighing against the idiocies of Washington like a good Republican."

His speeches made for such curious reading because his enemies, and reporters looking for a new angle, sometimes quoted them selectively. There is not a single recorded instance of Kennedy failing to follow a condemnation of urban violence with an equally strong denunciation of racial injustice. Yet his critics on the left and right repeated his "law and order" comments while omitting what he had said next, or ignored that since 1967, he had been condemning violence *and* racial injustice without regard to the racial composition of his audiences. During the tour, for example, he had told a black audience in Watts, "I run for President because I want to do something about violence in our streets," adding, "But I also run because I want citizens to have an equal chance for jobs and equal housing. . . . I want an America that understands this is a matter of simple justice—an America that begins to do justice to all its people."

The clearest statement of Kennedy's position on law and order is found in a half-hour television advertisement that he taped on April 17 and broadcast throughout Indiana. It showed him speaking extemporaneously to ordinary Hoosiers and responding to their unscreened questions. When asked, "Senator, some of the ideas you've stated, about resolving the problem of violence for instance, in cities, are going to take a long time to work out. What sorts of measures do you think might be necessary to maintain law and order?" he replied, "Well, I'm not sure first that it does take such a long time. But I think first in making it clear that we can't tolerate the lawlessness and violence of the riots that take place in our cities."

Had he wanted to pander to the backlash vote, he would have stopped here, just as other politicians, Republican and Democrat, incumbents and challengers, were doing in their own law-and-order speeches.* Instead, in a paid advertisement he could have easily edited, he followed this statement with a lengthy analysis of the causes of urban violence, arguing that white Americans must address black grievances. "I also know in the United States that there's no role and no place for injustice," he said. "I think a young man, or a child, is entitled to enough to eat. And I don't think in our society, where we spent $3 billion on pets, that there's any reason for a child to starve to death. And that still exists in the United States."

Critics who accused Kennedy of an opportunistic swing to the right also failed to acknowledge that his support for welfare reform, tax credits to encourage private enterprise to invest in inner-city neighborhoods, and giving more power to local institutions were all positions he had been espousing for several years. A *Newsweek* article based on John Lindsay's reporting got it right, pointing out that "the difference between the 'conservative' new Kennedy and the 'radical' old Bobby was more a matter of nuance and emphasis than of substance" and that "in truth, the antecedents of many of the positions he espoused in Indiana lay in speeches, newsletters, and his book *To Seek a Newer World*, produced before he became a declared candidate for the Presidency."

To Seek a Newer World was a distillation of his position on issues that he had been thinking, speaking, and writing about since 1965. The foundation of his urban policy was that inner-city neighborhoods must become thriving, self-sufficient communities instead of wards of the federal government or depopulated wastelands whose inhabitants had been dispersed to the suburbs. He believed the goal should be "community achievement," and said he hoped to see the day when a man could say, "I come from Bedford-Stuyvesant," and it would be considered a statement

---

*A survey of fifty congressmen taken after they returned from communing with their constituents during the Easter recess revealed that law and order had eclipsed the Vietnam War as an issue. One New England congressman told a reporter, "The red-neck Rotarian crowd in my district shows so little understanding of the racial crisis that I refuse to listen to them." The comments of the other legislators ranged from "They want law enforcement and not appeasement" to "We're headed right toward lynch law if the people can't get protection from local officials."

of pride and achievement. He believed this could only be accomplished through a program of community reconstruction that created new enterprises and dignified jobs in inner-city neighborhoods. Instead of a massive federal program, he wanted a partnership between private enterprise and community organizations that was the opposite of Johnson's Great Society programs.*

To imply that by reiterating these long-held positions Kennedy was pandering to conservative Hoosiers was unfair. If anything, his Indiana campaign proved the futility of arguing about whether he was a liberal, conservative, or triangulating moderate. Jack Newfield got it right when he called Kennedy's politics the product of "radical ideas and somewhat conservative values," or more specifically, "an iconoclastic mix of fundamentalist Puritan moralism, Jeffersonian individualism, and a marginally radical, new liberalism."

Instead of ideology, Kennedy was guided by a set of principles grounded in his upbringing, religion, and experience. Some of these principles struck liberals as conservative, so they distrusted him; others struck conservatives as radical, so they feared him. He believed in sacrifice, family, community, and love of country. He was skeptical that democracy and consumption were inseparable, or that there was a connection between economic growth and personal happiness. He was all over the map ideologically: worried that big government programs crushed individual initiative and committed to empowering local entities, yet convinced that the federal government had a responsibility to protect minorities from discrimination and serve as an employer of last resort. Whatever Kennedy was, he was not a compromiser searching for a middle road. Instead, his speeches in Indiana expressed his belief that poverty, discrimination, and starvation were wrong, sacrifice and moral courage were right, and it was the duty of a president to convince Americans of this fact.

---

*To prove his ideas were workable, in 1966 Kennedy founded the Bedford-Stuyvesant Restoration Corporation (Bed-Stuy) in the Brooklyn neighborhood of the same name. He hoped that its emphasis on physical renovation and job creation would serve as a pilot project and a model for similar organizations elsewhere. Bed-Stuy required an enormous amount of effort by Kennedy, and he personally persuaded business leaders such as William Paley of CBS, Thomas J. Watson of IBM, and George Moore of the First National City Bank to become involved.

He often clashed with aides over how much to stress his more conservative positions. At times, he seemed to be warring with himself. He wanted to focus on poverty and racial reconciliation, yet understood that any hint of "rewarding" blacks for the riots with more government funds and programs might alienate white voters. He wanted to win the presidency, but also to begin healing the racial wounds during his campaign, so he would not assume the leadership of a bitterly divided nation.

He told journalist Jules Witcover that whites in rural Indiana "don't want to listen to what the blacks want and need. You have to get them listening by talking about what they're interested in before you can persuade them about other matters." But he became so uncomfortable with what critics were calling "the new Bob Kennedy" that he once asked Martin and Dutton plaintively when he could have "a liberal day."

When Adam Walinsky scolded him for mentioning law and order so frequently, he countered that he always balanced his law-and-order remarks with a call for racial justice. He once became so exasperated with Walinsky's carping that he shot back, "You go up there before the crowd. I'll talk racial reconciliation for ten minutes and it's as cold as it can be. [Then] I'll talk about how we've got to pull this country together again. We've got to enforce the law, and they'll break loose. Now are we trying to win votes, or are we trying to drop dead here?"

He complained to Walinsky and Jeff Greenfield that their speeches were boring and said, "I'm tired of talking about the war and blacks all the time." But when they removed these topics from his next speech he asked, "Don't you think we should have something in here about Vietnam, or race?"

He asked Greenfield what the kids who were working for McCarthy—the "A Students" whom he so desperately wanted to recapture—thought about him. When Greenfield said they did not like it that he was talking about law and order and the riots so much, he replied, "Gene McCarthy doesn't have to prove he cares about white people. He's never done anything about civil rights. But [because] I'm the Negro candidate, I have to tell white people I [also] care about what they care about."

Most on his Washington-based campaign staff, including Ted

Kennedy, wanted him to talk more about law and order in Indiana. On the other side were Richard Wade and younger staffers such as Jeff Greenfield, Adam Walinsky, and Peter Edelman. In the middle was Fred Dutton, who was perhaps more sympathetic with the Martin/Ted Kennedy faction but believed he should play the role of mediator. In the end Kennedy listened to both sides, sometimes swinging one way, sometimes the other. He knew it was smart politics to reach out to working- and middle-class white voters in Indiana, but when faced with a needy black audience or a comfortable white one, he listened to his heart rather than his head.

His prepared speeches may have made for curious reading back East, but they were not all that Hoosiers were hearing from him, and transcripts of his extemporaneous remarks show him delivering lengthy riffs on poverty, racial justice, and reconciliation. Martin wrote in his diary, "What he [Kennedy] did and said was largely his own. . . . He went yammering around Indiana about the poor whites of Appalachia and the starving Indians who committed suicide on the reservations and the jobless Negroes in the distant great cities, and half the Hoosiers didn't have any idea what he was talking about; but he plodded ahead stubbornly, making them listen, maybe even making some of them care, by the sheer power of his own caring."

Kennedy did the same thing in Nebraska, leading Steve Bell of ABC to observe, "In Nebraska, we [the press] suddenly began to realize that Robert Kennedy had "a near obsession about the plight of the poor." Kennedy kept hammering away about the poor, Bell added, "when there was more chance for political loss than gain."

A good example of this came when Kennedy addressed a mixed audience of local residents and students at Fort Wayne's Concordia College on April 23. After delivering a dry little speech about education reform, he spent thirty minutes talking about poverty. He received a standing ovation but, concerned that he had still not moved this audience enough, he motioned for quiet and said in a soft voice, "Camus once said there will always be suffering children in the world and if you and I don't help them, who will?" Then, speaking almost in a whisper, he said, "Help us," and left everyone stunned into silence.

Martin believed the moment when Kennedy broke through to the people of Indiana came on May 1 at Purdue. The audience had been cold and unresponsive during his prepared speech. Then someone asked a question about poverty and he delivered an eloquent description of the life of a child growing up in a ghetto and spoke of "the almost impassable barriers between the poor and the rest of the country." When he finished, an audience that had listened to him with what one witness called "hostile disinterest" rose to its feet.

"He [Kennedy] spoke from the heart," Martin wrote, "and the sincerity and compassion wrapped around every word reached out and pulled that audience to its feet in a roaring, whistling, cheering standing ovation. You knew that the audience had discovered that this was not just a politician, but a man who cared and truly believed that we could do better." One Purdue student told Richard Harwood that the speech had moved her because Kennedy "*really* cares about the Negroes and poor people . . . [and] can put himself in their place," and one journalist told another as they were leaving the hall, "Scotty Reston [the *New York Times* reporter and columnist] always claimed that Jack Kennedy never educated the people on their country, but you've just seen as good an example of it as you'll see in American politics."

The more Kennedy campaigned through rural Indiana, the more he discovered that he liked its people and small towns. Just as he could not hide his discomfort when confronted by audiences of businessmen and conservative students, he could not conceal that he enjoyed visiting these towns.

No one meeting Kennedy and hearing him speak in these county seats recalls being captivated by his endorsement of the free enterprise system. Jim Osborne was impressed that when Kennedy addressed him he felt he was not interested in anyone else. Gus Stevens remembers that "anyone that he spoke to, he focused on, and his face tightened and he paid attention to every word." Bill Gigerich, who drove Ethel to numerous events in Indianapolis, says he was impressed "because when Robert Kennedy asked you a question he made you feel that he gave a shit about what you said. He'd go around the room asking, 'What do you think?' and he seemed to give equal weight to everyone's answers. Even a twenty-two-year-old kid." And Shirley Amick, who rode with him into Scottsburg on April 24, says, "I felt I was the only person in the car with him. A lot of time you're disappointed by politicians when you meet them, but he was exactly what I had expected."

A similar dynamic occurred between him and these rural audiences. Indiana's rural county seats are remarkably alike: most have a courthouse built on a rise, shady streets, rambling wooden houses with front porches, a war memorial, and some feed stores and cafés, but each is fiercely proud of what distinguishes it from the others. Wabash had its train, Vincennes had been the birthplace of Gimbels department store, Martinsburg was the nation's largest producer of goldfish, Peru was the former hometown of Wendell Willkie and Cole Porter. Astronaut Gus Grissom came from Mitchell, and Seymour was the site of the nation's first train robbery. Candidates are expected to mention local history, but most do it in a perfunctory manner. But by reading their hand-lettered signs out loud, even the hostile ones, by spending more time answering their questions than delivering a speech, and by taking time to banter with them, Kennedy convinced rural Hoosiers that despite his strange accent, city slicker entourage, opposition to a war some of them supported, and popularity with a racial group many of them feared, he was genuinely interested in them, and liked them.

Martin believed that Kennedy won the Indiana primary while campaigning in these towns, writing that "he must have touched something . . . pushed a button somewhere." Then, speculating about the nature of these buttons, he said, "The people [of Indiana] didn't want programs. They wanted leadership. They had programs running out of their ears and look at the mess things were in. They wanted a man. This was what ignited the Kennedy crowds."

ELEVEN

"FROM YOU!"

APRIL 26, 1968

A spectacularly rancorous encounter on April 26 between Kennedy and medical students at Indiana University had its genesis in an appearance he made at Columbia University during his senatorial campaign. Until then, he had been a lackluster candidate, remote, introverted, speaking in a high-pitched monotone, stammering, still mourning his brother, and frequently referring to him and his presidency. Instead of the idealistic Peace Corps types of the early sixties, many of the five hundred students filling the law school auditorium were future gray-flannel-suited attorneys—"snotty, wise-ass kids," according to advertising man Fred Papert, who had brought a film crew to the event.

As soon as Kennedy opened the floor to questions, a student asked if he agreed with the Warren Commission's conclusion that Lee Harvey Oswald had acted alone. Kennedy froze and turned away to hide his tears. The Warren Commission had published its report a few days earlier, leading him to cancel his appointments and closet himself in a hotel room. After regaining his composure he told the students that he agreed with the findings of the Warren Commission.

A girl wearing a turtleneck and heavy black-framed glasses said, "Could you tell us why you chose to run from New York rather than

Massachusetts, or Virginia, or somewhere else?" The audience whooped and applauded. Supporters of Republican incumbent Kenneth Keating had been attacking Kennedy for being an opportunist and carpetbagger and running on his dead brother's reputation. The *New York Times*, reflecting the animosity of liberal and reform Democrats in New York, had editorialized that "Mr. Kennedy appears to have decided his ambition will be best and most immediately served by finding a political launching pad in New York State."

Kennedy responded by telling a joke about JFK's wartime service. Then his expression suddenly hardened and in a clipped voice he said that he had lived in New York for the first twenty years of his life, longer than anywhere else, and if the election was going to be decided on whether he had a New York or Massachusetts accent, then maybe they should vote for someone else.

It was at this moment, when Kennedy finally lost patience with these students, that Papert believes he began turning around his campaign and establishing how he would handle hostile audiences like this one in the future. "Look at the film," Papert says. "You can almost *see* him thinking, 'Why am I jerking around with this woman?'"

Kennedy ended the exchange by saying, "If [the election's] going to be judged on who's lived here longest then my opponent has, but then maybe you should elect the oldest person in the state of New York."

A smug-looking young man wearing a suit and tie stood up and said, "I'd like to ask you a question that seems to go to the very heart of the matter, and if it seems blunt, so be it. Aren't you really using New York State as a jumping-off place for your own presidential ambitions?"

Kennedy's reply was equally blunt. "Let me say that I had really two choices over the period of the last ten months. I could have retired—and my father has done very well and I could have lived off him. Or I could have continued to work for the government." He pointed out that government had always been his family's major interest, saying, "I don't consider there's anything sinister in that we've all worked for the U.S. Government." Then, becoming increasingly exasperated, he snapped, "Frankly, I don't need the title. . . . I don't need the money. I don't need the office space." He quoted from Pericles' funeral oration:

"We differ from other states in that we regard the individual who holds himself aloof from public affairs as useless," and turned the question back on the student, charging that those enjoying greater educational advantages had a greater responsibility to enter public service.

Papert edited these exchanges into a thirty-minute film that was broadcast during the remainder of the campaign. It became a model for the spots that Kennedy ran in Indiana four years later. Many ran as long as thirty minutes and showed him answering challenging questions.

Columbia confirmed what Kennedy's advisers had suspected, that the question-and-answer format played to his strengths—his quick mind, sense of humor, and competitive instincts—and that he was at his best when sparring with a hostile audience. Kennedy came to realize this, too, telling former JFK aide Ken O'Donnell, "I don't come across well on set affairs. I do very well with questions and answers."

Kennedy believed that you could not change minds unless you engaged your opponents, and during his Free At Last Tour, he had frequently sought out people who looked hostile or skeptical and called on them. Fred Dutton believed that he sometimes went too far and ended up "chewing" on an audience rather than educating it. Jerry Bruno later said that unlike most politicians, who followed their audiences, Kennedy tried to lead his. The more they resisted, the more he liked it.

Telling people the opposite of what they want to hear, and making members of a sympathetic audience ashamed of themselves, is a reckless political strategy, but one that Kennedy pursued throughout his campaign. He told an audience of aerospace workers in California, "We should slow down the race to the moon." When a bellicose student in Oregon demanded that the government mount a military action against North Korea, he told him, "It's not too late to enlist." When poor whites in West Virginia complained that they had no jobs and nothing to do, he said, "Well, you could remove those wrecked cars from the side of the road." During a May 2 luncheon at the Indianapolis Real Estate Board, he was asked if he agreed that the new open housing law discriminated against homeowners attempting to sell their property. Although this was obviously the sentiment of most in the audience, Kennedy's dissent was blunt and uncompromising. He said: "I think if you are asking people to go fight for us 12,500 miles away . . . while we are all comfortably sitting in this room—and I am standing here comfortable—and tell them 'you can die for us but you can't buy a home' . . . it seems to me that is rather inequitable, don't you think?" The *Indianapolis Star* reported this statement receiving "mild applause."

Nothing got Kennedy chewing on the crowd more than the subject of student draft deferments. His exchange with students at the University of Idaho in Pocatello on March 26 would be typical of others to come. His charge that the Johnson administration was "sterile and tired" and had "embarked our nation on a course of national self-destruction" played well with the audience. But the applause stopped when he announced that he wanted to abolish the student deferments that had saved many of the male students in the hall from dying on a Vietnamese battlefield. He advocated a volunteer army, he said, but until the war ended he favored replacing student deferments with a lottery system. "Now I know—I realize—I think I can understand your disappointment with my stand," he stammered as boos and catcalls filled the hall. He appealed to their sense of justice, saying, "The fact remains that the major burden of this war is being carried by the poor—the youths who can't afford college. As I mentioned, 10 percent of Americans are Negroes, yet 20 percent of Americans killed in Vietnam have been Negroes. . . . What about the boy who simply wants to run a filling station, as opposed to one who wants to go to college? Why should he have to drop his plans and go? Is he not contributing to the betterment of our country with his determination and diligence? I say he is."

The roughest confrontation between Kennedy and students came when he spoke at the University of Indiana Medical School to the kind of privileged youths who had angered him at Columbia.

As he walked into the auditorium, a black janitor in the balcony shouted, "We want Bobby!"

Students seated below immediately chorused, "No, we don't!"

He was ashen-faced and hollow-eyed with fatigue. His hand trembled as he sipped a glass of water, and John Nolan, who had not seen him in weeks, assumed he was sick.

He began by poking fun at the sulfurous atmosphere, saying, "They've been trying to form a doctor's committee for me in Indiana, and they're still trying." Then he told students who had been training for years to become physicians that the American health system was in critical condition, their profession had failed the poor, and he wanted to restructure medical care to enable nonprofessionals to provide rudimentary services to the poor in neighborhood health centers funded by the federal government. He quoted Aristotle: "If we believe men have any personal rights at all, then they must have an absolute moral right to such a measure of good health as society can provide." He told them they had a responsibility to make "decent medical care something more than a luxury of the affluent," and said that health care and poverty were inseparable issues, arguing that "no program to improve the nation's health will be effective unless we understand the conditions of injustice which underlie disease. It is illusionary to think we can cure a sickly child—and ignore his need for enough food to eat."

He spoke for twenty-one minutes to an audience that a *New York Times* reporter described as "generally hostile." There was no applause when he finished, and nothing to prevent him from leaving, except that he had not changed a single mind.

He began the question period by calling on his most obvious antagonist, a gangly young man in the balcony holding a blue REAGAN balloon.

"Where does this money come from for the programs you suggest?" the boy shouted.

"The federal government will have to make some available."

"Money implies control."

"Barry Goldwater lost that struggle four years ago," he answered, explaining that he believed in funding social programs with federal funds but allowing local people to administer them.

A student called the neighborhood clinics that Kennedy was proposing unneeded and costly. Another asked why he wanted to increase social security payments to the elderly. Another questioned why it mattered that ghetto health centers were second-rate, since most

Negroes did not bother using them anyway. Another raised the issue of funding again, saying, "All these programs sound very fine and nice and all that, but where's the money gonna come from?"

As at Columbia, Kennedy had finally had enough. "From you!" he barked, pointing a finger at the student who had asked the question. He pointed at the youth with the Reagan balloon and said, "From you," then went around the hall, jabbing his finger and shouting, "From you! . . . You! . . . You! . . . You!"

He paused before saying, "Let me just say something about the tenor of that question and some of the other questions. The fact is that there are people who suffer in this country to whom we have some responsibility. I look around this audience here today and I don't see very many black faces of men who are going to become doctors. The fact is the poor have a very difficult time even entering your profession."

This was met by only a smattering of applause, but he continued. "It's incumbent upon a civilized society to make it possible for those who are not the most affluent party of our society to go to medical school," he said. "You don't find many boys or girls that come out of a ghetto or off an Indian reservation, or a Mexican-American or Puerto Rican or poor white from eastern Tennessee or Kentucky that end up in medical school. They have a very, very difficult time. I would like to make loans available so that they can go to medical school. Wouldn't you?"

Again there was no applause, and he joked, "This is one of the reasons I had trouble getting people to join my doctor's committee."

A student stood up and said he believed that it was the government's responsibility to make sure that children living on Indian reservations and in ghettos received an education.

Everyone was responsible for the state of schools in poor neighborhoods, Kennedy replied, and poor Americans deserved a decent education because they were doing most of the fighting in Vietnam. "Again, as white students sit here in medical school, and it's this way all across the United States," he said, "it's the black people who carry the major burden of the struggle in Vietnam."

The students booed and shouted, "We're going! We're going!" and

"They've already signed us up!" John Nolan thought things were spiraling out of control and that Kennedy might be booed from the hall.

"The fact is that the war is going on *now*," Kennedy said, and it might be settled before any of these students went to Vietnam. Meanwhile, blacks were suffering a disproportionate share of the casualties and he did not see many black faces in *this* audience.

A black nurse stood up and waved, and a black student shouted, "Hey, don't forget me!"

"I can see you," Kennedy said, "but you sure stand out."

A few of the students laughed, the tension eased, and Kennedy was asked if he advocated ending draft deferments for medical students.

"The way things are going here today, probably yes."

There was more laughter, and a student stood up and said, "A lot of us agree with what you are saying." Kennedy left to cheers and applause, but was under no illusion about what had happened. "Well, we'll get lots of votes here," he told Walinsky under his breath. During a flight from Indianapolis to Wyoming afterward, he kept shaking his head and saying, "They were so comfortable, so comfortable."

Three days later at Valparaiso University, McCarthy supporters heckled him, and he was assailed for advocating the use of federal funds to fight poverty. The attacks seemed to energize him and he said, "Well, you tell me something now. How many of you spent time over the summer, or on vacations, working in a black ghetto, or in eastern Kentucky, or on Indian reservations? Instead of asking what the federal government is doing about starving children, I say, what is your responsibility, what are you going to do about it? I think you people should organize yourselves right here and try to do something about it."

On the eve of Nebraska's May 14 primary, he spoke in the quadrangle of Omaha's Creighton University to a lunchtime crowd of four thousand largely white, middle-class students. The day was sunny and warm, and the students lay on the grass or sat in windowsills. He was in shirtsleeves and seemed more rested and relaxed than in weeks. He delivered a gentle speech encouraging the students to view their education as a tool for bettering the lives of the poor. Creighton was a Jesuit institution, friendly ground, and his message was well received.

The questions began on a lighthearted note when a boy asked what distinguished him from McCarthy. Charm and a sense of humor, he replied, adding, "I think he's occasionally ruthless." Then, unable to leave well enough alone, he advocated replacing student deferments with a lottery. When the quadrangle erupted in boos, he asked everyone who believed that students should be deferred from military service to raise their hands. A forest of arms shot up. "How can you possibly say . . . Look around you. How many black faces do you see here?" he asked, his voice rising. "How many American Indians? How many Mexican-Americans? The fact is, if you look at any regiment or division of paratroopers in Vietnam, forty-five percent of them are black. How can you accept this?"

Speaking over the boos, he said, "What I don't understand is that you don't even debate these things among yourselves. You're the most exclusive minority in the world. Are you going to sit on your duffs and do nothing? Or just carry signs and protest?" After scolding them some more, he shouted, "So there!"

A boy stood up and asked, "But isn't the army one way of getting people out of the ghettos . . . and solving the ghetto problem?"

Kennedy was stunned. "Here, at a Catholic university, how can you say that we can deal with the problems of the poor by sending them to Vietnam?" he asked. "There is a great moral force in the United States about the wrongs of the Federal Government and all the mistakes Lyndon Johnson has made, and how Congress has failed to pass legislation dealing with civil rights. And yet, when it comes down to yourselves and your own individual lives, then you say students should be draft-deferred." The *Washington Post* reported that by the time Kennedy had finished, he had shamed the Creighton students into "a red-faced silence."

Kennedy became so exercised over the issue of student deferments because they contravened a concept central to his patriotism: equality of sacrifice. Like JFK, he believed that Americans were not only created equal, but had an equal responsibility to participate in the nation's political process and fight its wars. He also viewed student deferments as an affront to his own family's wartime sacrifices. His eldest brother,

Joseph Kennedy, and his brother-in-law Billy Hartington had been killed in the Second World War, and JFK had also died in the service of his country. This principle of equal sacrifice explains why Kennedy opposed federal programs that did not encourage the participation of those being helped by them, why he believed that local businessmen and those living in inner-city neighborhoods should help to rebuild and revive them, and why students like those at the Indiana Medical School and Creighton disturbed him. The corollary to his belief in equal sacrifice was his insistence that Americans had a shared responsibility for what their government did in their name. His most impassioned expression of this idea had come in a speech in the Senate, when he had said, "It is we who live in abundance and send our young men out to die. It is our chemicals that scorch the children [of Vietnam] and our bombs that level the [Vietnamese] villages. We are all participants."

From Creighton, Kennedy drove by motorcade into the Omaha ghetto for a street rally at his campaign headquarters. It began raining, but he kept the top down so people could see and touch him. He turned a corner, saw a thousand supporters standing in the downpour, and shouted, "These are my people!" Instead of promising them government programs, he said, "Lawlessness, violence, or rioting make no sense in Omaha or anywhere else in America."

He sat next to reporter Jack Germond on a flight from Omaha to Columbus, Ohio, afterward. Germond asked what he had thought of "all those kids." Germond had meant the students at Creighton, but the only kids Kennedy wanted to discuss were the ghetto ones who had run alongside his car and listened to him in the rain.

When Germond said that their lives and prospects were obviously different from those of his own daughters, Kennedy asked *how* they were different. And where did Germond's daughters go to school? And how many of the kids in that Omaha ghetto would escape their neighborhood? And how would they do it? And look at my own kids, he said, rich children with every imaginable opportunity and nothing to fear from life.

He ordered a second bourbon and talked with Germond about

children for the rest of the flight. Their conversation was off the record. Instead of fishing for a flattering article, Kennedy simply wanted to discuss what moved him, and it was not the Creighton students, but children like the little black girl with the pink ribbons on her pigtails. "She seemed bright and had a great smile," he said. "But where does she end up?"

TWELVE

RIDING WITH
THE NEXT PRESIDENT

APRIL 27, 1968

Kennedy flew from the Indiana Medical School to Cheyenne, Wyoming, and addressed a friendly audience at the Frontier Pavilion. The next morning, on a gray day too cold to melt an overnight dusting of snow, he boarded a seven-car chartered Union Pacific train and began a twelve-hour, five-hundred-mile whistle-stop tour across Nebraska that speechwriter Jeff Greenfield considers the most successful day of the campaign, "when everything came together" and Kennedy began to believe that he could win the nomination.

The train had been organized by Don O'Brien, an Honorary Kennedy from Iowa who had stopped at the Justice Department after President Kennedy's funeral and left a note on Bobby's desk saying, "When you're ready, Robert, I'm ready to go." The week before the whistle-stop, he had taken a scheduled passenger train between Cheyenne and Omaha, calculating to the foot where Kennedy's train should stop at every station. In Omaha, he walked through the rail yards with a Union Pacific official, inspecting all the private business cars with open rear platforms, and learning that the line's best car, "The Arden," belonged to the family of Union Pacific founder E. H. Harriman. He contacted Averell Harriman, who dispatched the Arden to Cheyenne, and on April 27, Kennedy rode past the wheat fields and cattle herds, windmills and grain elevators of eastern Wyoming and western Nebraska in railway baron splendor: in a wood-paneled private car with a dining room outfitted with Union Pacific china and flatware, and an open rear platform surrounded by a polished grille. Traveling with him in the six red-and-yellow day coaches of the Robert F. Kennedy Presidential Special were hundreds of city slickers in business suits, campaign aides, Union Pacific executives who had competed for places on the train, and reporters from the same magazines that sat on many Nebraska coffee tables.

Before Johnson withdrew, Kennedy's advisers had been pessimistic about his chances in Nebraska. His traditional constituencies of blacks and blue-collar workers comprised, respectively, only 5 and 15 percent of its population. He had little experience or background in the subjects mattering most to Cornhuskers, ranching and agriculture, and could only campaign in the state for a few days because its primary fell a week after Indiana's, and two weeks before Oregon's. It was assumed that McCarthy's Midwestern roots, knowledge of agricultural issues, and low-key style would appeal to farmers. Meanwhile, supporters of Vice President Humphrey were organizing a write-in campaign, and Johnson's name remained on the ballot. During a discouraging swing through the state the week before, local college students in Scottsbluff had unnerved Kennedy with their heckling, and he had snapped, "Why don't you get bored and go home?" In Wayne, signs for McCarthy outnumbered his, and he drove into town under a banner proclaiming MCCARTHY IS NO OPPORTUNIST. Students waving Nixon signs greeted him in Norfolk, where its mayor presented him with a key to the city and said, "This doesn't mean I'm for him. It's a public gesture. . . . This is Nixon country, and I'm a Nixon man."

But when Kennedy's whistle-stop train made its first stop in Kimball, Nebraska, on April 27, a crowd of fifteen hundred turned out despite cold, drizzly weather. He looked down from the rear platform of the observation car and saw women in faded housedresses and leathery-faced men in faded overalls, arms crossed and expressions impassive. They looked up and saw a politician wearing a blue suit, white shirt, cuff links, tie pin, and folded breast-pocket handkerchief, and his wife dressed in an above-the-knees red coat and textured white stockings.

They saw a man who had never lived in a small town or on a farm, who opposed an American war, and who was a hero to black Americans. He saw a crowd of hardworking rural people who had spent their lives on farms and ranches, loathed the antiwar demonstrators, and might never have seen a black American. At Kimball he had fifteen minutes to persuade them that he understood them and cared about them.

"You may not know it," he began, "but I come from a farm state. New York is first in sour cherries."

The teenagers at the front laughed. A few of their parents cracked smiles.

Pointing to the Nixon signs he said, "Actually, Richard Nixon is speaking up at the front of the train. We thought that was fair. He has no crowd at all." This time, everyone laughed.

Hays Gorey was impressed by how quickly Kennedy won over these whistle-stop crowds, reporting that "They arrive with frowns. . . . Some of them arrive with sneers. A few leave the same way. But most are smiling before the candidate has even started to deliver the prepared portion of his speech."

Jeff Greenfield noted that when Kennedy began speaking, the adults—"Grant Wood characters"—would fold their arms and stare up at him, as if saying, "Okay, buddy, let's hear the guff," but within minutes Kennedy had won them over. It was the first time Greenfield had witnessed what he called Kennedy's "ability to command very different kinds of political constituencies," and his skill at relating to people "who had nothing in common with him at all." He called that day a revelation for Kennedy's press corps and aides.

There is no transcript of Kennedy's remarks at Kimball or any of the other whistle-stop towns, only press clippings and memories. At some stations he told the farmers and ranchers that they should support him because his family ate so much beef and drank so much milk, telling them, "You should see us at the breakfast table!" Sometimes he pointed to Ethel and said, "Now, you wouldn't want her to tell her friends, 'He lost in Nebraska,' a nice girl like that with all those children." Sometimes he let a sheet of paper slip from his hand, shouting as the wind carried it away, "Quick, someone grab that, it's my entire farm program!"

When a crowd was cold he said, "Break out in spontaneous applause whenever I make a point." When they did, he asked innocently, "Did anyone over twenty-one clap?" If there were signs for Nixon he reminded them that Nixon had beaten his brother in Nebraska and asked, "Now, you wouldn't want something like that to happen again, would you?" They chorused, "No!" and he said, "Then throw away your Nixon buttons. Stomp on them!"

After observing him interact with the whistle-stop crowds, Ward Just of the *Washington Post* decided that he possessed "the most spontaneously witty political style of any political candidate in this century." Comedian Alan King believed he went over so well in Nebraska and Indiana because his down-to-earth, self-deprecating humor made him a kind of "Midwestern New Englander."

Much of his humor was based on the premise that the rituals and insincerities of a political campaign were absurd and that his audiences were too smart to be fooled by them. His remarks about his farm program filling only a single sheet of paper, his requests to "break out in spontaneous applause," his claims to have come to a particular town only because Ethel had always dreamed of seeing it, were also a form of flattery, a way of letting an audience know that he considered them too smart to be conned by the usual political hokum. One of the best examples of this approach had come on April 16, when he stopped in Sioux Falls on his way to Pine Ridge and a local businessman asked if he would give priority to the city's application for urban renewal funds. Instead of feigning interest, or pretending to know about the application, Kennedy said, "Top priority! I was saying to my wife the other day that one of the first things I'm going to do if I'm elected President is to get that urban renewal grant for Sioux Falls." Instead of being offended, the crowd laughed and clapped.

Before leaving Kimball, Kennedy leaned over the railing of the observation car and asked a boy wearing a Nixon button if he had changed his mind. "Nope!" the boy said. But Kennedy must have changed some minds because on primary day turnout in Kimball County would be higher than usual, and he would win 68 percent of the vote, seventeen percentage points above his statewide average.

After Sydney, the Union Pacific tracks dipped into northeastern

Colorado and ran through Julesburg, a ranching and railway town where Fred Dutton's father had once practiced medicine on the second floor of a redbrick commercial building opposite the station. Ethel Kennedy had organized an elaborate prank for Julesburg. After the train made an unscheduled stop, everyone poured out of the coaches, waving FRED IS GROOVY! and SOCK IT TO 'EM FREDDY! signs, and chanting "We Want Fred!" Dutton played along, delivering a parody of a Kennedy speech from the rear platform, punctuated by cries of "This is not acceptable!"

After Julesburg Kennedy became even looser. He saw Nixon posters and exclaimed, "Ooooooohhhh, he doesn't care about you! He's taking you for granted. I thought he was running for Governor of California. Whatever happened to him?" He joked about his feud with Johnson, saying, "President Johnson once said to me, 'Go West, young man.' I thought he was trying to tell me something because I was in California at the time."

When he returned to Nebraska a week later, he told an audience at the dedication of Czech Village, a senior citizens center in Wilbur, "None of my children are Czech. But if things keep going as they are now, one of them may be. I don't know precisely what that means, but it brings us closer together." It was the kind of absurd comment that popped out when he was happy and relaxed, but it was also a good summary of what he was trying to do: eliminate every physical and psychological barrier between himself and an audience.

At the Ogallala station he asked if any of the other candidates had stopped there. The crowd roared, "No!" and he said, "Remember who was here first, who really cares about Ogallala. In fact, when I was asked why I wanted to campaign in Nebraska, I said, 'because I want to go to Ogallala!'" It was a corny line, but it reminded them that he really *was* the only candidate who cared enough about Ogallala to visit it.

As in Indiana, small-town Nebraskans were flattered that Kennedy was visiting them. An article in the North Platte *Telegram* reported that the newsmen from England, France, Japan, Canada, and other nations accompanying Kennedy had placed North Platte "in the international limelight." After his rally a *Telegram* reporter asked a "staunch Republican" why she was lugging a Kennedy sign home. "I'm surprised he would stop at a small town like this and give us his consideration," she said.

Before each stop Kennedy changed into a clean shirt and built suspense by waiting a few minutes before appearing on the rear platform. He let reporters know it was time to reboard by quoting George Bernard Shaw's "Some people see things that are and ask 'Why?' I see things that never were, and ask 'Why not?'" As the train pulled away, he stood alone on the platform, watching people chase him until they ran out of breath.

Between stops, he interrogated the politicians who were being cycled through his private car and gave interviews to reporters like Don Pieper of the *Omaha World-Herald*, who was surprised to hear him say, "I don't really thrive on this."

Hays Gorey found him sitting alone at the Arden's huge dining table, looking so exhausted that Gorey started backing out of the room. Kennedy motioned him over and launched into a monologue. "I don't think I'm tired," he said. "People say I look tired but I really think it's something else. You know—I'd really rather be doing other things [than campaigning]. . . . But you have to campaign if you want to win. People in small towns, for instance. People in Kimball and Sydney appreciate your coming there." Kennedy knew that McCarthy would try reaching these people with television, "but I still think it means something if people can see you in person," he said.

Gorey asked about race relations. "I think I can work with the Negroes as well as anyone can," Kennedy said. "I think I can get them to do things, to work together with the whites. You know, the Negroes and the poor—they aren't very numerous. But their situation is what's wrong with this country. Scotty Reston [*New York Times* columnist James Reston] says Hubert Humphrey is in the best position to unify the party and the country. But he's not talking about what the real divisions are. To bring labor and business together isn't the problem. They're already together. All the establishments are together—business, labor, politics. The alienated are the young and the poor and the Negroes. The problem is those divisions."

Reflecting on what distinguished him from McCarthy, Kennedy told Gorey, "I really want this [the presidency]. I'm willing to break my neck to get it, too." After a pause, he added, "I don't know what I'll do if I'm not elected."

Kennedy charmed the local politicians who rode with him. Jerry Micek, who headed his campaign in Platte County, joined the train at North Platte and disembarked four hours later in Columbus, where his family owned a popular tavern. His father was mayor and a Humphrey supporter, but Micek had told him he could only ride with Kennedy if he promised to vote for him. They argued for a week before his father capitulated. After spending several hours on the train, and joining Kennedy on the rear platform when he spoke in Columbus, Micek's father pronounced him "ahead of his time" and declared that he would be a better president than JFK, a surprising comment from someone who had idolized John Kennedy.

Doug German and Wilbur ("Doc") Kloeppering boarded at North Platte and rode with Kennedy to Lexington. German was a former Peace Corps volunteer who had organized the Lexington rally. He was meeting Kennedy for the first time and was shocked by how he staggered down the aisle, as if about to collapse from fatigue. Kloeppering, a burly German farmer, ran the minuscule Democratic Party in Dawson County, a GOP stronghold that had voted for Goldwater in 1964. Afterward he told German, "I knew he was solid when he shook my hand and I grabbed his biceps. Oh, he's solid, solid." As the train passed through his property, he said, "My God, it isn't often that you can check your cattle while you're riding along with the next President of the United States."

German and Kloeppering flanked Kennedy as he spoke at Lexington. Despite Dawson County's conservative reputation, he did not mute his criticism of the Vietnam War. He told the crowd that if the North Vietnamese refused Johnson's offer of negotiations, then American troops should withdraw to the major cities and let the South Vietnamese defend the countryside, adding, "If the South Vietnamese think Khe Sanh is so important, let them fight for it."

He concluded by asking the residents of each of the three Dawson County towns that were fierce athletic rivals to raise their hands and cheer. Then he said, "Everyone from Willow Island, raise your hand!" and everyone laughed because Willow Island was just a wide spot in the road with a population of five that included Kloeppering. German had briefed Kennedy on this, and imagined everyone thinking, "How the hell does Bob Kennedy know about *that* place?" When three Willow Island residents raised their hands, Kennedy said, "Well, that must be where all the Democrats live!" and the crowd of Goldwater Republicans laughed and cheered. "It was heady stuff, standing on that platform and hearing the next President of the United States use my material," German says. "That's what I remember most, that we all thought we were riding with the next President of the United States."

German believes that rural Nebraskans warmed to Kennedy because he came across as a tough little runt who opposed the big established institutions, and by 1968 many of them, particularly the farmers, were fed up with how those institutions had treated them. Kennedy showed his tough side by never allowing a hostile sign or an insult to go unchallenged. His rebukes were usually gentle, but could be barbed. When a small-town mayor wearing a Nixon button introduced him, he said, "I want you to know how pleased I am at the courtesy of the mayor, wearing his Nixon button, to come up here and introduce me."

Kennedy managed to convince these farmers that he genuinely liked them. After watching him campaign in Nebraska, aide Peter Edelman decided that he was at his best with rural people, quieter and more playful, like the shy and witty man he knew in private. Richard Harwood thought that by the time Kennedy reached Nebraska, he had become more candid with the crowds and with his own press corps. It was in Nebraska, Harwood believed, that he and other reporters decided that Kennedy had become "a pure candidate," and that "a kind of purity attached itself to his campaign."

Nebraskans liked Kennedy's Midwestern sense of humor, Midwestern disinterest in the trappings of wealth, and his promotion of Midwestern values such as hard work, responsibility, and love of family. They knew he was no agricultural expert, and were impressed that he did not pretend to be. At one stop, a farmer told Gorey that he liked Kennedy because "he sort of respects our intelligence." Instead of reciting a canned farm policy, Kennedy told the farmers he knew they were hurting, understood they were squeezed by declining prices and

rising credit costs, and praised their contributions to the nation's pros-
perity. He repeated himself, stammered, and came across as honest
and unpolished, the way farmers thought of themselves. He looked at
their pained faces, saw they were suffering, and added them to his list
of neglected, and hurting, Americans.

The romance between Kennedy and rural Nebraskans, like the one
between him and Native Americans, Chicanos, and urban blacks, was
grounded in his moral imagination—his ability to experience their
lives as if they were his own. His brother's assassination and his own
experiences among the poor had deepened his moral imagination so
that by 1968 he could imagine himself being a Nebraskan farmer, a
migrant farmworker, or anyone who was hurting, and when he spoke
to members of these aggrieved communities, they sensed a communion and intimacy that went beyond politics or pity.

Kennedy's moral imagination was the silent heartbeat of his campaign. It explained why black Americans considered him their "blue-
eyed soul brother," and former Wallace supporters told reporters, "I
like him. I don't know why, but I like him." It gave him the emotional
reserves to endure seventeen-hour days, and was why he resisted the
entreaties of his aides to "lay off the Injuns." It was why he argued
against draft deferments by pointing out that he could afford to send
his own sons to college but a poor family could not, and asked, "Why
should my sons be treated differently?" It even enabled him to sympa-
thize with his enemies. While he was touring a Ford plant in Indiana, a
white assembly-line worker had refused his outstretched hand and
said, "Get your fucking nigger-loving presence out of here." Kennedy
noticed that the man worked alongside several blacks, and remarked
afterward, "Imagine what he must be like inside! Imagine working next
to those people and feeling that way!"

WHEN KENNEDY'S WHISTLE-STOP was between North Platte
and Lexington, Vice President Hubert Humphrey finally announced
that he would also be a candidate for the Democratic nomination. At
the conclusion of a month more heartbreaking and troubled than any
since World War II, at a time when the Johnson administration was

waging a bloody and unpopular war, just three weeks after the assassination of Martin Luther King Jr. and the worst racial disturbances in U.S. history, and four days after students had occupied administration buildings at Columbia University, an event that would precipitate a bloody confrontation with police on April 30, Humphrey told an audience of labor officials and party regulars gathered in a Washington hotel ballroom, "Here we are, the way politics ought to be in America: the politics of happiness, the politics of purpose and the politics of joy! And that's the way it's going to be, too, all the way from here on out."

The Humphrey candidacy would be the last gasp of the Old Politics—the last time a major party candidate would try to win a presidential nomination without entering a single primary or participating in a single preconvention debate. Humphrey had the support of big labor and most Democratic congressmen and governors. So many members of the Johnson cabinet had endorsed him even before he declared his candidacy that he asked the others to refrain from announcing their support, to avoid being accused of using administration officials to further his campaign. He had already courted delegates in nonprimary states and held numerous backroom meetings with party bosses, so that by the time he announced his candidacy he was already close to winning the nomination.

His greatest weakness was that his support was shallow, a bloodless matter of the party faithful rewarding his loyalty. While Kennedy's and McCarthy's supporters were passionate, his were dutiful and motivated more by the fear of a Kennedy or McCarthy presidency than by their affection for Humphrey. He also carried some heavy baggage that included his disappointing showing in the 1960 primaries and his slavish defense of Johnson's Vietnam policies. Jesse Jackson would later call him "a grape of hope that has been turned into a raisin of despair by the sunshine of Lyndon Johnson."

Humphrey understood that his front-runner status was precarious. In an April 24 *New York Times* interview he had conceded that the greatest threat to his nomination would come from a series of overwhelming Kennedy victories in the Indiana, Nebraska, Oregon, and California primaries. These would give Kennedy what he called "media momentum." His best hope was that Kennedy and McCarthy would battle each other to a draw in the primaries while he traveled the country picking up delegates. McCarthy had no reasonable chance of winning the nomination, and it was assumed that when he withdrew his delegates would support Kennedy. Meanwhile, Kennedy needed to eliminate McCarthy from the race as quickly as possible so he could turn his attention to Humphrey.

Kennedy felt conflicted about Humphrey. He was a more formidable opponent than McCarthy, and strongest with the Democratic constituencies where Kennedy was weakest—the big-city bosses, unions, Southern governors, and Jews. Yet, despite this, and despite Humphrey's support for Johnson and the war, Kennedy preferred him to McCarthy because he believed that Humphrey cared more about the poor, and because he knew that after learning of JFK's assassination, Humphrey had put his head on his desk and wept for thirty minutes.

Kennedy read a transcript of Humphrey's Politics of Joy speech while he was still traveling across Nebraska. He told his next whistle-stop audience, "If you want to be filled with Pablum and tranquilizers, then you should vote for some other candidate. . . . If you see a small black child starving to death in the Mississippi Delta, as I have, it is not the politics of joy." He continued mocking the "Politics of Joy" throughout the campaign, although without mentioning Humphrey by name. Typical were his comments at a rally in Detroit, when he said, "For those who have affluence it is easy to say this is the politics of happiness, but if you see . . . the despair on the Indian reservations, then you know that everything in America is not satisfactory."

The absurdity of Humphrey's Politics of Joy was underlined by what occurred in Chicago on the afternoon of April 27. The same afternoon that he declared his candidacy, Chicago police assaulted six thousand antiwar protesters who had marched two miles from Grant Park to the Civic Center. The protesters were mostly white and middle class. They had obtained all the necessary permits for their march, and had done nothing provocative—no shouts of "Pig!," no North Vietnamese flags, and no rocks, eggs, or epithets. The police nevertheless pummeled them with nightsticks and sprayed them with Mace. They dragged long-haired young men out of the crowd and beat them, and assaulted innocent bystanders. It was a preview of the police riot that would unfold on a much larger and bloodier scale four months later during the Democratic Convention, turning Humphrey's victory into a pyrrhic one, and tarnishing the Democratic Party for decades.

KENNEDY'S WHISTLE-STOP ENDED in Omaha, where he was scheduled to address a rally in a twelve-thousand-seat auditorium. Omaha was notorious among Democrats for President Truman's disastrous appearance during the 1948 campaign, when he had addressed a very small audience in a very large auditorium, and photographs of rows of empty seats had appeared the next day on front pages across the nation. Kennedy was wary of the city because he had only drawn a crowd of 750 while campaigning there for his brother in 1960. His fear that the hall was too large for the crowd he would attract seemed confirmed when his aide Bill Foley, who had been advancing the rally, boarded the train at Omaha's Union Station, shouting, "Don't let him off the train! You've got to hold him. . . . We've only got 500 people in the audience. It's not going to fill up! It's not going to fill up!"

Kennedy exploded, and Fred Dutton would later point to this moment as a good reminder that "just sweetness and light wasn't the real Bob Kennedy." But as Kennedy was being driven to the auditorium, an additional seven thousand people turned up. As he walked into the hall he turned to Foley and said, "You should have had more faith in me."

Before he began, a young man cupped his hands over his mouth and bellowed, "You just don't have it!" Hecklers sometimes unnerved Kennedy, but tonight he seemed relieved that there was someone there to boo him. "I've just learned that the election in Nebraska is not going to be unanimous," he said. "Oh, well."

David Breasted of the New York *Daily News* believed that Kennedy was always on edge before a large audience. He appeared relaxed from the front, but Breasted, who was sitting to one side in Omaha, noticed him grinding his jaw, "bearing down and drawing on everything he had."

Kennedy's speech was an argument for reason over ideology, and employing conservative strategies to accomplish liberal goals. He mentioned the corrosive influence of welfare on family life, but said he also believed that "it is both compassionate and right for our Government . . . to help those who cannot care for themselves, or who have the need of assistance." The shortcomings of federal programs were "not failures of goodwill or intentions, but failures in judgment and understanding."

During the flight back to Washington, Breasted played the guitar and Ethel led everyone in singing "The Sloop John B" and "Radio S-A-V-E-D." Kennedy walked down the aisle stirring a bourbon on the rocks with his index finger, stopping to speak with newsmen.

AP reporter Joe Mohbat remarked that the crowd at Union Station had almost crushed Ethel against a pillar and asked Kennedy if he ever worried about being injured. Kennedy acknowledged that his style of campaigning was risky, but said it was more important for people to be able to get close to him and touch him. Then, encouraged by the relaxed atmosphere and Kennedy's high spirits, Mohbat posed the great unasked question of the campaign: "Have you ever considered that you might be assassinated?"

"There's just no sense in worrying about those things," Kennedy replied evenly. "If they want to, they can get you. . . . Well, let's not talk about that."

But then he sat down next to Mohbat and did talk about it. After mentioning President Johnson's bubble-topped, bulletproof limousine, he said, "I'll tell you one thing: if I'm elected President you won't find me riding around in any of those God-damned cars. We can't have that kind of country, where the President is afraid to go among the people." He paused before adding, "Of course I worry about what would happen to my family, to the children. But they're well taken care of, and there's nothing else I can do, is there? So I really don't care about anything happening to me." After a long silence, he said, "This really isn't such a happy existence, is it?"

THIRTEEN

MOTHER INN

MAY 3–14, 1968

In 1861, a train carrying President Abraham Lincoln stopped at Greensburg, Indiana, for ten minutes on a day the official town history calls "proudly recalled forever after." It is not what Lincoln said that is remembered, but that the crowd sang "Flag of the Union," and Uncle Joe Doakes, a beloved local character, handed him a big red apple. Robert Kennedy's visit to Greensburg on May 3 was similar in that locals like Jim Ryle are less likely to remember the speech he delivered than how he looked and what he did, memories that Ryle has preserved as lovingly as the 1968 Oldsmobile convertible he keeps in mint condition because Kennedy rode in it.

Ryle was shocked by how exhausted Kennedy looked when he arrived at the Greensburg air strip, and amazed at how quickly the crowd revived him. He noticed Ryle's teenage daughter standing with some friends on the tarmac, lit up "as if someone had flipped a switch," Ryle says, and spent several minutes chatting with the kids. He saw a farmer in overalls and rubber boots, holding a sheet of yellow legal paper with questions about agricultural issues, and spoke with him at length while everyone waited. He slipped the man's questions into his pocket, telling Ryle as they drove into town, "You know,

I get a lot of form and typed letters, but when I get a handwritten one, I better pay attention."

A mob of teenagers waving SOCK IT TO ME, BOBBY! signs met him in the courthouse square. He began by saying, "I hope there's someone here who can vote." The *Indianapolis Star* routinely discounted his crowds on the grounds that they consisted mostly of students. Although most of Greensburg's seven hundred high school students were at the courthouse, many had excused absences, meaning that in this Republican town their parents had given them signed permissions to attend a Kennedy rally.

He asked how many in the crowd knew how to milk a cow. After dozens of hands shot up, and he said, "I have no idea how to milk a cow, but I have a farm program." A light rain began falling, but no one left. He promised that when he became president he would return to Greensburg, where they had listened to him in the rain.

Before leaving Greensburg, Kennedy ducked into Keilor's restaurant for coffee and doughnuts with a women's club and stopped at the offices of the *Daily News* and posed for a photograph with its editor in chief. (The next edition of this Republican newspaper would contain an adulatory account of his visit under the headline, "Screams, Squeals Welcome Kennedy.") As he was climbing into Ryle's convertible, a boy with a broken arm asked him to sign his cast. He shook his head and said, "I don't want to put my name on any injury or misery."

He flew to three more county seats on May 3. After a fourteen-hour day during which approximately fifty thousand people had seen, touched, and heard him, he boarded the chartered Electra that his staff and press corps had taken to calling "The Mother Ship," and returned to "The Mother Inn," the Indianapolis airport Holiday Inn.

For the last several weeks, he and his entourage had been flying across Indiana on this plane, returning every evening to sleep at this same hotel. The arrangement encouraged an extraordinary intimacy among his press corps and staff. Sylvia Wright called the Mother Inn "our home," and when Dick Harwood returned to Indiana after visiting his family in Washington, she threw her arms around him and whispered, "Welcome home. We've missed you. I've got a husband

and family back there somewhere. But this is our real home." When Harwood's daughter asked him what campaigning with Robert Kennedy was like, he had told her, "We all just live together and it's like being at home. And we don't have Mommys and Daddys 'cause we're all old and the same age; but it's a little like all are our brothers and sisters, and we love them the same."

Ethel was the Mother Ship's cruise director, ordering birthday cakes, encouraging sing-alongs, and pulling practical jokes. After CBS correspondent Roger Mudd reported heavy drinking on the Mother Ship (the flight attendants poured generous drinks, and the heaviest drinkers could be found among the press corps), Ethel appeared wearing an apron bearing a picture of the legendary prohibitionist Carrie Nation, and fixed a plaque over the bar announcing that drinking was prohibited by order of Provost Marshal Roger Mudd. Kennedy mingled freely with the press on the flights and at the Mother Inn. Harwood decided that he won them over by drawing a circle around himself "so big that it took us in." Within it, family, class, color, and wealth disappeared, Harwood said, and "you were just people together in a loving and tolerant place."

Like Harwood, Loudon Wainwright of *Life* had initially been lukewarm about Kennedy. He changed his mind after hearing him recount how a study of the artwork of white and black children had revealed that when poor black children drew a house they seldom put a sun overhead. Turning to Wainwright, he asked, "Have you ever noticed that the faces of poor kids are much more alert and bright than the faces of kids who are more comfortable?" He added that once those poor children moved into adolescence all the curiosity and expectation had vanished from their faces. Later, Wainwright wrote, "A candidate who remarks on such matters is going to get harder to hate."

Columnist Joe Kraft was impressed that Kennedy had won over what he called "the old, tired . . . Willy Lomans of our trade." Tom Wicker of the *Times*, who managed to resist Kennedy's charm, called him "an easy man to fall in love with . . . if you were a reporter, and too many people did."

The romance between Kennedy and the press was surprising because he had entered the campaign with a reputation for being prickly and difficult. John Lindsay, who had accompanied him to West Virginia during the 1966 midterm elections, remembered him being "wooden as a stick" and "very cold," with an irritating habit of gazing out the window for several minutes when asked a question.

Harwood called the Kennedy campaign a "fun enterprise." Charles Quinn of CBS remembered it as a "huge, joyous adventure," adding, "It was an important adventure and had great significance. But we weren't exactly sure how it was all going to turn out, and neither was Kennedy. . . . It was really a lot of fun." Wainwright believed by early May that the Kennedy press corps had become "a partisan band, obsessed with the fortunes of our candidate . . . concerned to the point of anxiety about his safety and success." When the *San Francisco Examiner* published an article that was critical of Kennedy, *New York Post* columnist Jimmy Breslin bought all the *Examiners* from the machine outside his motel and burned them in the street. Some reporters, fearing that the enthusiastic crowds might injure Kennedy, pitched in to help manage them. Joe Mohbat sometimes found himself gripping Kennedy around the waist to prevent him being yanked from a convertible. Mohbat knew he was crossing a line, but could not bear the thought of Kennedy being hurt.

AFTER RETURNING TO the Mother Inn from campaigning in Greensburg on May 3, Kennedy ate a late dinner with a group of reporters and aides including Jim Tolan, Warren Rogers of *Look*, director John Frankenheimer, David Brinkley of NBC, and speechwriter Richard Goodwin. He viewed these dinners as a way of learning more about what had gone on during his rallies, and he often sought the advice of the still photographers and television cameramen, asking what they had seen, and what he could do to engage and move his audiences. Jim Stevenson of *The New Yorker*, who had attended several dinners like this one, recalled that reporters and aides would try to entertain him, "but it was 12:30 at night, and his face was exhausted. And he would smile and try to respond and be nice. Then he would turn and look out the dark window, out at the Indiana night, and he would be miles and miles away."

On May 3, the conversation revolved around whether Kennedy should continue campaigning in the streets or rely more on a media campaign, as some advisers were urging. One man argued that television could be a force for good, helping to "throw the rascals out." Another countered, "But what about the rascals it throws in?" and mentioned Governor Ronald Reagan. After several patrons had badgered Kennedy for autographs he appeared to switch sides, saying that perhaps he should just campaign from a television studio and avoid these kinds of hassles. But Richard Goodwin, who usually argued for a greater use of television, said, "No. You have to go out there . . . and you have to show that you don't have contempt for them, that you value who they are."

Kennedy polled the table, framing the choice as one between continuing with the rallies and motorcades that enabled tens of thousands of people to see him every day, or relying on what he called "slick, packaged TV pitches."

Warren Rogers accused Kennedy of preferring the streets because he was good at it. "If you were as good as McCarthy on TV you'd be arguing for that technique," he said.

"Yeah, I guess you're right," Kennedy conceded, rubbing one hand over his face as he spoke to stay awake. "But we're still going to do it my way."

"You're a political dinosaur, the last we'll probably ever see," Rogers replied, predicting that in the future, candidates would run from television studios.

"That may be. But you know something? I just can't campaign that way."

Kennedy preferred campaigning in the streets because he knew it worked. He knew that when he appeared before a skeptical audience, the applause was always louder at the end than at the beginning, and he had noticed that people watching his motorcades seemed as moved as those hearing him speak. He knew that the same qualities hurting him on television—his halting speech, shyness, and stridency—made him seem more human and approachable in person and that going into the streets was the best way to reach the poor, who were more likely to turn out for a candidate they had met and touched. He also understood that because his charisma was more tactile and mystical than physical and rhetorical, he had to let people see, touch, and commune with him.

His wordless communion worked best with children. Photographer

Burt Glinn sometimes brought his wife along while covering Kennedy. She was struck by the gentle way he brushed a child's face with the first two fingers of his hand, or just touched their fingers with his fingers, and was impressed that he refused to kiss youngsters, as other politicians did. Instead, he liked to touch them gently on their heads, as if trying to feel their thoughts.

Two days earlier, Kennedy had made the obligatory pilgrimage to the gloomy Victorian home of famed Hoosier poet James Whitcomb Riley in Indianapolis. Afterward, he walked next door to a nursery where children from broken homes were playing in a scruffy playground. They ran over when they saw him and pushed their fingers through a chain-link fence. Then he walked into their playground, and according to David Murray of the *Chicago Sun-Times*, "Two little girls came up and put their heads against his waist and he put his hands on their heads. And suddenly it was hard to watch, because he had become in that moment the father they did not know or the elder brother who couldn't talk to them. . . . The word that came on strongest as he sat and listened to the children and made a quiet remark now and then, was the word 'compassion.' This is because—and anyone who has ever dealt with five-year-olds knows this—you can fool a lot of people in a campaign. . . . But lonely little children don't come up and put their heads on your lap unless you mean it."

Kennedy needed crowds for the energy he drew from them and the way they revived him, "like a couple of drinks" according to Fred Dutton.* He believed that letting voters see him in person was the only way to prove that the "ruthless" epithet—one Theodore White said had "seared his spirit"—was unwarranted. If an audience was enthusiastic and responsive, then he became more forceful and eloquent. If it was small and flat, then he was, too. He liked sending aides into crowds to conduct informal polls, and Dutton sometimes found himself jogging alongside a motorcade, peppering spectators with questions and sprinting back with a report.

---

*According to John Nolan, who scheduled many of his appearances, "He liked kids, and he liked black people, and he liked Indians, and he liked crowds—crowds most of all. He really liked crowds."

Some of the energy flowing between Kennedy and a crowd was sexual. Photographer Bill Eppridge, who had covered the Beatles' first American tour, sensed the same sexual tension that had existed between the Beatles and their audiences. Joe Mohbat, who spent more time in closer physical proximity to Kennedy than anyone in his press corps, believes that because Kennedy stirred up such deep passions, reporters who wanted to fool around on the campaign trail discovered that he had, quite literally, done the foreplay for them. Mohbat noticed a glazed, almost rapturous look crossing Kennedy's face as he motorcaded past miles of outstretched hands and ecstatic faces, and is certain he was experiencing a joy that was almost sexual. At an outdoor rally in San Diego, a young female volunteer who had been standing close to the stage suddenly uttered a loud moan as he was speaking. Her knees buckled and, Mohbat says, "I'll be convinced until the day I die that she was having a climax."

Small crowds upset Kennedy more than hostile ones. When Cesar Chavez tried to apologize for an unruly audience of farmworkers he told him, "The important thing is that they're here." He noticed Bill Barry chopping away at outstretched hands as if they were vines and shouted, "No. No. No. Don't hurt them."

Because Kennedy was a shy man, campaigning this way was hard for him, and he sometimes appeared to be steeling himself before diving into a crowd. Journalist Gail Sheehy asked him how he endured the mob scenes. "I remove myself," he said. "My mind is somewhere else a lot of the time."

But did he like campaigning this way? she wondered.

"I'd rather be home, or anywhere else. That being touched all the time, I don't like it. But people can hear everything about a candidate, and it's the touching him they never forget."

He took risks by making himself so accessible. A woman in Mishawaka, Indiana, yanked him from the back of his convertible and he chipped a tooth against the curb. A woman in Kalamazoo, Michigan, stole a shoe, a boy in Los Angeles stole two and wore them to his prom.

Some people cursed him, tried to hurt him, and shouted questions such as "Can you tell us what is the difference between you and your brother Jack, other than he is dead and you are alive?" and "If your name was anything but Kennedy, could you mount a campaign for the presidency on any grounds other than opportunism and ruthlessness?"

Comedian Alan King warned that by making himself so accessible, he was giving his enemies a chance to hurt him. "Well, so many people hate me that I've got to give the people who love me a chance to get at me," he replied.

Folk singer John Stewart, the campaign's unofficial troubadour, was shocked by how Kennedy would sit on the trunk of his convertible, not holding on to anything while traveling at breakneck speed through the countryside. Then he would stop in a small town, Stewart says, and plow into the "redneck crowds." Kennedy was "almost laughing in their faces," he remembers. "Not, you know, jeering them, but feeding off this danger."

The way the crowds swarmed over Kennedy reminded Fran Martin, John Bartlow Martin's wife, of the relationship between the famed Spanish matador Manolete and his voracious fans. Martin agreed with her, recalling that Manolete's biographer, Barnaby Conrad, had written that his fans kept demanding more and more and he kept giving it, "until there was nothing left to give but his life, and he gave them that."

Kennedy's advisers disagreed over the wisdom of his crowd-centered strategy. Fred Dutton believed that if Kennedy wanted to stop the war, educate Americans about poverty, and unite black and backlash votes, "he had to see the people. He had to be with them. . . . You can lead other human beings only if you're out there. If you're in front of them. If you've got courage." But Arthur Schlesinger predicted in a prescient April memorandum that 1968 would witness "the death of the old-fashioned political organization." He argued that Humphrey would be the last candidate of the big-city machines, Southern governors, and labor and farm leaders, whereas McCarthy's languid style was perfect for the New Politics in which "two minutes on the Cronkite show before fifty million people is more important than the hysteria of twelve hundred people in a hall." He concluded that while McCarthy disappointed his live audiences, he came over as reasonable and thoughtful on television. Kennedy, however, was great with a live audience, "but will very likely seem emotional, pressing too hard, even demagogic in a two-minute excerpt before the great audience."

Kennedy's television spots in Indiana were long and talky affairs, versions of the thirty-minute spot that Fred Papert had crafted from his 1964 appearance at Columbia. They showed him fielding questions from students, veterans, housewives, and senior citizens. He sat with students in an elementary school classroom and instead of reading them a story, told them how poor children lived. He described conditions in inner-city schools to housewives sitting in a suburban living room, warning, "We're destroying the lives of these people." He offered veterans an apology for involving America in Vietnam, saying, "The administration of which I was intimately associated is also going to have to share the responsibility when blame is assessed—not just the administration, but me personally." He never mentioned his opponents by name, or questioned their character or patriotism.

AFTER DEBATING THE merits of campaigning in the streets versus television, Kennedy left the restaurant and took a walk with Jim Tolan. He wondered out loud if he really might be a dinosaur, the last candidate to campaign this way. The possibility disturbed him because he believed a politician had a duty to make himself accessible to voters, whether or not he was good at it. He told Tolan, "Just as de Tocqueville said that the people in a democracy reign supreme as the deities in the universe, and just as you go to church to worship your deity—your God—so, too, when you seek the highest laurels in the country, you have to go before the people, where the power is. And you can't just do it by sitting in front of a TV camera . . . that's not what it's all about. You become isolated from the wants of the people."

De Tocqueville would have liked political motorcades for the same reason Kennedy did: because no other form of campaigning enabled a candidate to go before so many people in such a short period of time. Slow-moving motorcades in open cars have fallen out of favor, not only because of the risk of an assassination, but because, unlike people attending rallies or "town meetings," those lining a highway are impossible to screen or manage, and anyone can turn up and boo or wave a nasty sign, and appear on the evening news.

On May 6, the eve of the Indiana primary, Kennedy embarked upon the longest and wildest motorcade in U.S. political history, a nine-hour, hundred-mile trip across northern Indiana that reporter Jules Witcover called "one of the most incredible outpourings of sentiment for a political candidate in all the annals of American campaigning."

He started the day with a breakfast meeting in Indianapolis, an airport rally in Evansville, and a flight to Fort Wayne where a boisterous crowd at the courthouse cheered his "we cannot accept violence or injustice" line. On his way back to the airport he insisted on stopping when he noticed a sign at Zoli's Continental Restaurant for HUNGARIAN PIZZA. Throughout the Indiana Kennedy had been telling aides, "I'm *going* to win the blue-collar vote . . . I'm *going* to win the blue-collar vote . . ." and making unscheduled stops at factory gates, Catholic churches, and restaurants like Zoli's. Proprietor Zoltan Herman, a former Hungarian freedom fighter, opened a bottle of wine that he had put away for a special occasion, and Kennedy had a lunch of beer, pizza, and apple strudel. After seeing Dutton and Barry nervously checking their watches, he stood on the seat of one of the booths and said, "As George Bernard Shaw once said . . ." Reporters laughed and bolted their drinks. Kennedy arrived at the airport almost two hours late.

Kennedy was supposed to cover the hundred miles from South Bend to Chicago in three and a half hours and make brief stops in La Porte and Whiting. Instead, his motorcade traveled so slowly and stopped so often that the trip took nine hours, and it was almost midnight when he finished.

Huge crowds lined rural highways in St. Joseph and La Porte counties, forcing him to travel so slowly that boys on bicycles were able to keep pace with his car. He tossed a basketball back and forth with a boy jogging alongside, and some young women greeted him at one crossroad, then raced down back roads and met him at the next, repeating the feat a dozen times. He stood on the backseat, holding out both hands so people could slap and grab them.

The brilliant spring afternoon turned chilly and at sunset, as the motorcade neared Gary, Kennedy's car suddenly swerved off the road. Reporters in the press bus became nervous when they saw people crouched down in the backseat, but Ethel Kennedy had simply become cold and was bending down to slip on an overcoat.

Kennedy's motorcade took a circuitous route through Gary and Hammond, rattling over level crossings, passing underneath tangles of high-tension wires, and driving past hulking mills and smokestacks shooting flames. He sped through industrial neighborhoods and crawled down streets lined with brick and wood-framed bungalows. White neighborhoods sat jammed against black ones, black against Hispanic. Black, brown, and white arms waved like grain as he passed. If you shut your eyes it was impossible to know if you were in white Hammond or black Gary because the cheering was as loud in both.

He stood on the backseat of the convertible, sandwiched between Richard Hatcher, the first black mayor of an American city, and Tony Zale, the "Man of Steel," a Polish-American two-time middleweight boxing champion who was Gary's most celebrated white resident. Instead of delivering a televised speech in front of a backdrop of white hands grasping black ones, or traveling through the black neighborhoods with Hatcher, and the white ones with Zale, he rode with his arms around both men's waists, past crowds changing from black to white to black again, through Gary's decaying downtown and into its suburban Miller district where the white holdouts lived. It was a dramatic but risky tableau. If black militants had gone on a rampage that evening, he would have been blamed for inciting them. If he and Hatcher had been booed by whites, or if he and Zale had been booed by blacks, Mayor Daley would have heard about it, since Lake County was in his backyard.

Zale and Hatcher remained with Kennedy when he crossed into Hammond and picked up Mayor Joseph Klen. After riding through Hammond with Kennedy the week before, and witnessing his popularity, Klen had shocked the crowd at a rally at St. Michael's Ukrainian Hall by introducing him as the "next President of the United States of America." Klen had previously declared that he was neutral, and

Richard Wade believes it was the first time that a politician had changed his mind about an endorsement while addressing a rally.

Kennedy made fifteen unscheduled stops in Hammond and Whiting. He chatted with a priest in St. Casimir's Church. He noticed three children in pajamas sleeping on a mattress strapped to the roof of a car, woke them, and had coffee with their parents and neighbors. When a woman told him that her mother had suffered a stroke, like Kennedy's father, he stopped the motorcade and climbed a hill to the house where the afflicted woman was living. He told Hammond's whites what he had told Gary's blacks: poverty was indecent, welfare was destructive, jobs were better than handouts, and only negotiations could end the Vietnam War.

France Soir correspondent Adalbert de Segonzac had found Kennedy to be maddeningly silent and monosyllabic during their interviews, until de Segonzac hit on a subject that moved him. Then, he said, "it all came out; [and] you felt it came from very, very deep inside him . . . all the things he believed in." De Segonzac noticed the same thing happening as Kennedy spoke to working-class whites in cities like Hammond. It was so obvious that he believed what he was saying that even those disagreeing with him found themselves applauding.

Whiting, Kennedy's last stop, was a tidy blue-collar village of Eastern Europeans and Appalachian whites living in two-story homes on postage-stamp-sized lots hemmed in by refineries, Lake Michigan, and the Illinois state line. There is not a single black face in the 1968 Whiting High School yearbook, and blacks working in the nearby refinery were discouraged from lingering in town, so the fifteen hundred people filling the street in front of the Whiting High School and City Hall were presumably all white and had been waiting almost four hours to greet him. They mobbed him when he arrived and cheered when he joked about the town's notoriously polluted air. Whatever he said must have touched them, since Whiting would be among the more unlikely towns that he would win the following day.

He arrived back in Indianapolis after midnight, missing his own election eve party. After shaking thousands of hands, delivering dozens of speeches, and being seen by an estimated one hundred thousand people, he was too keyed up to sleep. He wandered into the bar at the Mother Inn, stopping at a table where reporters Jules Witcover and Jack Germond were having a nightcap. "Well, I've done all I could do," he said. "Maybe it's just my time. But I've learned something from Indiana. The country is changing."

He invited some aides and reporters to join him for a late dinner at Sam's Attic, the only restaurant in Indianapolis open after midnight. They pushed two tables together and he launched into a disjointed monologue about the campaign. "I like Indiana. The people here were fair to me. They gave me a chance. They listened to me," he said. "The people here are not so neurotic and hypocritical as in Washington or New York. If they don't like you, they let you know; if they do like you, they let you know that, too. They're more direct. I like rural people, who work hard with their hands. There is something healthy about them. I gave it everything I had here, and if I lose, then, well, I'm just out of tune with the rest of the country."

He described the faces of the farmers and steelworkers he had seen during the motorcade, and told them about the children sleeping on the roof of the car. But throughout dinner he kept returning to a man who had run alongside his car waving a sign saying, YOU PUNK! His face had been twisted with hate and anger, Kennedy said, and he had grabbed his outstretched hand in a bone-crushing grip, "as if he was trying to break every bone in it." Why would someone want to hurt him? he asked. Why did some people hate him so much?

It was not the first time that an unpleasant incident had spooked Kennedy, and he had dwelled on it. Some reporters thought he was thin-skinned. But none of them knew what it was like to excite such hatred in a stranger, or face an adoring crowd that could conceal someone who wanted to harm you.

KENNEDY WON THE Indiana primary with 42 percent of the vote. Branigin received 31 percent; McCarthy 27 percent. It was not the 50 percent plurality that he had wanted and the press had set as his goal. Nor was it decisive enough to eliminate McCarthy or prove to Daley and the other bosses that Kennedy had the kind of wide-spectrum appeal that would make him a stronger candidate than Humphrey. Still, given the obstacles he had faced—his late entry into the contest, the large backlash vote, the opposition of the powerful Democratic machine and the state's most influential newspaper—it was an encouraging victory.

He had won ten of the state's eleven congressional districts, and fifty-one of its ninety-two counties, including most of the former Klan strongholds. He had won Governor Branigin's home county, town, and precinct, and seventeen of twenty-five counties in its southern tier, a region containing a sizable population of first-generation white migrants from below the Mason-Dixon Line.

The results seemed to vindicate his insistence on campaigning in the streets. He took all of the counties in the southeastern corner of the state where he had campaigned, all of the rural counties that he had whistle-stopped through on the Wabash Cannonball, and all but one of the counties he had driven through on the Lincoln Trail. He had also won cities like Muncie, Logansport, Fort Wayne, Terre Haute, and Kokomo that had large populations of blue-collar workers and union members. In Lake County, he had won 85 percent of the black vote, and 46 percent of the total vote, bettering his statewide margin by four percentage points, and earning the votes of some former Wallace supporters.

After declaring victory, he told Larry O'Brien, "I've proved I can really be a leader of a broad spectrum. I can be a bridge between blacks and whites without stepping back from my positions."

Many reporters and political experts agreed. *Newsweek* observed, "The way Kennedy won was more significant than the cold statistics," and reported him sweeping the black vote while also piling up big leads among backlashy white working men. The *New York Times* credited him with assembling "an unusual coalition of Negroes and lower income whites," and reported him doing well "with blue collar workers in the industrial areas and with rural whites." Columnists Evans and Novak wrote that he had won some Polish precincts in Gary and South Bend by a two-to-one margin, citing St. Adelbert's parish in South Bend where he had taken 65 percent of the vote. An analysis of the results by pollster Lou Harris showed him easily winning the cities, running even with Branigin in small towns and rural areas, and losing only the college towns and most educated and affluent voters to McCarthy. Harris concluded that his victory "went a long way toward establishing his claim as perhaps the likeliest Democrat in 1968 who can deliver both the Negro and the lower-income white urban vote."

In 1970, two former Kennedy campaign aides, William vanden Heuvel and Milton Gwirtzman, questioned this interpretation of the Indiana results in *On His Own: RFK 1964–68*, a generally laudatory account of the last four years of Kennedy's life. They concluded on the basis of the returns from Lake County, "His [Kennedy's] message of reconciliation had been powerfully articulated, but those whites who needed to hear it most desperately were not listening." They based this conclusion on their interpretation of the Lake County results, justifying their narrow focus on the grounds that Lake County was usually cited as proof that Kennedy had succeeded in forging a coalition of black and lower-middle-income white voters. They said that their own study of the Lake County returns showed Kennedy had lost fifty-nine of Gary's seventy overwhelmingly white precincts, and had won only two of Gary's Polish precincts by two-to-one margins. They pointed out that Kennedy's 15,500-vote margin in Lake County had come entirely from Gary, where he had won 80 percent of the vote in the black community, while in the seventy precincts where Gary's white voters lived he had received "only" 34 percent of the vote.

Kennedy debunkers such as Ronald Steel would later embrace vanden Heuvel and Gwirtzman's analysis of Lake County. Steel identifies Kennedy's purported success at winning votes from working-class whites as a "central part of the Kennedy legend," and writes in *In Love with Night: The American Romance with Robert Kennedy* (2002) that "on analysis it [this success] has turned out to be a combination of wishful thinking, misperception, and spin control." To back up this statement Steel cites vanden Heuvel and Gwirtzman's analysis of the Lake County returns.

Roger Dooley, author of *Robert Kennedy: The Final Years* (1996), also relies on vanden Heuvel and Gwirtzman for his conclusion that "the truth, however, was that Kennedy had depended on blacks for nearly half of the votes he took to win the Indiana primary, and that support [for Kennedy] from 'white backlash' areas was not impressive at all."

But vanden Heuvel and Gwirtzman's analysis is not only too narrow a foundation for such sweeping pronouncements, it is also flawed. They ignore that approximately 10 percent of the 700,000 votes cast in the Indiana Democratic primary were cast for McCarthy or Branigin by Republican crossover voters, and that otherwise Kennedy would have won almost 50 percent of the vote. They state that "in the seventy precincts of Gary where all the white voters live, Kennedy received only 34 per cent of the vote." The word *only* implies that this was a disappointing result. But considering that Gary was the most racially polarized city in the North, that in 1967 over 95 percent of white voters in these same seventy precincts had supported the white mayoral candidate rather than Richard Hatcher, that it was a strong union town where the United Steelworkers Union had mounted a vigorous anti-Kennedy campaign, that the eighty-thousand-member-strong AFL-CIO Central Labor Council of Lake and Porter counties had endorsed Branigin, and that Kennedy had once prosecuted popular Gary mayor George Cacharis on corruption charges—considering all this, winning a third of the vote in Gary's white precincts was a considerable accomplishment. And losing fifty-nine of those seventy white precincts was not the damning statistic that vanden Heuvel and Gwirtzman implied. These precincts were not winner-take-all propositions, like states in the electoral college. The ones where Kennedy was weakest and McCarthy strongest were middle-class ones on Gary's southern perimeter, the kinds of suburban neighborhoods where McCarthy always did well.

Vanden Heuvel and Gwirtzman also erred by focusing solely on Gary, and assuming that because Kennedy had not done well among its backlash whites, at least by their reckoning, he had also done poorly among similar white voters elsewhere in Lake County, and across Indiana.

In fact, Kennedy won the all-white city of Whiting, other former backlash cities outside Lake County, and even took rural Scott County, once considered the most racist in Indiana, by thirteen hundred votes to only nine hundred for Branigin and five hundred for McCarthy. He had also demonstrated surprising strength among rural whites, taking two thirds of the counties in southern Indiana and every one of the seven counties that Wallace had won in 1964.

New York Times columnist Tom Wicker pointed out that Kennedy's victory was not just won among the blacks of Gary and Indianapolis, but that he had "carried the Southern-oriented counties along the Ohio river, scored a clear majority among the Slavic minorities in the industrial cities . . . carrying rural and urban [counties] alike." Kennedy's strong showing in the pro-Wallace counties coincided with a May 7 Gallup poll reporting the "strong possibility" that if the general election was held now, Wallace would capture enough electoral votes to prevent either the Republican or Democratic candidate from winning the presidency—a poll making Kennedy's success with former Wallace voters even more significant.

Kennedy's appeal to backlash whites had more to do with character than policy. Jim Tolan believed they liked him, despite his identification with black aspirations, because he came across as a "tough Irish cop." Steve Bell of ABC had been stunned to discover that many of the blue-collar workers he interviewed outside a factory gate in Wisconsin before that state's April 2 primary had no intention of voting for Johnson or McCarthy. Instead, they told him they could not decide if they were for Kennedy or Wallace. Bell decided that the only rational explanation was that Wallace and Kennedy were both tough guys who were going to stick it to the establishment.

Columnist and Honorary Kennedy Art Buchwald reached a similar conclusion, and after interviewing people who later voted for Wallace in the 1968 general election but had previously supported Bobby, he decided that they had identified both as "strong individuals who would protect their individual rights."

Kennedy confirmed his appeal to rural white voters by winning the May 14 Nebraska primary with 51 percent of the vote. He took eighty-eight of ninety-three counties in a state even more conservative and white than Indiana. These included twenty-four of the twenty-five counties where he had campaigned, 60 percent of its farm vote, and 60 percent of the blue-collar vote. McCarthy, who had written off

Nebraska after polls showed him doing poorly, got 31 percent, President Johnson, whose name could not be removed from the ballot, had 8 percent, and Vice President Humphrey, 6 percent, despite an energetic write-in campaign waged by his supporters and his appearance as the featured speaker at the Omaha Jackson–Jefferson Day dinner.

Kennedy had a sound organization in Nebraska, had received good advice from Ted Sorensen's brother, former Nebraska lieutenant governor Phil Sorensen, and had campaigned in every town with a population over eight thousand. The *New York Times* said, "Equally important is the fact that he ran well among farmers and in small towns as well as in the cities," and *Time* magazine, not usually a friendly publication, concluded that Nebraska had "crushed the argument that his appeal is restricted to city dwellers, the black and the poor."

An event almost as significant as Kennedy's two primary victories occurred when he met members of the uncommitted Ohio delegation in Columbus on the evening of May 13. Kenny O'Donnell, a former adviser to JFK and Bobby's former Harvard classmate, had arranged the event. He called Kennedy throughout the day, begging him to be on time and telling him, "They [the delegates] don't care how many crowds you get. They want to know whether you can win the election and what kind of guy you are. As of right now they don't like you! Don't be late for this meeting, because they think they're 'King for a Day.' "

Kennedy landed in Columbus ahead of schedule. Instead of driving to the Neil House Hotel where the delegates were waiting, he detoured through a black neighborhood. Wall-to-wall crowds engulfed him, creating epic traffic jams. One local political observer said he "could not recall a more exuberant demonstration for a political candidate in this city's history."

Kennedy arrived at the hotel almost three hours late, shirttails flapping and cuff links missing. He walked into a room filled with angry, sullen, and inebriated delegates, and saved himself by delivering what O'Donnell called "the best damn speech I have ever heard in my life."

He began by distancing himself from his late brother, saying, "I'm not asking favors. I'm not asking your support on the basis that you were friendly to a relative of mine eight years ago." He continued, "Look, if I were you fellows I'd be doing just what you're doing, be uncommitted. . . . Bob Kennedy may go out to California and get murdered [Kennedy was presumably speaking metaphorically]. . . . If I can't get elected president of the United States I don't want you to vote for me, and if I can't win in California, I can't be elected president of the United States. All I am here for is just to ask if you would please wait and give me a chance to talk to each one of you individually and tell you what I am going to do if I am president."

O'Donnell was ecstatic, saying later, "He knew just what they wanted to hear and acted as if he loved being there. . . . He just handled himself beautifully. He was his brother. It was fantastic. The women just went ga-ga over him. They were unanimous—all the old pros were just taken aback by how much they liked him. This was not the Bob Kennedy they had read about. This was not the ruthless arrogant young fellow. All they kept saying was, 'He's just like Jack! He's just like Jack!' I knew he could go all the way, then. Once he had California in his pocket, he would have Daley and all the pros were going to love him. I was never worried about the general election."

He was not "just like Jack," at least not any longer. But he wanted to win the nomination as badly as Jack had, and because he did, he charmed these delegates just as Jack would have. After he left, 80 members of Ohio's pivotal 115-vote delegation announced that they would wait until the primaries concluded before declaring for a candidate. Kennedy's performance in Columbus had proved that when he told Hays Gorey that he would "break his neck" to win the presidency, he had meant it.

PART IV

THE
WEST COAST

FOURTEEN

"THIS IS PEANUTS"

MAY 15–28, 1968

After spending an entire day campaigning in Portland on May 15, Kennedy realized that he might lose Oregon to Gene McCarthy. He received a cool reception from a midday audience of businessmen at the Portland City Club, then stopped at a chain-saw factory where the workers shunned him, and at a nursing home whose residents ignored him. The turnout at an antipoverty center was so disappointing that he muttered, "I'm glad the police are here to keep them back."

As soon as he returned to his suite at the Benson Hotel he called John Nolan, Joe Dolan, Larry O'Brien, and other seasoned advisers, told them he was in trouble, and ordered them to Oregon. That evening he attended a mock political convention at Sunset High School. After telling the students that they probably did not want to hear what he had to say, he said that although their city had escaped the racial conflicts devastating other U.S. cities, they could not ignore these conflicts because America did not belong to one geographic area, religion, or race. High school students were usually his most fervent supporters. But after he left, these students nominated Hubert Humphrey, even though he was not on the Oregon ballot.

Some of Kennedy's difficulties stemmed from the fact that unlike in

Indiana, where the party establishment had opposed him and he had relied on cadres of honorary Kennedys, in Oregon he enjoyed the support of party leaders such as the strong-willed congresswoman Edith
Green, who proved to be an inept campaign manager. Oregon's
demographics were also not in his favor. Organized labor was influential, particularly in Portland, and union officials still nursed grudges
over Kennedy's bruising interrogation of labor leaders during the
McClellan Committee hearings. The state had a robust antiwar
movement and because many Oregonians had been early opponents
of the war, they felt a natural affinity for McCarthy. The Catholic
vote was small, the Hispanic population negligible, blacks were less
than 1 percent of the population, and the Portland ghetto comprised
five city blocks. The state had a large population of the kind of
educated, middle- and upper-middle-class white suburbanites who
tended to be strong McCarthy supporters. Kennedy's frenzied campaign style frightened them; instead of a blue-eyed soul brother or a
tough antiestablishment Irish cop, they saw a rabble-rousing demagogue.

McCarthy ran a smart and energetic campaign in Oregon while
Kennedy arrived exhausted from eighteen-hour days in Indiana and
Nebraska, and missed the adoring crowds that had rejuvenated him
elsewhere.

He understood his handicaps. During a flight to Portland after an
exhilarating day in California, he roamed down the aisle, griping that
Oregon was one big suburb, saying, "Let's face it. I appeal best to people who have problems." Over dinner in Portland with folk singers
John Stewart and Buffy Ford, he said, "I just can't get a foothold here
in Oregon. . . . Everyone is too comfortable here" and reported that
students canvassing for him in one neighborhood had been unable to
find a single supporter. "I can't understand why people hate me," he
said in despair. "In some towns that I go to there's no need for a psy-
chiatrist because they get their hatred out on me."

Stewart asked what would happen if he lost.

"Then it's all over. I *have* to prove that I can win in every state."

Although Kennedy understood why he might lose Oregon, and believed that a loss would be devastating, he seemed incapable, or unwill-

ing, to concentrate on winning votes rather than changing minds. In a state whose inhabitants tended to be joyful and happy, he continued attacking Hubert Humphrey's Politics of Joy. In a state with a minuscule black population, few racial problems, and little desperate poverty, he banged on about the poor and race relations, holding Oregonians' feet against what must have seemed to them a nonexistent fire. Tom Wicker of the *New York Times* reported crowds listening to his jeremiads about race and poverty "with no particular interest or engagement." When Kennedy delivered his usual call for action and sacrifice to people in a shopping center who had probably never seen a ghetto or an Indian reservation, Dick Harwood noticed that everyone was smiling.

Many of Kennedy's attempts to connect with Oregon voters were halfhearted and ill-conceived. He condemned the high cost of living while touring factory floors, but got little response from workers who seemed satisfied with their salaries. He praised the state's natural beauty and spoke about timber issues, but audiences sat on their hands. He told a crowd at a rally in suburban Portland that he could not participate in a politics of happiness when thousands of soldiers were being summoned to Washington to confront rioters, and received only polite applause. He spent a morning cruising down the Willamette River on a sightseeing boat, discussing environmental and maritime issues with local officials, but failing to meet a single voter. "I've got a problem here," he told reporter Jules Witcover as he disembarked. Witcover asked what he meant. "You're a political writer," he shot back. "You can look around and see what it is."

In the days preceding the primary, he oscillated between extremes, becoming within the space of a few minutes tender and sullen, giddy and morose, withdrawn and exhilarated. He delivered a string of self-deprecating jokes and jazzy riffs on poverty and sacrifice, then tumbled into despair. After one long and disappointing day, he ran into his aide Dick Drayne in the lobby of the Benson and asked, "How about giving me some jokes?" Drayne said he was funnier when he made up his own. "Well, I don't feel very funny right now," he replied.

He was like a drowning man grasping for a life preserver that remains just out of reach. He jumped up during a rally in Portland and sang a duet of "There Is a Rose in Spanish Harlem" with former pro football star Roosevelt Grier, but the audience was unmoved. He stripped down to his boxer shorts while walking along a beach in Astoria and jumped into the cold surf, but Oregonians, who never swam this early in the year, viewed it as a reckless stunt confirming that he misunderstood their state and lacked presidential gravitas.

As it became more likely that he would lose, he became moodier, retreating to the camaraderie of his campaign plane and taking comfort in his encounters with children. One of the most poignant came during his whistle-stop tour through the Willamette Valley. As he was speaking, a little girl's face suddenly popped up over the edge of his observation car's platform. He stopped and said, "Hello, what's this?" The girl wordlessly handed him a box of chocolate-covered cherries. He opened it and asked if she would like one. She nodded, ate the cherry in a gulp, and he did the same. After noticing another child standing nearby, he suggested they give him a cherry, saying, "He looks awfully cross." The one-sided conversation and cherry eating continued for several minutes as the audience waited.

Whenever Kennedy left Oregon to campaign in California his mood improved. After speaking to sparse crowds in suburbs south of San Francisco on May 21, he drove back to the city over the Twin Peaks through largely empty streets, becoming increasingly morose. Then his motorcade turned onto Castro Street and he ran into a huge crowd. As Mexicans holding out plates of tortillas and Irishmen waving shillelaghs rushed toward his car, he turned to Jim Tolan and shouted, "I'm home! I'm home!" It was at this moment, Tolan believes, that Kennedy decided that if he only concentrated on exciting voters who already liked him, he could win California.

He was so elated after his reception in the Castro that during an appearance at the San Francisco Press Club he blurted out what he was thinking, telling reporters, "If I get beaten in any primary, I am not a very viable candidate." Later, he tried to back-pedal, claiming he had only been trying to encourage his supporters to work harder, but the damage was done.

He left Oregon again three days later, flying to Los Angeles on Friday, May 24, to attend a Hollywood for Kennedy fund-raising gala at the Los Angeles Sports Arena. His West Coast charter flights had become an airborne version of Hickory Hill, filled with a boisterous roster of celebrities, family members, honorary Kennedys, and Ethel's "pals" and "sparklies." As at Hickory Hill, Ethel pulled the pranks and organized the fun. On the flight to Los Angeles she threw a surprise birthday party for bodyguard Bill Barry, decorating the plane in red, white, and blue crepe paper, filling it with red and silver balloons, and ordering a birthday cake with a picture of Bobby and Bill drawn on the icing. It was a happy occasion until a balloon burst and Kennedy, believing it was a gunshot, threw his hands over his face.

The Hollywood for Kennedy gala was one of many times that spring when Kennedy would be haunted by his brother's presidential campaign. The 1960 Democratic Convention had been held in the Los Angeles Sports Arena, and the gala would be the first time since then that he had been inside.

Actress Raquel Welch introduced him by saying, "I just felt that if there was a man who could unite the country where it's divided, John—his brother Robert F. Kennedy is the man," a slip of the tongue guaranteeing that Bobby would remember 1960.

Kennedy took the stage looking weary and grim. After delivering some jokes written by others, he listened as Andy Williams, Mahalia Jackson, and the Byrds sang in the same cavernous hall where he had last seen delegates waving posters with his brother's photograph. In the middle of a speech decrying young lives wasted in Vietnam and children starving in Mississippi, he stopped abruptly and said, "So do not ask for whom the bell tolls, it tolls for thee." A hush immediately fell over the glittering audience.

After the gala, Kennedy went to a television studio for a taping while reporters and aides returned to his plane and sang. Sylvia Wright had grown up in a fundamentalist family, and Richard Harwood and John Hart of NBC were clergymen's sons, so they knew all the Baptist and Methodist hymns. John Stewart and Buffy Ford knew the folk songs. They poured drinks, took off jackets, rolled up sleeves, sang "Onward Christian Soldiers," "I Come to the Garden Alone While the Dew Is Still on the Roses," and "What a Friend We

Have in Jesus," repeating it as "What a Friend We Have in Bobby." They sang "Oh, Lamb of God, I Come, I Come," the hymn that had left mourners weeping at King's funeral, and "It's a Grand Old Flag," "I'm a Yankee Doodle Dandy," and "The Battle Hymn of the Republic."

Kennedy returned at two a.m. "Oh, Bobby! You don't know what you missed," Ethel said. "I've been lying here for three hours, and the kids have been singing. You *must* hear them sing 'Battle Hymn of the Republic.'"

He changed into a sweater and slacks and asked them to sing all the songs again. He joined in singing "The Battle Hymn of the Republic." When they came to the verse, "In the beauty of the lilies, Christ was born across the sea," Wright and Harwood slowed it down, as a church choir would, but Kennedy charged ahead. "If you'll keep quiet, Kennedy, we'll show you how it's done," Harwood said. They all sang it again slowly. "It was very pretty," Wright remembered, "and made Kennedy very sad."

It is difficult to sing in harmony while sitting in rows of airplane seats, so Kennedy moved into the aisle and sat on the floor. The others joined him. They leaned against the seats and one another. As they sang, Kennedy pulled gently on Sylvia Wright's pigtails and absentmindedly fingered strands of Buffy Ford's blond hair. They finished with "Where Have All the Flowers Gone," repeating it several times because they knew it was one of Kennedy's favorites.

As the sky lightened, they fell asleep in a huddle. Wright remained awake, unable to move because Harwood lay across her. She watched Kennedy struggle to his feet and go around the cabin collecting blankets and overcoats. After throwing them over everyone he snapped off the lights above their empty seats. Then he stood in the aisle for a long time, staring down at them.

Hours after landing in Portland, Kennedy began a twelve-hour day that would take him to two high schools, five rallies, and an art center, shopping center, and nursing home. Before leaving the Benson Hotel, he and Dutton discussed his decision to reject McCarthy's invitation to participate in a televised debate. McCarthy had increased the pressure with radio and television advertisements accusing Kennedy of cowardice. He had also purchased a half hour of television time that evening and had challenged Kennedy to join him in the studio. But after winning Indiana and Nebraska, Kennedy had decided to ignore McCarthy and concentrate on Humphrey. The problem with this strategy was that Humphrey was not on the Oregon ballot, and polls showed Kennedy locked in a tight race with McCarthy.

For the past week Adam Walinsky, Pat Lucey, and other aides had been urging Kennedy to change his mind and debate McCarthy. Kennedy refused. He knew that McCarthy came across well on television, and also feared that McCarthy, a notoriously leisurely campaigner, would arrive at the studio fresh and rested, while he would be exhausted. Dutton believed that after the gala and all-night hootenanny, Kennedy was too tired to make a good showing in a debate that evening.

Kennedy was also opposed to debating because he knew it was something that McCarthy wanted, and by May 25 he was in no mood to make him happy.

The men had never been friends. McCarthy had told speechwriter Richard Goodwin (who later defected to the Kennedy campaign) that the Kennedys had never "appreciated" him, and Kennedy had privately dismissed McCarthy as unfit for the presidency. By the time they arrived in Oregon, their vague contempt for each other had metastasized into a bitter loathing. Kennedy had come to see McCarthy as lazy, arrogant, and dishonest, and McCarthy viewed Kennedy as a spoiled rich boy. They had little in common, aside from being observant Catholics and skilled grudge-nursers. Kennedy cultivated reporters and enjoyed their company; McCarthy distrusted them. Kennedy was an energetic campaigner; McCarthy was aloof and lazy. Kennedy poked fun at himself in public; McCarthy took himself seriously. Kennedy courted minority and blue-collar voters; McCarthy avoided black neighborhoods and factory floors and was strongest where Kennedy was weakest, in the suburbs and university towns. Kennedy believed in collective guilt and redemption; McCarthy never told his audiences that they bore any responsibility for Vietnam or racial injustice.

McCarthy had a large ego, and Kennedy had repeatedly bruised it by ignoring him. McCarthy struck back during a May 22 speech at the San Francisco Cow Palace. After linking Kennedy to the Vietnam policies of his brother's administration, he dismissed him as a practitioner of the Old Politics. He even made fun of his cocker spaniel, saying, "I have not been able to understand how bringing Freckles out really helped to make it easier to choose on the basis of the issues."

During one Oregon press conference McCarthy dismissed Kennedy's supporters as intellectually inferior to his own, citing a Gallup poll showing that more educated voters preferred him to Kennedy. He belittled Hoosiers for rejecting him, telling an audience of academics in Corvallis, "They [Hoosiers] kept talking about the poet out there, I asked if they were talking about Shakespeare or even my friend Robert Lowell. But it was James Whitcomb Riley. You could hardly expect to win under those conditions." To students at Oregon State he said, "It is necessary that a refined judgment be made on the character of the men who seek the Presidency in 1968," the implication being that voters in Nebraska and Indiana had been incapable of making such a judgment.

McCarthy made one comment during his Oregon campaign that Kennedy must have considered unforgivable. McCarthy often spoke tongue in cheek, and the most generous explanation is that he was joking when he told reporters, "I suppose that we'll also read next that Bobby Kennedy's people will leak a story that there's been an attempt on his life."

Kennedy heard about the comment when Dick Tuck came into his bathroom the next morning and read him a selection of press clips while he was soaking in the tub. When Tuck reached McCarthy's comment, he stopped in mid-sentence, knowing it was a subject that the Kennedys never joked about. Kennedy immediately became suspicious and insisted that Tuck continue. Afterward he fell silent, devastated by McCarthy's remark.

When Kennedy returned to the Benson Hotel on Saturday afternoon after attending several disappointing rallies, Walinsky, Lucey, Salinger, vanden Heuvel, and others begged him to change his mind and debate McCarthy. He called Congresswoman Edith Green, who reiterated her long-standing opposition to participating in a debate, then summoned Larry O'Brien, a veteran of many Massachusetts political wars. Although O'Brien favored a debate, he did not think it would have much effect on the vote and did not push it. "Do you think it's down the drain?" Kennedy asked, referring to the Oregon primary. O'Brien said it might be, and left believing Kennedy would not debate because he believed it would be viewed as an act of desperation.

Kennedy announced that his decision stood and kicked everyone out of his suite so he could take a nap. But Walinsky and others, believing he was committing a fatal error, went to Dutton and begged him to reopen the issue. They returned, woke Kennedy, and reargued their case. Kennedy refused to budge. Finally, Dutton said, "I think there's some stage or other [when] you've just got to bring this to an end. You can't keep rehashing the whole thing."

After Kennedy ordered them out again they stood in the corridor, talking loudly and laughing. He stomped into the hall and, directing his comments at Walinsky and the absent Jeff Greenfield, said, "If my speechwriters don't have anything better to do than stand around hotel corridors and laugh I think they should be out ringing doorbells and making phone calls. Besides that, I don't see why my speechwriters have to carry guitars around everywhere." Kennedy often snapped at staff when he was annoyed, but no one could recall him being this angry and brutal. He was probably mad because he realized that he probably should be debating McCarthy.

The day before the primary Kennedy flew to Roseburg, a county seat in southern Oregon where he hoped to duplicate his successes in rural Indiana and Nebraska. His briefing sheet identified gun control as the major local concern, and warned he might face opponents of proposed federal legislation to regulate the sale of mail-order guns. McCarthy's opposition to this bill was helping him in Oregon. But it was not an issue on which Kennedy could show much flexibility since Lee Harvey Oswald had assassinated his brother with a mail-order rifle purchased under an assumed name.

The propeller planes bringing Kennedy and his entourage to Roseburg almost collided while landing, and he disembarked to face men in lumberjack shirts waving signs saying PROTECT YOUR RIGHT TO KEEP AND BEAR ARMS. Gun control opponents also dominated the crowd at the Douglas County Courthouse in downtown Roseburg. Considering his family history, Kennedy remained remarkably calm. He said, "I see signs about guns. I'm wondering if any of you would like to come up and explain." A burly man identifying himself as the director of the Association to Preserve Our Right to Keep and Bear Arms argued that the bill would lead to a blanket registration of all guns.

"All this legislation does is keep guns from criminals, and the demented and those too young," Kennedy replied. "With all the violence and murder and killings we've had in the United States, I think you will agree that we must keep firearms from people who have no business with guns or rifles."

Some in the crowd booed. One man shouted that Nazi Germany had started with gun registration. Kennedy continued arguing for the bill. But instead of pointing out that black rioters and militants could easily order guns by mail, an argument that might have appealed to this audience, he defended the legislation as narrowly drawn and guaranteeing that anyone purchasing a gun through the mail was competent to handle it. "So protect your right to keep and bear arms," he said. "The legislation doesn't stop you unless you're a criminal. I don't think the registration of cars and the registration of drug prescriptions destroyed democracy, and I don't think the registration of guns will either." As he left, some of the men carrying signs cheered.

He spent primary day campaigning in California. His press corps expected a defeat and treated him gently. But columnist Joseph Alsop, who had just arrived from Washington, D.C., and had argued against him running, felt no such compunction. During the flight to California that morning, Alsop said, "Oregon looks bad, California is turning against you. You are going to destroy yourself politically. Why did you do it?"

Kennedy was in no mood to second-guess himself. He shook his head and said, "I don't want to talk. I want to sing with my friends." He turned to Bobby Darin, who was sitting nearby with his guitar, and they sang folk songs for the rest of the flight. Kennedy sometimes complained that Bob Dylan's songs were depressing, but he liked the way Darin sang "Blowing in the Wind," and they sang it again and again.

His last event that day was a motorcade through Oxnard. As he stood on the backseat of a convertible shaking hands, someone shouted, "That guy has a gun!" An aide ran back to Kennedy's car, shouting, "Get down! Get down!" An armed man was wrestled to the ground. His weapon was a toy, but Kennedy had not known this, and had refused to duck.

As he was boarding his chartered plane to return to Portland, a reporter said, "Bad news, Bob." The polls were still open, but network projections showed McCarthy with an insurmountable lead.

"That's too bad," Kennedy said in a quiet voice.

Some passengers were surprised by how gracefully he took defeat and by the absence of what Harwood called "hand-wringing or bewailing the fact that he was the first Kennedy to lose an election." (The final count would show him losing by six percentage points, breaking a family record of twenty-seven straight primary and general election victories.) When someone blamed his aides for bungling Oregon, he said, "That's a lot of malarkey. If I'd won it, it would have been my victory, and I've lost it and it's my defeat."

Rather than hide out, he sat with reporters and speculated about why he had lost. "I sometimes wonder if I have correctly sensed the mood of America," he said. "I think I have. But maybe I'm all wrong. Maybe the people don't want things changed." He admitted having underestimated McCarthy and said, "I think he hates me so much he'd rather stop me than . . ." but trailed off without finishing his sentence.

Hays Gorey asked if he would change his strategy in California.

"No. I have a program I believe in, and I'm going to press forward with it. I may have misjudged the mood of America, but I don't think so."

He was asked what would happen to poor and minority Americans if he lost the nomination, and whether he thought Humphrey or McCarthy had the best rapport with these groups.

"I don't think either one of them has it," he replied.

He was smiling as he walked down the aisle to comfort Ethel. How could he look so happy after what had just happened, she asked. "Because I had such a good day," he said, mentioning the mariachi bands that had greeted him in Oxnard.

Some reporters tried to cheer him up by singing hymns, and Dick Tuck chanted "Catholic Action," a parochial school marching song that went, "Our hearts are pure, Our minds are sure: No sin our gleaming helmet taints. . . . We're captained by God's unconquered saints. Yet peace we bring, and a gentle King, Whose law is light and life and love." When a reporter asked Tuck how Ethel was taking the defeat, he said, "She knows about adversity. This is peanuts."

FIFTEEN

RESURRECTION CITY

MAY 29, 1968

The *Los Angeles Times* described the Oregon results as "a body blow" for Kennedy. The *Wall Street Journal* said Humphrey had been the real winner in Oregon. A *New York Times* editorial called McCarthy "The Quiet Man" and "Gene the Giant Killer" and said his victory had made him a serious contender for the nomination. The *New York Times* accused Kennedy and "his entourage" of having been "too aggressive and too relentless in their single-minded pursuit of power," and his campaign of having "too much money, too much glamour, and a faintly overbearing air of natural superiority." It praised McCarthy for avoiding "bombast and conventional oversimplification," and for relying instead on "the intellectual thrust, the witty aside, the reflective understatement—and poetry," a sentence speaking volumes about the estrangement within the Democratic Party between liberal intellectuals and working-class voters.

The next morning, Kennedy flew back to Los Angeles to begin a last week of campaigning in California. At an airport press conference, he was unnecessarily honest, calling Oregon "a setback . . . which I could ill afford," and saying he had agreed to debate McCarthy because "conditions have changed." Asked if he still believed that losing a single primary meant he was no longer "a viable candidate," he said he had changed his mind. Asked if California was now "the ultimate test" of his candidacy, he replied, "That would be very close to describing how I feel."

In previous years the winner-take-all California primary had proven to be pivotal, capable of crippling front-runners and resuscitating a struggling campaign. Senator Barry Goldwater's slim victory in California in 1964 had given him enough momentum to win the nomination, despite his loss of earlier primaries to Governor Nelson Rockefeller. Robert Kennedy came into the state in a stronger position than Goldwater. Although some informal delegate counts showed Humphrey with almost enough votes to capture the nomination, his support was soft, and the leaders of several large state delegations, including Daley, were waiting to see how Kennedy performed in California.

Daley and Wade had met as planned on the Wednesdays following the Indiana and Nebraska primaries. Both times Daley had seemed pleased that Kennedy had won, winking broadly, congratulating Wade, and reminding him that "the primaries count . . . the primaries count . . . the primaries count."

Wade was so confident that Kennedy would win Oregon that he had arranged to be away on business the following Wednesday. That evening Daley called and said, "I missed you yesterday. I want to see you." Wade assumed that Daley wanted to inform him that after Kennedy's loss in Oregon he was backing Humphrey. The next morning he went to Daley's office and apologized for missing their meeting. Daley waved a pudgy hand in the air and said, "Don't worry about it." Wade assumed he meant, "Don't worry about the meeting." But when he said, "The primaries cut everything. If he's all right in California, he's going to be all right," Wade realized he was saying that Kennedy should not worry about losing Oregon, and that everything now depended on California. He left their meeting convinced that Daley was hoping that Kennedy would win California so he would have a reason for supporting him.

The dozens of honorary Kennedys who descended on California during the final week of campaigning believed that a convincing Kennedy victory would eliminate McCarthy and win over some of the uncommitted Democratic leaders. Like Kennedy, they understood that even a narrow loss to McCarthy would be fatal to his candidacy and might cripple his political career, putting the nomination out of reach in 1972.

These high stakes made a campaign that was already emotional and intense enough even more so. Raising the temperature still further was the fact that Kennedy was loved and hated more passionately in California than anywhere else. In a *Saturday Evening Post* column titled "Why Do They Hate Him So?" political columnist Stewart Alsop speculated that Kennedy frightened middle-class Americans by using fierce words such as *indecent* and *immoral* and wearing his hair just long enough to give the impression of him being "a sort of angry, over-aged hippy." He believed that Kennedy's most implacable foes could be found among the upper and upper-middle classes and the business community, and that they did not hate him for being a left-wing ideologue, which he was not, but for being an idealist who was serious about tackling poverty and whose election, Alsop said, "could lead to major redistribution of income in the United States."

Meanwhile, left-wing radicals in California dismissed Kennedy as an establishment sellout who might derail their revolution. They brought SELL-OUT WITH BOBBY and WHO KILLED YOUR BROTHER? signs to rallies and disrupted one of his motorcades.

The most unpleasant confrontation of the entire campaign had occurred when Kennedy spoke at the University of San Francisco on April 19. As he walked through the audience to the podium, a student spat in his face and screamed, "Fascist Pig!" ("There was this guy screaming 'fascist pig' and spitting at me," Kennedy told a friend. "And I was looking around to see who he was talking to, and he was talking to me!") When he began speaking, members of the Peace and Freedom Party chanted, "Victory to the Vietcong!" and "What about Huey Newton?" He finally put away his speech and took questions, shouting into a microphone to be heard over the heckling. After he said he opposed student deferments and amnesty for military deserters, a boy bellowed, "You're a bum, Kennedy!" Asked if he believed in "My country, right or wrong," he replied, "As Camus said, I love my country, but I love my country in justice the most." [Camus had said, "I love my country too much to be a nationalist."] He gave up and told them, "This happy time—this happening—must come to an end. I was about to say it's been a pleasure, but I'm glad I didn't make that mistake." Some students applauded; others pelted him with apple cores.

On May 15 he had spoken at Los Angeles Valley College. Tolan had hoped that adults from the surrounding towns would fill many of the seats. Instead, the students arrived early, packed the hall, and greeted Kennedy with screams of "Where were you in New Hampshire?" Afterward he exploded at Tolan, shouting, "How many times must I tell you I don't want to go to universities anymore, and then you put me in a university." As they drove away, people standing on an overpass pelted his open car with a shower of small objects. Tolan assumed they were pebbles. They turned out to be candy kisses, but Kennedy's assailants had been throwing them hard, trying to hurt him.

No group in California loved Kennedy more than its Chicano farmworkers. They loved him because they were Catholics, and he was the brother of the first Catholic president, and because he had been the first important Anglo politician to pay attention to them, and support their union, the United Farm Workers (UFW). Its leader, Cesar Chavez, had met him when he visited Delano in 1966 as a member of the Senate's migratory labor subcommittee that was holding hearings to determine if the UFW qualified for union status under the terms of the National Labor Relations Act. There was no compelling reason for a senator from New York to champion the cause of farmworkers in California. The Anglo growers opposing the union were wealthy and influential, while many of the Chicanos were aliens, and even those with citizenship seldom voted in large numbers. (Governor Ronald Reagan, reflecting the prevailing wisdom of the state's GOP establishment, had remarked that Chicanos were ideally suited for stoop labor because they were "built close to the ground.") Kennedy had been reluctant to involve himself, but once he saw the farmworkers' housing and the picket lines and heard testimony from the growers and workers, he knew why he was there and proved that his reputation as a ruthless interrogator of the corrupt and powerful was deserved.

Kern County sheriff Roy Gaylen had arrested picketing farmworkers based on rumors that scabs employed by the growers were preparing to assault them. Asked by Kennedy to justify this policy, Gaylen replied, "Well, if I have reason to believe that there's going to be a riot started, and somebody tells me that there's going to be trouble if you don't stop them, then it's my duty to stop them." After more back and forth, Kennedy said, "This is a most interesting concept, I think, that you suddenly hear talk . . . about somebody's going to get out of order, perhaps violate the law, and you go in and arrest them, and they haven't done anything wrong. How do you go arrest somebody if they haven't violated the law?" Gaylen said, "They are ready to violate the law, in other words—" Kennedy cut him off. "[Can] I suggest during the luncheon period that the sheriff and the district attorney read the Constitution of the United States?" Farmworkers in the audience cheered, and news of the exchange quickly spread through the Chicano community. After the hearings concluded, Kennedy joined the UFW picket line.

When Kennedy returned to Delano on March 10, 1968, to join Chavez in breaking his fast, four thousand Chicanos had lined the road leading to the park where he was speaking, waving their baseball caps and shouting "Bobby! Bobby! Bobby!" Men with tears running down their cheeks grabbed at his clothes as he walked to the platform, kissing him on the hands and mouth and shouting "Un gran' hombre! Un gran' hombre!" Dolores Huerta, who was escorting him through the crowd with Peter Edelman, feared he would be injured and shouted, "Get back! Get back!" But Edelman, knowing Kennedy wanted to be touched, said, "Don't tell them anything! Don't worry about it. It's alright."

California's large population of Chicanos, blacks, students, and working-class whites—the kinds of "people with problems" whom Kennedy counted among his base—should have made it a good state for him. But its large size and population also made it poorly suited for his going-into-the-streets style of campaigning, and made running from a television studio more logical. It was also a challenging state for someone promising to bridge America's many gaps and divisions, since nowhere was the generation gap wider, campuses more radicalized, youth more alienated, or blacks angrier.

As in Oregon, his California campaign had drifted during the early days of his candidacy, and an internal April 25 memorandum described it as "standing still." Some staffers blamed Jesse Unruh, the formidable speaker of the California State Assembly, who had been the most influential national Democrat to endorse Kennedy. Instead of confronting the mercurial Unruh, the Kennedy people set up a parallel organization called Volunteers for Kennedy and operated independently. Unruh wanted to mount a traditional California campaign of direct mail and television spots targeting suburban voters. He dismissed courting blacks and Chicanos as a waste of time because, he claimed, their votes could easily be bought. He argued that sending a Kennedy motorcade through Hispanic neighborhoods was futile because they did not respond to that kind of campaigning, and that sending one through black ghettos was unwise, because it might alienate suburban whites.

Some of the native Californians on Kennedy's staff agreed that Kennedy was lavishing too much attention on minorities who would vote for him anyway, and too little on the million registered Democrats in suburban Orange County; spending too much time in liberal San Francisco and too little in the rest of the state. Like Unruh, they wanted him to campaign from television studios and court middle-class voters.

Ed Guthman, a former Kennedy Justice Department aide who had become an editor at the *Los Angeles Times*, recommended cutting back on the rallies and motorcades and holding a series of reassuring, low-key conversations about race relations with small groups of white suburbanites that could be broadcast across the state. Had Kennedy won Oregon he might have been more receptive to this advice, but after losing one overwhelmingly white and suburban state, he was reluctant to place his political future in the hands of the same kinds of voters again. Instead, during the final week he largely suspended his efforts to awaken the consciences of middle-class voters and concentrated on encouraging those who already liked him to turn out to vote for him. He did not entirely abandon the rest of the electorate. He handed the campuses and Beverly Hills drawing rooms over to East Cost Honorary Kennedys like Arthur Schlesinger, Pat Moynihan, and George Plimpton, and made a few forays into the suburbs. Nor did he ignore television, and on many days he appeared in all three of the state's major media markets, San Francisco, Los Angeles, and San Diego, so he could make the evening news in each. But he continued with the whistle-stops, motorcades, and street rallies that excited minority voters.

Whether Kennedy's frenetic campaign style encouraged his assassin is unknowable. But it seems probable that if he had won Oregon he might not have pushed himself as hard in California, engaging in the kind of frenzied campaigning that excited his base, but also increased the hysteria in a state that was already hysterical enough. And it is possible that his strategy of encouraging those who loved him to love him still more may have had a similar effect on those who hated him, and on California's considerable population of the disgruntled, disturbed, and alienated.

Journalist Theodore White, who traveled with him during this final week, believed that his intensity sometimes disturbed the peace of those who wanted to be left alone, writing that residents of Beverly Hills and Pasadena would see a televised clip of Kennedy campaigning in Watts—see his "exhausted outburst to a minority group"—and feel threatened. White thought that, more than elsewhere, Kennedy came across in California as someone who wanted to churn the political waters rather than calm them: "He was the disturber. . . . He meant what he said. If he were elected, he would perform as he promised and the country would change."

During a Los Angeles symposium in 2000 marking Robert Kennedy's seventy-fifth birthday, Ted Sorensen blamed himself for contributing to a situation that had prompted Kennedy to campaign so passionately and recklessly, and drew an oblique connection between the way he ran for president and his assassination. "I find it hard to talk about the '68 campaign for many reasons, and I'm sure some of them are reasons of guilt," Sorensen said, adding, "It's no secret that I was opposed to Bobby running. . . . I have since worried and wondered as to whether or not that delayed his entry into the presidential race. I have wondered whether that delay made the race that much more frantic and difficult, and whether something better might have come out of it all." By "something better," he presumably meant Robert Kennedy surviving.

THE MOST FRENZIED event of Kennedy's last week was its first one, his May 29 motorcade from the airport to downtown Los Angeles.

He concluded his airport news conference by telling reporters, "I think I probably have to win here. I have to go now because I have thousands of fans waiting for me—I hope," then climbed into a convertible and began a two-hour, thirteen-vehicle motorcade through black and Mexican-American neighborhoods and downtown Los Angeles that ended at the Beverly Hilton. His May 6 Indiana motorcade had been the longest in the annals of American politics. His one through Los Angeles on March 24 had been the wildest in that city's history, but the one on May 29 was even wilder. People filled the streets in minority neighborhoods, slowing his motorcade to a crawl, thrusting scraps of paper at him for autographs, and screaming his name. The moment he shook one hand, several more gripped his wrist, his fingers, his arm, anything. Sometimes he gave a brief speech, shouting through a bullhorn and encouraging them to vote. As they cheered and swirled around his car he pumped his fist in the air and shouted, "These are my people! These are my people!" At one point, he dashed back to the car carrying the photographers, yelling, "From now on Los Angeles is my Resurrection City!"

He had never needed his people more, and they knew it. A middle-aged woman in a chorus-girl costume chased his car for blocks, screaming "Piss on Oregon! Piss on Oregon!" Chicanos shouted "Viva Kennedy!" as they stroked his hair. A boy poked his head into the window of the press bus and yelled, "Remember my name, Ernesto Juarez!" as if seeing Kennedy had suddenly made him important. A Chicano crowd pulled Kennedy from his car and a uniformed LAPD sergeant attempted to rescue him. Kennedy yelled, "We're all right, can't you leave us alone?"

Kennedy disliked being surrounded by uniformed officers, but he and his aides recognized that he needed the police to halt traffic and close streets for his motorcades. Police departments had provided this service in other cities, but the Los Angeles Police Department (LAPD) refused on grounds that Kennedy was, as one official put it, "nobody special." His campaign hired a squad of retired LAPD motorcycle officers who usually managed traffic for movie studios and funeral homes. But despite their presence on May 29, an LAPD spokesman accused the Kennedy motorcade of committing a hundred traffic violations, mostly running stop signs and red lights. On orders from Mayor Sam Yorty, police issued the campaign twenty-three tickets.*

When Kennedy's motorcade reached the narrow, urban streets of downtown Los Angeles, office workers showered him with cut-up newspapers and phone books. His shirt was soaked with perspiration and stuck to his back. He stood on the backseat of a convertible, punching his fist in the air as a blizzard of paper swirled around him and shouting, "I need your help! I need your help!"

"You've got it! You've got it!" the crowd screamed. "Sock it to 'em, Bobby!"

"Will you give me a hand on June 4?" he yelled.

"Yes! Yes! Yes!"

At the Beverly Hilton, he told his campaign workers, "If I died in Oregon, I hope Los Angeles is Resurrection City." Hays Gorey, who was in the audience, thought he seemed more nervous than usual; he detected "a slight but real lessening of confidence, a bit more stammering," and concluded that "Oregon had shaken Kennedy— severely."

After leaving the Hilton, Kennedy spent eight hours motorcading through middle-class and working-class towns in the San Gabriel Valley and in San Bernardino and Riverside counties. He opened a campaign headquarters and spoke in a high school auditorium and at street rallies. This was not supposed to be friendly territory. After the Watts riots, Californians had voted to repeal the state's antidiscrimination housing law, and a recent poll showed 61 percent believing that "Robert Kennedy spends most of [his] time courting minority groups." But although San Bernardino mayor Al Ballard had equipped city fire trucks with shotguns during the Watts riots and had become notorious for urging residents to arm themselves, he gave Kennedy a rousing introduction. Kennedy did

---

*The traffic tickets were the final fruit of a Yorty–Kennedy feud that had begun in 1960 when Yorty crossed party lines to support Richard Nixon. Just as Kennedy had cemented his popularity with Chicanos by his interrogation of Sheriff Gaylen, he had turned Yorty into an enemy while interrogating him during hearings on the 1965 Watts riots. After Yorty testified that every problem contributing to the riots had not been his responsibility, Kennedy had snapped, "The Mayor . . . [should] stay here through all of these hearings, and I think he could safely do so, because as I understand from your testimony, you have nothing to get back to."

not finish campaigning until midnight. He had again lost his shoes to a souvenir hunter. After returning a borrowed pair, he limped down the aisle of his chartered plane. As he passed John Lindsay he put a stockinged foot on the armrest of Lindsay's chair and said, "Don't tell me the people of this country don't love me. . . . On the other hand, perhaps all they wanted was a shoe."

SIXTEEN

"THE LAST OF THE GREAT BELIEVABLES"

MAY 30–JUNE 3, 1968

When Robert Kennedy whistle-stopped up the San Joaquin Valley on Thursday, May 30, he saw the same vineyards, fields, and orchards that his brother had seen while campaigning down this same valley by train in 1960. He spoke at the same stations, addressing some of the same people, and collecting similar offerings of fruits, vegetables, and nuts, so that his private car, like his brother's, resembled a traveling grocery store. But here the similarities end. He was campaigning for a nomination that his brother had already won, and he was five days away from the most important election of his career, while his brother had two months until the general election. Even so, he was much looser than his brother, joking about his large family and making fun of the usual campaign folderol.

He told a crowd in Turlock, "Turkey Capital of the World," that his family lived on Turlock turkey, saying, "We even had turkey for breakfast!" then asked, "Has Nixon eaten Turlock turkey?—No! Has he eaten a Turlock pizza?—No! Has he eaten Turlock grapes?—No! That's what I thought. Well, I have!" When someone yelled, "Nixon is better looking!" he shot back, "We all have our bad days."

He asked the crowd at the Fresno station, "Will you help us on Tuesday?" They shouted, "Yes!" He asked if they had read his book. They shouted "Yes!" He laughed and said, "You lie!"

After the jokes and banter came speeches directed at those who worked the land rather than owned it. The audience in Fresno, largely black and Chicano, cheered when he demanded decent jobs, homes, and schools "for all segments of American society," and cheered again when he condemned "violence, and riots and lawlessness." Dave Murray of the *Chicago Sun-Times* was so moved by Kennedy's communion with the whistle-stop crowds that he stopped taking notes and became a spectator. As Kennedy jabbed a finger in the air and delivered a message Murray summarized as "Look, I'm going to take you to the top of the mountain and show you what our country can really be like if we only put our backs into it," Murray found himself thinking, "Go, baby! Go!"

JFK had spoken to trackside crowds numbering in the hundreds; Bobby's were in the thousands. JFK had whistle-stopped on an overcast weekday; Bobby had a sunny Memorial Day holiday. JFK's prepared speeches had been somewhat cold and perfunctory, and he seemed unaware, or unconcerned, that the fruits and vegetables filling his car had been harvested by people performing backbreaking labor for pitiful wages. Instead of better working conditions, he offered his audiences Cold War victories. In Modesto, he had said that America should be concerned with "meeting its responsibilities to freedom around the world" and, in Merced, that "the United States must be concerned with what happens in Colombia, in the Congo, and in Indonesia." Perhaps this explains why Cesar Chavez estimated that for every Chicano who worked for JFK in 1960, fifty worked for Bobby in 1968.

All spring the campaign had traveled to a sound track of rock, gospel, and folk music. Walinsky and Greenfield strummed guitars and sang Dylan and the Beatles. Reporters composed a faux folk song, "The Ruthless Cannonball," that they sang during his Wabash Cannonball whistle-stop. By the time Kennedy reached California, folk singers John Stewart and Buffy Ford became the campaign's troubadours. Stewart was a former member of the Kingston Trio who had written "Daydream Believer" for the Monkees. Ford had a crystalline voice and long blond hair. They sang on Kennedy's charter flights, warmed up his crowds, and kept him company late at night in hotel suites while he ate bowls of chocolate ice cream smothered in chocolate sauce.

On May 30, Stewart and Ford stood on the rear platform of the San Joaquin Daylight, belting out "If I Had a Hammer," "Blowing in the Wind," and "We Shall Overcome." As the train chugged through some of the richest farmland in the world, they sang "This Land Is Your Land." As it approached stations they sang, "I'd hammer out justice, I'd hammer out freedom." As cheering farmworkers, themselves just beginning to enjoy economic freedom, ran toward the train from every direction, and as Kennedy leaned over the railing of the observation car and shook a forest of black, brown, and white hands, they sang, "This man is your man."

When the friends, campaign aides, and reporters riding with Kennedy on this gorgeous afternoon heard these folk anthems, and heard Kennedy promise sacrifice, reconciliation, and a noble future, and saw the shining faces of the young and the hopeful faces of the farmworkers, they were also witnessing a final sunlit moment of the optimism that John Kennedy had launched with an inaugural address delivered seven years before on a wintry day in January.

Stewart composed "Clack Clack / The Oldest Living Son Medley" on the San Joaquin Special and began singing it between stops. One stanza began, "Clack, clack, clack, the train is rolling down the track; to carry me home, back where I belong." Another ended, ". . . but there ain't nowhere to run, the oldest living son . . ." Stewart later realized that he could have sung it on the funeral train.

Another of his ballads, "Lincoln's Train," began with a small boy collecting fireflies as the train carrying Abraham Lincoln's body approached his town. The boy said, "And over the voices I can hear the train / that is taking Mr. Lincoln to the prairie once again." The chorus went, "And the train has a dream for the great San Joaquin . . . It's the thirtieth of May / I'm going to ride it all the way / It's all the way with RFK / On the train to California . . . As the train passes by / Sing a dream that never dies / Like the grass in my home, California." The idea, Stewart says, was that Kennedy was going to fulfill Lincoln's dream, not share his fate.

While Stewart and Kennedy were standing together on the rear platform, watching the crowd fall away as they left a station, he reminded Kennedy of his remark that it was "all over" if he lost Oregon.

"Well, if we could only win California . . ." Kennedy said, his voice trailing off. Stewart's last conversation with Kennedy is etched in his memory. As the train was leaving Lodi, a boy on a bicycle began pedaling furiously alongside to keep up. Bobby leaned over the rail and shouted, "Don't ever run for P-P-P-President!" stammering out the last word before adding, "It's very tiring."

Kennedy concluded one of the longest days of his campaign with one of his most acrimonious events, a meeting with several hundred Bay Area black leaders and activists at Taylor Memorial Methodist Church in West Oakland. John Seigenthaler, a former Kennedy Justice Department aide who was heading his campaign in Northern California, had organized the Taylor meeting with help from the Northern California Black Caucus, and had enlisted Assemblyman Willie Brown to serve as moderator, hoping that he might keep the event from spinning out of control. The militant Black Panther Party had its headquarters in Oakland, and the city had experienced several violent confrontations between its police force and the Panthers, most recently a ninety-minute gun battle on April 6 that had left Panther Bobby Hutton dead. Seigenthaler expected militants to attend the meeting and attack Kennedy, but he thought the risks were justified because Kennedy had handled himself so well during similar encounters in Indianapolis and Atlanta, although those had been small private gatherings in hotel rooms.

Kennedy himself had misgivings about the event. He told Seigenthaler, "It's going to be a very disorganized meeting and there's going to be some anger." He decided to go because most of the Bay Area's prominent black leaders were coming, and he wanted to show them that he was not taking black voters for granted.

Former astronaut John Glenn had spent May 30 campaigning with Kennedy and rode with him to the West Oakland meeting. Kennedy steeled himself for a difficult encounter, telling Glenn, "This won't be a pleasant experience, John. These people have a lot of hostility towards whites and lots of reasons for it. . . . They're just going to tell me off, over and over. I've been through these before, and you don't do anything. You listen and try to respond thoughtfully. But no matter how insulting they are, they're trying to communicate what's inside of them."

The meeting had been scheduled for ten, but the whistle-stop had run late and it was after eleven when Kennedy arrived. He walked down the aisle and stood leaning against the altar rail, facing an audience of Black Panthers, attorneys, teachers, and government workers, NAACP (National Association for the Advancement of Colored People) moderates and SNCC (Student Nonviolent Coordinating Committee) activists. Some seized on his tardiness as a sign of disrespect, and the meeting started badly, with the first questioner accusing the government of building concentration camps for blacks. When Kennedy denied their existence, there were shouts of "We don't believe you!"

He was told that whites only came into black neighborhoods when they wanted something. He was asked, "Why don't you just take your family fortune and redistribute it to the people?" "Why did you tap Dr. King's telephone?" "What do you think about black people, Senator?"

"I like some. Some, I don't like," he said evenly, adding that he felt the same way about white people.

A man in a red sweater jumped up and shouted, "Talk, talk, talk, talk, talk; go ahead, baby, talk, talk talk, talk," then launched into a vicious attack on the entire Kennedy family.

Willie Brown interrupted and asked that Kennedy be allowed to reply. He was shouted down and called a Technicolor Nigger. Rafer Johnson said, "I've had enough," and apologized to Kennedy for the rough treatment.

"No. Just be quiet," Kennedy said. "These people have come to tell me things."

The roughest questions came from Curtis Baker, a tall community activist known as Black Jesus who carried an imposing cane and wore a gold cape, a black turban, and a tangle of amulets and necklaces. After complaining that Kennedy had ignored his letters, he demanded that he and members of his family open a bank in West Oakland and each deposit a million dollars in it. When Kennedy tried to respond, he said, "Look, man, I don't want to hear none of your shit! What the goddamned hell are you going to do, boy. . . . You bastards haven't did nothing for us, we wants to know, what are you going to do for us? You want this vote? . . . Put up a black bank and let us borrow this money."

Kennedy described his Bedford-Stuyvesant project and said that a similar organization might work in Oakland, but refused to make any promises. He endured almost two hours of similar attacks before Willie Brown called for a last question. After answering it, he said, "You know there are two other people who have their hands up. Could I answer those questions?" Brown was impressed by his willingness to continue. "I'll never forget those last two questions," he said. "When I wanted to let him out of that trap, he didn't want to escape from it."

On the way back to San Francisco, Kennedy asked Glenn and Seigenthaler for their impressions of the meeting. Glenn just shook his head in despair. Kennedy smiled and said, "That's the kind of situation I really enjoy."

Seigenthaler said, "I think you had all the votes you were going to get when you went in there."

"Well, I'm glad I went. I feel better because . . . [now] they know that, while there's nobody that's going to solve their problems overnight, that I'll at least be here to listen and that I won't make any false promises to them."

As they walked into the lobby of the Fairmont Hotel, Seigenthaler told Brown he thought the meeting had been "pretty rough." Brown disagreed. "We're going to do very well over there," he said. "Everybody who was there tonight will help." He was right. The next day many of those at the church called Tom Berkley, a Kennedy supporter who published the Bay Area's most influential black newspaper, offering to work for the campaign and open store-front offices. On primary day, some black precincts in Oakland gave Kennedy 90 percent of the vote, with turnout approaching 100 percent.

As Kennedy walked through the lobby, he turned to Seigenthaler and said, "Gosh, I'd like some ice cream." The Blum's parlor had closed, but a hotel worker reopened it. After an eighteen-hour day Kennedy sat with Glenn, Dutton, and Seigenthaler, eating ice cream and insisting that he was really, really glad he had gone to West Oakland.

The next day he delivered a speech at a Commonwealth Club luncheon on Vietnam. Although the war had become a less urgent issue after Johnson's March 31 speech, it had been receiving more attention as the peace talks in Paris moved at a glacial pace, and American casualties mounted.

Kennedy acknowledged that Johnson's suspension of the bombing of North Vietnam and willingness to negotiate had seemed to be "a watershed in our war policy," a reason to believe that "at last the futile military escalation would come to an end." But he said he was concerned that America appeared "fated to six more months of futile destruction" and accused Johnson of dragging out negotiations, either hoping for a military victory or buying time until January 20, 1969, when he could hand over the war to his successor. After telling Commonwealth Club members "we still seem to hold a naive faith in our military power" and "we must abandon the futile dream of crushing the enemy's forces or his will to continue the struggle," he proposed measures aimed at shifting the burden of fighting to the South Vietnamese army, and pulling most American forces back to positions where they were less likely to engage the enemy—withdrawing them from the battlefield without, for the time being, withdrawing them from South Vietnam.

Kennedy's schedule for May 31 had been drafted before he lost Oregon and included visits to San Jose and Long Beach. Instead, he decided to return to Oakland.

He drove through the city by motorcade, stopping at intersections, small parks, and in front of public buildings, delivering short speeches, singing "There Is a Rose in Spanish Harlem" with Roosevelt Grier, and letting one hundred thousand people see him and several thousand touch him. His motorcade ended at a rally in Defremery Park that was the largest in West Oakland history.

He was met by McCarthy supporters waving signs and passing out flyers and Black Panthers pumping their fists into the air and chanting "Free Huey!"—a reference to jailed Panther leader Huey Newton. To reach the platform he had to be carried hand over hand over the heads of the audience. When he began speaking, people shushed the Black Panthers, and the McCarthy supporters put down their leaflets. Any resentment due to his tardiness turned into what Hector Lopez, an Oakland community activist, later described as "enthusiasm, joy, and just passion." These were not starstruck high school students in rural Indiana, or blue-collar Catholics who looked at Bobby and saw JFK. They were residents of one of the poorest and angriest inner-city neighborhoods in America.

There is no transcript of what Kennedy said, only newspaper articles and passing mention of the event in oral history interviews. Fred Dutton and Jim Tolan, and reporters like Joe Mohbat, had witnessed so many similar rallies that they later found it difficult to differentiate them. Journalist Theodore White, who witnessed them, conflated them in *The Making of the President—1968*. So it is possible he was describing the Defremery Park rally when he spoke of black Americans boiling up "like a volcanic cone about Kennedy's car, shouting, 'Bobby, Bobby, please! Oh, Bobby, Bobby!' in a sighing, near-sexual orgy of exultation," At these rallies, White reported, Kennedy often asked, "How many of you are registered? Up with your hands." If only a few hands went up, he would shout, "Shame on you! Get registered. How many are going to vote? Up with the hands. And get your husbands to vote, and your neighbors."

When Kennedy finished, he was trapped by thousands of people, all "trying to touch this one, crazy, son-of-a-bitching white man," according to Lopez. A photograph taken from above shows Kennedy caught in a web of black arms. Hands reach from every direction, pulling on the sleeves and collar of his white dress shirt. One can almost hear the fabric ripping. Afterward, Lopez decided that black Americans had really believed Kennedy. For them, he was not "the last of the great liberals" but "the last of the great believables."

The Black Panthers who had heckled Kennedy the previous night pushed people back and cleared a path to his car. Curtis Baker walked in front, wearing his cloak and turban and carrying his cane, raising his hands and parting the crowd like Moses at the Red Sea while shouting, "I'm Senator Kennedy's personal representative."

Kennedy invited him to join him in the car and offered him a beer. Baker replied that he would prefer what Kennedy was drinking so they passed a cup of Bourbon back and forth while crossing the Bay Bridge.

(Baker was something of a fabulist, but his account of his ride with Kennedy is believable because he got so many of the details right, saying, "That's the first time I knowed he had a cocker spaniel dog in the car and he liked Bourbon, not Scotch.") When they parted in San Francisco, Kennedy asked Baker to join him in Los Angeles on primary day, and spoke of a position in his administration. "You'll be up with me, I won't forget you," he said. "I won't let you down . . . or your people."

THE LONG-AWAITED debate between Kennedy and McCarthy was as dull and disappointing as might be expected of an exchange between two politicians who agreed on most issues. More interesting is the casual way that Kennedy prepared for it, and the controversy surrounding one of his remarks.

His staff had prepared extensive briefing books. At nine-thirty a.m. on Saturday, June 1, Mankiewicz, Sorensen, Edelman, Unruh, and Dutton filled his Fairmont suite and began peppering him with questions. Ted Sorensen, who had prepared JFK for his debate with Nixon, tried imposing some discipline on the session by ticking off the points he should make. But Kennedy was curiously detached. He lay curled up on a long couch in a silk kimono, saying little, and distracted by the gorgeous weather and stunning views of San Francisco Bay. He was "floating almost all alone," according to Walinsky. The session petered out after ninety minutes, and he went to Fisherman's Wharf to sightsee and eat clam chowder, JFK's favorite dish.

During an afternoon session, he resisted William vanden Heuvel's attempts to educate him about the gold flow and special drawing rights. "I'll tell you what I'm going to do" he said. "I'll say, 'That's a very interesting question . . . and I will now ask Mr. vanden Heuvel to come out and give you my answer.' "

While he was in the green room at the television studio preparing to go on the air, John Frankenheimer irritated him by repeatedly saying, "What you've got to do is be yourself."

"Well, who am I going to be if not myself?" he asked.

Reporters scoring the debate declared him the winner on points. A telephone poll by the *Los Angeles Times* showed him beating McCarthy by two and a half to one.

McCarthy was tense and heavily made up, Kennedy loose and tanned. Kennedy's worst moment came when he was asked to give a concluding statement. His summary of his qualifications was halting and unconvincing, while McCarthy delivered an elegant, prepared statement. He told Dutton and Newfield that when the producer announced that time was up, he had not understood that he was expected to give a concluding statement. "You won't believe it, but I was daydreaming," he said. He claimed he had been wondering where to take Ethel for dinner. It was an amusing excuse, but not a convincing explanation for why a man who excelled at extemporaneous repartee had been caught so flat-footed, or why he had not prepared a concluding statement, since after witnessing his brother's debates with Nixon he must have known it was part of the format.

He offered a better explanation the next morning while riding with a reporter to Sunday mass, saying, "How do you tell people to vote for you? How do you stand up there, or sit there, and just tell them you're the greatest? You just can't do that."

"Well, you just *tell* them," the reporter replied. "You're the candidate. I'm just from the press."

"How do you tell people?" he shot back. "It's by action that people have to come to learn what you stand for, what you're going to do. . . . 'Why you should vote for me' really is meaningless. It's rhetoric, whereas the most important thing is the action."

The Kennedy–McCarthy debate is remembered for an exchange that would lead to charges that Kennedy had made a racist appeal to white suburban voters.

It began when McCarthy characterized Kennedy's plan to bring jobs and housing to ghetto neighborhoods through a partnership between government and the private sector as "a kind of apartheid." Instead, McCarthy proposed moving people from urban ghettos to the suburbs, and allocating five to six billion dollars a year of government funds to house them. This was a red flag for Kennedy, who had spent years promoting the revitalization of inner-city neighborhoods. He responded by saying,

> I am all in favor of moving people out of the ghetto. We have 14 million Negroes who are in the ghettos at the present time. We have here in the state of California a million Mexican-Americans whose poverty is even greater than many of the black people. You say you are going to take 10,000 black people and move them into Orange County. The people who graduate from high school . . . and the ones who graduate from high school have the equivalent of an eighth grade education. . . . If you are talking about 100 people that is one thing. But if you are talking about hitting this problem in a major way, to take these people out, put them in the suburbs where they can't afford the housing, where their children can't keep up with school, and where they don't have skills for the jobs it is just going to be catastrophic.
>
> I want to move as the groups have moved in the United States, that as they get the job and get the training, then they themselves can move out into other areas of the United States and will be accepted and will find jobs and employment.
>
> But that does not exist. That does not exist. Those are not the conditions we are facing in this country at the present time.

The most controversial passage in this response, "You say you are going to take 10,000 black people and move them into Orange County," was unfair to McCarthy, who had never specified how many people he wanted to move, or said that he planned on sending them to Orange County. The sentence struck even Arthur Schlesinger as demagogic, although he conceded, "It was not so demagogic as it sounded, however, because it had been Kennedy's consistent position."

In fact, there was nothing that Kennedy had said in public or private to suggest that he opposed McCarthy's plan in order to exploit the fears of white suburban voters in Orange County. Instead, he opposed transferring blacks to the suburbs because he considered it unwise and unrealistic. On May 31, the day before the debate, he had issued a paper titled "Meeting the Urban Crisis," a visionary document calling for inner-city enterprise zones, health care reform, and welfare payments that rewarded those who found work. The following passage was underlined to give it greater weight: "It must be understood that the building of a truly integrated society depends on the development of economic self-sufficiency and security in the communities of poverty, for only then will the residents of these areas have the where-withal to move freely with the society." The report went on to say, "Those who speak of ending the colonialism of the ghetto must there-fore recognize that the economic and social development of that com-munity is at the heart of any policy creating full mobility."

Kennedy had been impressed by the theater company and writing workshop that author and Honorary Kennedy Budd Schulberg had founded in Watts after the 1965 riots. Schulberg had introduced Kennedy to community leaders in Watts, and accompanied him when he campaigned there. While motorcading through Watts on May 29, Kennedy had turned to Richard Goodwin and said, "You know, if any-thing happens to me, there'll never be another white politician they'll trust." Then, referring to the richness of black culture, he added, "Suppose we do succeed, and the whole country becomes just one big middle class, do you know how much we'll lose?" When he said this, he was expressing his fear of the damage that could be inflicted on African-American culture if blacks were suddenly dispersed to white suburbs.

THINGS HAPPENED DURING the final days of the campaign in California that would not be remembered, at least in the same way, had Kennedy lived.

Jim Tolan considers it noteworthy that although Kennedy often attended religious services during the campaign, he could only remem-ber him taking mass once, on June 2 in San Francisco. John Lewis re-members watching Kennedy motorcade through Watts on June 3 unprotected and engulfed by adoring crowds, and thinking, "This is just too much for Senator Kennedy to travel around like this . . . somebody will try to take his life." George Plimpton recalled that on June 2, during a radio program he was hosting for the campaign, a caller asked, "Is Bobby Kennedy ready?" Plimpton replied, "Ready for what?" and the caller shouted, "Ready to be killed. He's doomed! He's doomed!"

Hays Gorey wrote, "There was something about Monday, June 3," and called the day "strangely gloomy and disorganized." Jules Witcover described it as another day marking the Kennedy campaign as "among the most emotional and exhausting [days] in the annals of presidential elections." While canvassing in Delano, Cesar Chavez remembered meeting a woman who said that she loved Kennedy but could not bring herself to vote for him. "I don't want to be guilty if anything happens," she explained.

Earlier in the campaign, Hays Gorey had reported, "We [Gorey] have earlier expressed a view which we now repeat: Kennedy couldn't possibly be play-acting in all the concern he expresses for Negroes, Indians, the young, the poor, etc. Not in all of it. Of course there's some political advantage. . . . But he just isn't the great actor he would have to be to fake all this. He picks up and cuddles Negro children, some of them filthy dirty. He never shrinks. You can watch his facial expression. There is no look of distaste. He is tortured. He is driven. He is consumed by his desire to be President." During these final days, Kennedy became even more driven and consumed, and those near him sensed him reaching the limits of his physical and emotional stamina. The lines in his face became fissures. His bloodshot eyes stared from cavernous sockets. He stuttered, fumbled sentences, and lost his train of thought. His hands shook during the day and bled at night. His emotions were so close to the surface that when he spoke about hunger and poverty, he shook.

During this week, Richard Harwood told his editor at the *Washington Post*, "I'm falling in love with the guy," and requested to be taken off the campaign. Explaining his decision later, he said, "I think we [the Kennedy press corps] were getting partisan. We hadn't quite become cheerleaders but we were in danger of it."

Theodore White collapsed, taking to his bed in the Ambassador Hotel and blaming his exhaustion on the emotion and intensity of the campaign. For the next several mornings, Kennedy visited with him for several minutes, teasing him for staying in bed and giving him a summary of the previous day's events. White saw a man who probably should have been in bed, too. He believed that Kennedy was testing "the limits of physical and emotional exertion," had "let his passion outrun his energies," and was campaigning by "simple will of spirit."

On June 3, the day before the primary, that will finally failed Kennedy. He woke to news of a last-minute poll that showed him leading McCarthy 39 percent to 30 percent, with 13 percent preferring an "uncommitted" slate of delegates (who were presumed to be pro-Humphrey) and 18 percent undecided. In earlier primaries, the undecided voters had broken for McCarthy.

He began the day by flying to San Francisco. Jim Tolan and Tim Hannon, who had organized a motorcade through Chinatown, met him at the airport dressed in rented Chinese coolie costumes and standing next to a rickshaw. Dutton, who disembarked first, told them, "This is going to be the best thing in the world or it's going to really bomb because he's really uptight." But Kennedy laughed and the prank put him in a good mood.

Tolan warned Bobby and Ethel to expect fireworks. Three blocks into Chinatown, a string of firecrackers exploded near their car. Ethel clutched her chest, flinching with each bang, and collapsing onto the floor of the car. Bobby twitched, but so briefly one has to watch a film of the incident several times to see it. Kennedy asked Richard Harwood, who had been jogging behind the car, to sit with Ethel and calm her. The motorcade ended at Fisherman's Wharf where "Italian-Americans for Kennedy" were holding a lunch at DiMaggio's Restaurant. The event was muted, and Jack Newfield thought Kennedy was "in a state beyond fatigue." But while driving to the airport afterward, the Kennedys belted out a song in Japanese at the top of their voices.

Kennedy flew to Long Beach and spoke at a large rally. A man standing next to the platform unnerved him by chanting, "Who killed your brother? Who killed your brother?" His speech was barely coherent, and as he left to motorcade through Compton, Watts, and Venice, Fred Dutton said gently, "You had a little trouble with some words that time."

Most of Kennedy's southern California motorcades had occurred in brilliant sunshine. But on June 3, the skies were leaden and smoggy, and the crowds in Watts were smaller than usual, partly because Kennedy was following a back-street route designed to spare him the usual battering and avoid some of the wild scenes that appeared so frightening on the evening news. Still, spectators hurled themselves in waves against Kennedy's slow-moving convertible, and as hundreds of hands slapped his, his body jolted, as if shocked by an electric current. It took three men—Bill Barry, Rafer Johnson, and Rosey Grier—holding on to one another's waists in a chain, to prevent him being yanked into the street. An inebriated young man with a goatee leapt onto the hood and rode for blocks while screaming "Make way for Kennedy!"

Kennedy stopped frequently so he could ask the crowds, "Are you going to vote for me tomorrow? ["Yes!"] Are you just going to wave to Mr. Kennedy and then tomorrow, when I'm gone, forget about me? ["No!"] Or are you going to vote? ["Yes!"]" When he finally sat down his face was expressionless and his eyes unfocused. A five-year-old black girl, whom he had earlier pulled into the car to keep her from falling under the wheels, sat in the backseat playing with a huge stuffed white rabbit. He placed her between his knees and began whispering into her ear. Finally, he stopped the motorcade. He and the girl got out and stood together at dusk in the middle of a wide boulevard, the girl clutching Kennedy with one hand and the stuffed rabbit with the other, waiting until a car could be found to return her to her parents.

After leaving Watts, Kennedy complained of feeling nauseous. Dutton dashed into a grocery store and returned with some ginger ale that revived him. The motorcade ended at the Los Angeles airport. Kennedy told Tolan and Hannon that they looked exhausted and should take a break after the primary. Tolan said that they were flying to upstate New York that evening to begin advancing his appearance at Niagara Falls on Friday. "You know where these kooks are going? They're going to Buffalo!" Kennedy shouted to Ethel, adding, "I'm due in Buffalo on Friday."

In San Diego, so many people had come to the El Cortez Hotel to see Kennedy that his staff had to divide them into two groups. During his first appearance he spoke so fast that his speech made little sense. Finally, after weeks of being cursed by the Kennedy-haters, kissed on the mouth by weeping Chicanos, reminded of his murdered brother, imagining guns between him and the White House, and giving Californians everything he had, he had nothing more to give. Ashen-faced, shaking, and racked with nausea, he abruptly stopped speaking. His knees buckled, and he sat down on the edge of the stage and buried his head in his hands.

Barry, Johnson, and Grier lifted him up and led him to the men's room. He vomited and returned thirty minutes later to address the second audience. He held a flower as he spoke. Singer and Honorary Kennedy Rosemary Clooney noticed that it never stopped shaking. When he finished, Harwood and others in his press corps yanked the plugs on the television cameras that a local news crew had set up in the lobby. They wanted to spare him the embarrassment of being filmed and interviewed while he was sick and disoriented.

Kennedy climbed into his bunk and slept for most of the thirty-five-minute flight back to Los Angeles. Ethel sat between Richard Harwood and another reporter. She nervously asked what they thought would happen tomorrow. Harwood told her to relax. The last-minute polls showed Bobby beating McCarthy. "I know you think so," she said. "But you see so many of the crowds and the people who love him. You don't hear the others."

"Stop worrying," one of the men said, "Tomorrow night at this time, you'll feel good."

SEVENTEEN

"SO THIS IS IT"

JUNE 4–5, 1968

Kennedy spent a smoggy and overcast primary day relaxing at the Malibu beach house of director John Frankenheimer. During an interview that morning with AP reporter Saul Pett, he said, "If anyone wanted to shoot the President of the United States, it is not a very difficult job. All one has to do is get on a high building some day with a telescopic rifle and there is nothing anyone could do to defend you."

The sea was rough but Kennedy dashed in and out of the surf with his children. A huge wave enveloped him and twelve-year-old David Kennedy. When they emerged from the water he was gripping his son's hand and had bruised his forehead.

During the afternoon he learned that early CBS polls showed him leading McCarthy in California by seven percentage points. He told Theodore White that if he could take urban California and rural South Dakota on the same day he could win over the Democratic bosses.

Speechwriter Richard Goodwin stopped at Frankenheimer's house, looked through a glass door onto the patio, and saw Kennedy stretched out on two chairs pulled together next to the pool, his head hanging limply to one side. For a split second, Goodwin thought he was dead. When he realized he was only sleeping, he thought, "God, I suppose none of us will ever get over John Kennedy."

Kennedy decided to skip the usual election night hoopla of ballrooms jammed with supporters, suites filled with friends and staff, and mobs of people wanting to confer, congratulate, or at least be in the same room with him. After months of making himself endlessly available to strangers and friends, he wanted to spend the most important evening of his political life watching the returns in Malibu with his family and close friends. He ordered television sets delivered to Frankenheimer's house, but the networks protested that they had already stationed their crews and correspondents at the Ambassador Hotel. Kennedy capitulated and after an early dinner, Frankenheimer drove him to the hotel. They were late and he encouraged Frankenheimer to speed. But after they missed a freeway exit he said, "Take it easy, John. Life is too short."

The last five hours of Kennedy's conscious life, between his arrival at the Ambassador at 7:15 p.m. and 12:16 a.m., when he was shot in a pantry corridor, were also a turning point for his campaign, when even the most skeptical reporters and aides began believing that he might win the nomination.

He spent most of these five hours in the hotel's fifth-floor Royal Suite, a spacious apartment with a long hallway, living room, and two bedrooms. His campaign had rented a second room across the corridor, but the in-the-room syndrome was in play, so supporters, aides, celebrities, newsmen, and friends jammed the Royal Suite, adding to the bedlam of jangling phones, shouted conversations, and blaring televisions.

Kennedy paced between the living room and bedrooms, watching the returns and giving informal interviews. People followed him, asking questions, and offering advice, all wanting a piece of him, like the crowds at his rallies.

Minutes after arriving, he received a call from Bill Daugherty, who was in a hotel in Sioux City, South Dakota, with campaign workers. Daugherty reported that partial returns showed him winning over 50 percent of the vote (the final count would give him 50 percent, followed by the Johnson-Humphrey ticket with 30 percent, and McCarthy with 20 percent). It was a stunning defeat for Humphrey, who had made several well-publicized trips to the state, even delivering a commencement address at his former high school. His supporters had mounted an expensive advertising campaign urging South Dakotans to put one of their own in the White House by voting for a slate of delegates that, although listed under Johnson's name, had pledged to vote for Humphrey at the convention. The vote was the largest ever cast in a South Dakota presidential primary. The next day, the conservative *Rapid City Journal* declared that despite the "intense battle" waged by the Humphrey people, Kennedy had won a "smashing triumph," distinguished by "crushing victories" in blue-collar precincts that had been expected to go for Humphrey.

Senator George McGovern also telephoned Kennedy, congratulating him on his victory and apologizing for implying that his candidacy had been "an impossible dream."

Kennedy called Daugherty back so he could thank his supporters over a speaker phone. Daugherty taped the call and later transferred it onto a CD. The recording is remarkably clear. Kennedy sounds youthful and exhilarated, and says he is looking forward to meeting everyone at his inauguration. Daugherty tells him, "We had a great Indian vote. Our trip down to Pine Ridge did a lot of good." Kennedy replies, "I'm very grateful to the Indians," adding, "I always thought there was some question of whether the white man should live here . . . particularly whether he should have gone all the way to Oregon."

Kennedy talked about South Dakota all evening, even after network projections showed him ahead in California. When Warren Rogers of *Look* and photographer Stan Tretick (who had shouted "He's going all the fucking way!" at Kansas State) arrived at his bedroom while he was changing into a suit, his first words were, "Have you heard about the Indian vote?" He poked his head into a room and asked reporters, "You want me to tell you about the Indians? In one county in South Dakota there were 858 Indian votes. I got 856, Hubert Humphrey got two." Then a wicked grin crossed his face, and he added, "McCarthy got none."

The returns from California came in slowly, delayed by punch card voting machines being used for the first time in Los Angeles. The suburban vote was tallied first. Early results showed McCarthy ahead, but CBS projections gave Kennedy a comfortable lead, and reported that black and Hispanic voters had turned out in record numbers, and had voted overwhelmingly for him. The final count would show Kennedy taking almost 95 percent of the vote in many Hispanic precincts, and winning one with 100 percent.

With a double victory in California and South Dakota seeming likely, Kennedy's suite became even more chaotic. Aides and reporters helped themselves to drinks, and conversations were shouted and repeated. A reporter asked Kennedy how he planned to celebrate. He said, "Have a drink. Maybe three." He took one reporter after another aside to invite them to his postelection party at a trendy Los Angeles discotheque until he had finally invited his entire press corps. He told aide Peter Smith, "We did pretty well here, didn't we?" and Smith saw a man "beside himself with enthusiasm." Ethel kissed the journalist who had insisted that Bobby would win California. Someone said, "Maybe people don't dislike this husband of yours as much as people think." Jabbing him with her finger, she said, "*I* never thought people disliked my husband."

During an impromptu hallway press conference, Kennedy was asked if he was angry about McCarthy distorting his Senate record. "You should read Lord Tweedsmuir on politicians and politics," he said, referring to one of John Kennedy's favorite authors. He pointed out that Tweedsmuir had called politics "an honorable adventure," adding that although there was nothing honorable in distorting records, "I like politics. I like politicians."

By 10:30 p.m. enough returns had come in from Los Angeles County to confirm that Kennedy's support from black and Chicano voters had overcome McCarthy's suburban strength. CBS declared him the winner with over 50 percent of the vote, and final returns would show him beating McCarthy 46 percent to 42 percent.

How Kennedy had won South Dakota and California was even more remarkable than the victories themselves. He had won South Dakota despite spending only two days there. Instead of making the customary pilgrimage to Mount Rushmore, he had tramped around Wounded Knee with Christopher Pretty Boy; instead of pretending to know about agricultural issues, he had cheerfully admitted his ignorance.

He had won California despite disregarding the advice of professionals like Jesse Unruh. Instead of campaigning from a television studio and the suburbs, he had whistle-stopped through the San Joaquin Valley, motorcaded through Watts and Oakland, spent hours fielding hostile questions in Oakland. He had won California and South Dakota, as he had Indiana and Nebraska, by following de Tocqueville's advice to treat the citizens of a democracy "like deities who reigned supreme in the universe," and without exploiting the affection voters felt for his martyred brother. He had campaigned differently than JFK would have, addressing different issues, so that by June 4 the greatest similarities between them were their Massachusetts accents and their belief that patriotism and sacrifice were inseparable.

Unruh urged Kennedy to go downstairs to the Embassy Ballroom and declare victory before the networks left the air on the East Coast. First, Kennedy took Goodwin and Dutton into a bathroom, closed the door, and talked strategy. He was concerned that while he was battling for votes in the June 18 New York primary, Humphrey would travel around the country picking up more delegates. "I've got to spend that time going to the states, talking to delegates before it's too late," he said. "My only chance is to chase Hubert's ass all over the country. Maybe he'll fold." Earlier in the campaign, he had dismissed Goodwin's suggestion that he offer McCarthy the post of secretary of state in exchange for leaving the race. It was the kind of political horse-trading he disliked, and his low opinion of McCarthy's temperament and capabilities made it a particularly loathsome bargain. But now, believing himself close to winning the nomination, he resurrected the idea himself, taking Goodwin aside and whispering, "I think we should tell him [McCarthy] if he withdraws now and supports me, I'll make him secretary of state."

Moments before heading downstairs, he telephoned Kenny O'Donnell, who was watching the returns at the Mayflower Hotel in Washington with Dan Rostenkowski, an influential Illinois congressman who was close to Mayor Daley. O'Donnell congratulated him and said he appeared poised to win the nomination.

"I think I may," Kennedy replied, adding, "I feel now for the first time that I've shaken off the shadow of my brother. I feel I made it on my own."

Kennedy asked Rostenkowski for his support. Rostenkowski said, "Daley is my guy. I do what Daley tells me. . . . You win California, you get Daley, we all come along."

O'Donnell had also been in touch with Daley and believed, as Richard Wade did, that he would back Kennedy if he won California. Now Rostenkowski had confirmed that the Illinois delegation would fall in line behind Daley.

O'Donnell took the phone back from Rostenkowski and said, "Bobby, you did it, you son of a bitch! See you tomorrow."

The two most deliriously happy moments of Kennedy's campaign occurred at its beginning and end: after his raucous reception at Kansas State, when it seemed possible he might "go all the way," and after his victories in South Dakota and California, when going all the way seemed even more likely. On both occasions, he had felt a sense of liberation: in Kansas, from months of caution and cowardice; in California, from his brother's shadow. On the flight back from Kansas he had said that he felt "Free!" and "Like a new man!" After winning South Dakota and California, he lit a cigar and paced around his suite, pounding his fist into his palm and saying, "I'm going to get Humphrey . . . I'm going to *make* him debate me . . . I'm going to chase his ass all over the country." *Look*'s Warren Rogers, who had never heard him speak so crudely, put it down to nerves and excitement. "For what it's worth, I think you can do it now," he told him. "I didn't think so before, but now I do. I think you can beat Humphrey and get the nomination." Kennedy grinned and said, "Glad to have your endorsement at last. Welcome aboard the bandwagon."

Kennedy retreated to a corner of the living room, squatting on his haunches and puffing on a cigar while watching the televised returns. Budd Schulberg came over and urged him to acknowledge the importance of the black vote in his victory statement. "Well, of course, you know who won this election for you," he said.

"You're going to give me that speech about eighty-five or ninety percent black vote, and the Chicanos practically one hundred percent," Kennedy replied.

"Bob, you're the only white man in the country they trust."

Kennedy and Schulberg spent several minutes discussing Schulberg's Watts Writer's Workshop and Douglas House Theatre, comparing them with Kennedy's efforts to encourage the private sector to invest in Bedford-Stuyvesant. Kennedy thought inner cities needed both kinds of projects. "We have to encourage not just mechanical skills and jobs in those areas, but creative talent," he said. "I saw it in Watts, at the Douglas House—so much talent to be channeled, strong self-expression. I'd like to see it on a national scale, with federal help. I'll do everything I can."

Before leaving to go downstairs Kennedy told John Lewis, "You let me down today. More Mexican-Americans voted for me than Negroes." Everyone in the room laughed. "Wait for me," Kennedy said. "I'll be back in fifteen or twenty minutes." Lewis remembered him looking so happy that "he could have floated out of the room."

Some of Kennedy's friends and aides remained in his suite to watch his victory speech on television rather than endure the noise and chaos of the Embassy Ballroom. But enough insisted on accompanying him downstairs to create gridlock in the corridor leading to the elevators. He ran into his eleven-year-old daughter, Courtney, and while everyone waited, spent several minutes quizzing her about her day. He stopped for another conversation with columnist Joseph Kraft, who had recommended that he abandon the primaries and support McCarthy, then when McCarthy lost the nomination to Humphrey, support Humphrey in the general election. Kraft had argued that after Humphrey lost to Nixon, Kennedy would be left in control of the party. "Now you're trapped," Kraft joked, meaning that now that he had won California, he would have to see the campaign through to the convention. Kennedy, understanding what Kraft meant, smiled and nodded.

Because the returns had been slow, many in the Embassy Room had been waiting several hours. The mood had slipped from one of exuberance into a near hysteria, and some would recall a crowd "full of animal energies" and "frightening suppressed violence." By midnight, when Kennedy finally took the stage, his young campaign workers were dancing in conga lines, shouting "Sock it to 'em, Bobby!" strumming guitars, singing "This man is your man. This man is my man. This man is Robert Kennedeee!" and leaping into the air.

He addressed them for about fifteen minutes, speaking off the cuff, sometimes consulting notes supplied by Frank Mankiewicz. His speech had the rambling quality of an Academy Awards acceptance speech, with him thanking in random order Jesse Unruh, his sister and brother-in-law Steve and Jean Smith, his mother "and all of those other Kennedys," his dog Freckles, and Ethel. He joked about acknowledging Freckles before his wife, repeated his pledge to help "those who still suffer within the United States from hunger" and, worried he was talking too long, said, "If I can just take a minute or two minutes more of your time."

He followed Schulberg's advice and thanked "all my friends in the black community." After mentioning Cesar Chavez and Dolores Huerta, he said, "We have certain obligations and responsibilities to our fellow citizens which we talked about during the course of this campaign," and promised to fulfill them when he became president. Finally, smiling broadly and standing next to Ethel, he said, "So my thanks to all of you, and on to Chicago and let's win there." Because these would be his last public words, and so perfectly captured this triumphant moment, they were rebroadcast for days and have become a staple of documentaries about the sixties.

After flashing a Churchillian V-for-Victory sign, he left the stage to chants of "We want Bobby! We want Bobby!" Then he broke his own rule of always leaving a hall through the crowd and allowed assistant maître d'hôtel Karl Uecker to take his arm and guide him toward the pantry.

Bill Barry had assumed that Kennedy would exit through the auditorium and had already started moving through the crowd to clear a path. When he noticed him heading for the pantry he doubled back and followed.

Why Kennedy chose this route is unclear. Perhaps the frenzied crowd had unsettled and frightened even him, or perhaps after being pummeled by people for eighty-two days, he simply wanted a break, or perhaps he was impatient to hold a scheduled news conference for print journalists in the Colonial Room and head for his victory party at the Factory discotheque. Dutton blamed himself for not contesting Kennedy's last-minute decision to leave through the kitchen, saying later, "I've always taken responsibility for it."

As Kennedy was heading toward the kitchen, he saw Paul Schrade, the regional director of the United Auto Workers and an early supporter, and said, "Paul, I want you and Jess with me." Schrade took this as meaning that he wanted them to join him in the Colonial Room. As he followed Kennedy into the pantry, he thought, "This is really what we've been fighting for. We're going to have a president."

As Kennedy was leaning across one of the pantry worktables to shake hands with a member of the kitchen staff, a young Palestinian man with the same first and last names, Sirhan Sirhan, reached out from the crowd, pointed a revolver at Kennedy's head, and fired.*

The shots reminded some of the firecrackers in Chinatown, although no one mistook them for that. "I had been in the infantry in World War II," Dutton said later, "and I immediately knew what it was." Sirhan used a .22-caliber pistol, a weapon that is not necessarily fatal even when fired at close range—and certainly not the weapon of choice for a professional assassin. He was close when he fired, and a surgeon who operated on Kennedy reported that if the fatal bullet had hit him a centimeter further back he would have survived and spent several weeks recuperating before resuming his campaign.

When the shots rang out there was already a crush of people in the pantry, and more immediately rushed in. Frank Mankiewicz leaned against someone's back and wept. George Plimpton, Bill Barry, Rafer Johnson, and Roosevelt Grier wrestled with Sirhan. Grier finally pinned him down and disarmed him.

John F. Kennedy and Martin Luther King Jr. had been shot at long distance by high-powered rifles, like prize stags. Bobby's assassination was less surprising than theirs, but more intimate, and gruesome. He was slaughtered at close range, like a farm animal, in a claustrophobic and abattoir-like room filled with metal tables and knives. Almost

---

*Sirhan Sirhan was a twenty-four-year-old Palestinian who had lived in the United States for twelve years. Four decades after the assassination he continues to serve a life sentence in a California penitentiary. It has been claimed that he killed Kennedy because he was angry over Kennedy's support for Israel (an explanation that could have prompted him to murder any number of presidential candidates), or because, in a *Manchurian Candidate* scenario, he had been brainwashed by the Mafia, CIA, or Aristotle Onassis. The most likely explanation is that he was a disturbed young man who sought to become famous by killing someone who already was.

eighty people stood only a few feet away. Five others were wounded, and the shooting was recorded, taped, and filmed by radio newsmen, still reporters, and television cameramen, except for Jim Wilson of CBS who smashed his camera against the wall so he could not film the tragedy. JFK had been killed during a routine political excursion to Texas, after serving as president almost three years. Dr. King had been shot in Memphis while supporting a strike by sanitation workers, at a time when his legacy was assured. But Bobby was assassinated moments after his greatest political triumph.

Because so many people were standing nearby when he was shot, there are numerous first-person accounts, photographs, and film clips. The most dramatic is a recording made by Andrew West, a mutual radio network reporter who was interviewing Kennedy as he walked into the pantry.

West begins by asking a garbled question: "Senator, how are you going to counter Mr. Humphrey and his backgrounding you as far as the delegate votes go?"

Kennedy says, "It just goes back to the struggle for it . . ." There are gunshots and screams, then West says, "Senator Kennedy has been shot—Senator Kennedy has been shot. Is that possible? Is that possible? It is possible, ladies and gentlemen. Is it possible? He has. Not only Senator Kennedy—Oh my God—Senator Kennedy and another man—a Kennedy campaign manager—and possibly shot in the head. I am right here and Rafer Johnson has hold of the man who apparently has fired the shot. . . . He still has the gun. The gun is pointed at me right at this moment. I hope they can get the gun out of his hand. Be very careful. Get the gun . . . get the gun . . . stay away from the gun . . . stay away from the gun.

"His hand is frozen . . . get his thumb . . . get his thumb . . . Take a hold of his thumb . . . and break it if you have to. . . . Get away from the barrel. . . . Look out for the gun. OK—all right. That's it. Rafer, get it. Get the gun, Rafer. OK, now hold on to the gun. . . .

"Ladies and gentlemen they have the gun away from the man. . . . I can't see the man. I can't see who it is. Senator Kennedy right now is on the ground. He has been shot. This is a—this is—wait a minute. Hold him. . . . We don't want another Oswald. . . . Hold him, Rafer.

Keep people away from him. . . . This is a—make room, make room, make room, make room. The Senator is on the ground. He's bleeding profusely . . . apparently the Senator has been shot from the frontal area, we don't see exactly where the Senator has been shot."

After Sirhan Sirhan had been subdued, the screams gave way to tears, and the curses to cries of "Get back!" and "Give him some air!"

After everyone moved back Kennedy could be seen lying on his back on the concrete floor, bleeding from a head wound. He held a rosary given him by a busboy. His tie had been loosened, his shirt opened, and his head rested on a folded suit jacket. Ethel knelt by his side and whispered in his ear. His chest moved and his breathing was labored. He regained consciousness, and lost it, regained it and lost it again. His eyes were blank, then clear and focused. His lips moved.

He asked the busboy, "Is everybody else all right?"

According to another version he asked, "Is Paul [Schrade] okay? Is everybody all right?"

Richard Harwood saw him raise one of his legs. British photographer Harry Benson heard him say, "My head," and heard Ethel tell him, "I'm with you, my baby." Someone else heard him murmur, "Jack . . . Jack."

As ambulance attendants transferred him onto a stretcher, he whispered, "Don't. Don't lift me."

Charles Quinn thought he cried, "No, no, no, no, no . . ." and was reminded of a rabbit, "squealing at the end of his life."

The most shocking thing about Robert Kennedy's assassination was that no one was shocked, including Kennedy. Hays Gorey wrote that, "gazing up from the floor . . . Robert Kennedy, still lucid, wore a haunting expression that no one who knew him will ever forget. . . . [He was] fully aware of what had happened." Reporter Pete Hamill saw a "sort of sweet kind of acceptance" crossing his face as he lay on the floor. As usual, his eyes told the story. Instead of asking "What happened?" they seemed to be saying, "So this is it."

POSTSCRIPT

For many of his supporters, Robert Kennedy's campaign ended with the shots in the pantry. For the members of his staff who had remained upstairs in his suite, it ended when they watched the assassination unfold on television. For Walter Fauntroy and Hosea Williams, who told themselves, "If he survives this, we'll make him President," it ended with his death on June 6. For others, it ended with his funeral services, or when pallbearers carried his casket to his grave, past thousands of mourners holding twinkling candles and singing "America the Beautiful." For the bridesmaids standing in that Delaware meadow it ended when they tossed their bouquets at his funeral train.

For his press corps, the campaign may have ended on Friday, June 21, when Ethel Kennedy invited them to Hickory Hill for a farewell party before she and her children left for Hyannisport. They met her at Arlington and drove in a motorcade to his grave, Ethel going first in a convertible packed with Kennedy children holding bunches of flowers. They prayed, left the flowers, and went to Hickory Hill for a cookout. The reporters swam with the kids, and there were drinks and steaks. You could almost imagine, Sylvia Wright recalled, that it was "another [campaign] activity." They concluded by singing Bobby's favorite song, "Where Have All the Flowers Gone," singing about soldiers gone to graveyards and graveyards covered with flowers. Six months later, some of the reporters returned to Hickory Hill on Christmas Eve and sang carols in the pouring rain. When Ethel invited them in, as they knew she would, they refused, preferring to make this last gesture and leave.

For filmmaker Charles Guggenheim, the campaign ended on an afternoon in late August, when he and Fred Dutton wheeled a cart containing a projector and his film of the Kennedy campaign into a freight elevator at Chicago's Conrad Hilton Hotel. Students and police had already fought the street battles that would tie the Democrats to violence and lawlessness for decades, and Guggenheim and Dutton were bringing the film to Hubert Humphrey's suite so that his aides, who were nervous about a last-minute attempt to draft Ted Kennedy, could view it before deciding whether and when to screen it. "That was that last scene, that was the last effort," Guggenheim said. "Everyone else had gone home. And we were just picking up the pieces." Guggenheim's film was shown after the balloting. When it concluded, the delegates wept.

For the aides who had arranged and typed an eleven-page schedule describing to the minute what Bobby Kennedy would have done between June 7 and June 17—a document that is perhaps the most heartbreaking in the Kennedy Library, and there are numerous contenders for that title—Kennedy's campaign may have ended when their schedule did.

Imagine that Kennedy leaves the Embassy Ballroom by a different route, or moves his head a centimeter forward as Sirhan fires. Then instead of lying in a mahogany coffin in the nave of St. Patrick's Cathedral in Manhattan on June 7, he rises before dawn in the Royal Suite, and flies to St. Louis for a luncheon with delegates to the national convention. He continues to Niagara Falls, where on a gorgeous spring afternoon, with the falls crashing behind him, he delivers a speech launching his campaign in the New York primary. He flies to Long Island and, standing on a flatbed truck in the parking lot of the Walt Whitman Shopping Center, addresses several thousand upturned white middle-class faces, telling them about suicidal Native-Americans and hungry children. He is driven to his Manhattan apartment, changes into black tie, and attends the Uniformed Firemen's Association Dinner Dance at the New York Hilton, where he and Ethel dance. The next morning, they bike through Central Park with their older children—"Family Recreational Manhattan. Central Park Bicycling," his schedule says. Photographs show them flashing their toothy Kennedy smiles and riding five or six abreast past hundreds of outstretched hands, like Tour de France cyclists. That afternoon he marches in the Bayshore, Long Island, Puerto Rican Day parade in his shirtsleeves, hearing cries of "Viva Kennedy!" as mothers hold up infants. During the next seven days he shakes hands with commuters disembarking from the Staten Island Ferry and delivers a commencement address at Yeshiva University. Lunchtime shoppers at Macy's mob him, and he hops by small plane between the same upstate cities where in 1964 the *New York Times* reported him being "cheered, mobbed, pawed, and jostled" by crowds of "unprecedented size." They are now even larger. He flies back to Niagara Falls on Monday, June 17, and drives to Buffalo in a motorcade. When he campaigned here in 1966 for Democratic candidates, 150,000 people filled the streets and policemen had trouble keeping their motorcycles balanced, and when he returns all this happens, and more. At 7:45 p.m., he climbs into a waiting convertible at La Guardia Airport and is driven to Harlem. As high pressure from Canada sweeps away the clouds blanketing the city, he motorcades down 125th Street and his romance with black Americans reaches its apogee. Crowds break through police as he shouts, "I need your help!" until he is hoarse. Again, his hands are scratched and bleeding, and crumpled notes cover his lap. His motorcade turns south on Columbus Avenue, picking up speed as it heads downtown. As he enters Madison Square Garden for a fund-raising gala the audience roars. Then the doors close, the sound becomes muffled, his schedule ends, and he becomes a more elusive ghost, materializing during presidential election years and on the five-year anniversaries of his birth and assassination, hovering specter-like over the Democrats' internecine feuds, sometimes conjured up by politicians claiming to be channeling his spirit.

President Clinton attempted this in his autobiography, writing that Robert Kennedy was "the first New Democrat, before Jimmy

Carter, before the Democratic Leadership Council, which I helped start in 1985, and before my campaign in 1992," and arguing that Kennedy had "understood in a visceral way that progressive politics requires the advocacy of both new politics and fundamental values." But when Clinton signed a welfare reform act that, among other things, cut food stamps to poor children and quoted Robert Kennedy at the signing ceremony, claiming that the new legislation was in concert with Kennedy's spirit, his daughter Rory Kennedy, who was born after his assassination, accused Clinton of "bastardizing" her father's name and legacy. Peter Edelman resigned from his position in the administration and criticized Clinton for "hijacking and twisting" Kennedy's words, adding, "What I would call Robert Kennedy's new progressivism is largely absent from our politics now."

During the November 2005 commemoration of Robert Kennedy's eightieth birthday, the issue of who most resembled him echoed through tributes offered by John Kerry, Hillary Clinton, Barack Obama, and others. Obama said, "If he were here today, I think it would be hard to place Robert F. Kennedy into any of the categories that constrain us politically," and argued that whatever Kennedy had been, he had not been "a centrist in the sense of finding a middle road," meaning that he would have been uncomfortable among the New Democrats and triangulating Clintons.

During a "How Is Robert F. Kennedy's Vision Relevant Today" panel discussion, moderator and former speechwriter Jeff Greenfield summarized Kennedy's political philosophy as "Take your foot off the other guy's neck!" He recalled that whenever Kennedy told an audience the opposite of what it presumably wanted to hear, "you could almost *hear* people thinking and changing their minds." And when Greenfield said this, one could almost hear people in the conference room asking themselves what politician in his right mind would do that now.

Congressman Rahm Emanuel, the chairman of the Democratic Campaign Committee, was on the panel as a "Keynote Listener." He contended that Kennedy had not faced the kind of "values issues" bedeviling current Democrats because abortion had been illegal in 1968 and there was no gay rights movement. He added he was promoting a Democratic "values agenda" consisting of curfews for teenagers, school uniforms, and V-chip Internet censorship. It was thin gruel compared to hunger and poverty, Kennedy's "values issues."

Emanuel also declared that neither President Clinton nor Carter had run on their religious beliefs, presumably like many Republicans, nor had they run away from them, presumably like some Democrats. The implication was that Robert Kennedy had not run away from his religion, either. Jeff Greenfield shot back that although Kennedy's faith had influenced some of his positions, he had never "run" on that faith. In fact, Greenfield said, he could only remember him mentioning God once during the campaign, when he remarked that "The only person who can solve our problems is God, and she isn't running this year."

In fact, candidates from either party could run today on the same issues and champion the same causes that Kennedy had in 1968, since little has been done since to address them. A June 2007 *Washington Post* article titled "A Slow Demise in the Delta" reported that less than 5 percent of federal subsidies meant to boost farmers' incomes and invigorate the economy of the impoverished Mississippi Delta had gone to poor black farmers, while the rest went to large, white-owned commercial farms. Also in June 2007, a *New York Times* article headlined "Indian Reservation Reeling in Wave of Youth Suicides and Attempts" reported that tribal officials in the Rosebud, South Dakota, reservation, which adjoins Pine Ridge, had declared a state of emergency after an epidemic of teenage suicides. *Times* reporter Evelyn Nieves said, "What is happening at Pine Ridge is all too common throughout Indian Country," adding that the suicide rate for Native American and Alaskan Native youth was more than three times the national average, the same rate as it had been in 1968.

SEVERAL DAYS AFTER Kennedy's assassination Charles Quinn of CBS interviewed a group of Southern men who were attending a

Wallace for President rally in Memphis. They all appeared to be fierce Wallace supporters, but told Quinn that if Kennedy had lived they would have voted for him instead. They were unable to explain why. "I just liked him," one said. "I thought he would have made a good President."

Whether Robert Kennedy would have made a good president is unknowable. All that is certain is that during his campaign he convinced millions of Americans that he was a good man, perhaps a great man. The Wallace supporters, Delaware bridesmaids, Gary steelworkers, Nebraska farmers, and Chicano farmworkers mourned him so fiercely because they sensed that he had tried to educate rather than manipulate them, reconcile rather than divide them, engage them in a dialogue rather than feed them the message of the day, appeal to their better angels instead of their wallets, and demand sacrifice instead of promising comfort. They mourned him because they ached for a leader who could heal their wounded nation and restore its tarnished honor, and because they ached to feel noble again.

President Nixon adopted some of the policies Kennedy had advocated during his campaign, such as a draft lottery and volunteer army, and responded with surprisingly liberal legislation to an increased public awareness of issues that Kennedy had championed, such as hunger and Indian rights. But Nixon's Vietnam policies and his bombing of Cambodia hardened the nation's divisions and deepened the moral wounds. The war ended for America with the 1973 Paris Peace Accords, but without the national reconciliation and moral awakening that Kennedy believed was necessary to heal the national soul. As a result, Vietnam remains a painful and divisive issue for the generation that fought it and protested it.

In the final year of Ronald Reagan's presidency, Arthur Schlesinger wrote in an introduction to *Robert Kennedy: In His Own Words*, "Soon the dam will break, as it broke at the turn of the century, again in the 1930s, again in the 1960s. Sometime around the year 1990, if the rhythm holds, we can expect a breakthrough into a new and generous epoch in American life. When that time comes, the Kennedy ideals will no longer seem so exotic." That dam has still not burst. Perhaps the mortar of complacency, selfishness, and cynicism holding it together is indestructible. But if it ever does burst, then Robert Kennedy's ideals, and his campaign, will suddenly seem very relevant.

Notes

Abbreviations

AS: Arthur Schlesinger Jr., *Robert Kennedy and His Times*. Boston: Houghton Mifflin, 1978.

CBS: Transcript of CBS News Special, June 7, 1968.

GUGPRO: Transcript of Guggenheim Productions Sound Rolls in RFK Presidential Campaign Papers, John F. Kennedy Library.

HGP: Hays Gorey Papers, University of Utah.

JBMP: Papers of John Bartlow Martin at the Library of Congress.

JFKL: John F. Kennedy Library, Boston.

JFKLOH: Oral Histories, John F. Kennedy Library.

JSOH: Oral Histories compiled by Jean Stein and George Plimpton, John F. Kennedy Library.

NYT: *New York Times.*

RFKCONF: Robert F. Kennedy Conference, John F. Kennedy Library, November 18, 2000.

RFKCP: Robert F. Kennedy Presidential Campaign Papers 1968, John F. Kennedy Library.

RFKCS: Edwin O. Guthman and Jeffrey Shulman, eds. *RFK: Collected Speeches.* New York: Viking Press, 1993.

RFKMEM: Memorial event marking what would have been Robert Kennedy's eightieth birthday.

WP: *Washington Post.*

Prologue

PAGE

2 "the generous impulses . . .": RFKCS, p. 331.

2 "a way in which . . .": RFKCS, p. 338.

2 Crowds were expected: Description of the funeral train and crowds lining the tracks: NYT and WP, June 9, 1968; *Life*, "The Kennedys," Special Edition, June 1968; Fusco, *Funeral Train.*

3 "It was only . . .": White, *1968*, p. 214.

3 "Where, dear God . . .": Salinger et al., p. 134.

3 "the same thing . . .": AS, p. 857.

4 "You look at . . .": JSOH, Papert, p. 8.

4 "I hope this train . . .": Bruno and Greenfield, pp. 131–32.

5 "Marvelous crowds . . .": AS, p. 915.

5 Adalbert de Segonzac: JSOH, de Segonzac, pp. 1, 4; WP, June 9, 1968.

5 "It may not have had . . .": WP, June 9, 1968.

5 "the only white . . .": JSOH, Brinkley, pp. 19–20.

6 Mohbat and Miller cry: Mohbat interview.

6 Gertrude Wilson: *Amsterdam News*, June 15, 1968.

6 Wedding party: JSOH, Wright, p. 48; *Life*, Special Edition, June 1968.

6 "a wound that . . .": Newfield, p. 7.

6 "My heart ached . . .": Cornelius interview.

7 "I had a dream . . .": WP, June 4, 1988.

7 "The year after . . .": RFKCONF, p. 33.

7 "What would . . .": Lewis interview.

7 "because Bob Kennedy was . . .": Mankiewicz interview.

7 "The music died . . .": German interview.

7 "It's over . . .": JBMP, p. 75.

7 "It was like all of our lives . . .": Bruno interview.

7 "When you get to the pinnacle . . .": Eppridge interview.

7 "I fell in love with . . .": Tolan interview.

8 "I can still see him . . .": Mohbat interview.

8 Hugh McDonald mentioned: interviews with Dutton, Eppridge, Mankiewicz, Tolan.

8 Later, he wandered the corridors: McDonald's life after the assassination is described by Craig Colgan in the *Citizen Patriot* (Jackson, Mich.), May 31, 1998.

8 Rafer Johnson: Johnson, p. 205.

9 Clooney: Clooney with Strait, pp. 36–37.

9 "metaphysical illumination": Evanier, p. 190; *Beyond* magazine, July 1969.

9 "I have no doubt . . .": JBMP, p. 78.

9 "I can feel history . . .": Lewis interview.

9 "I thought that if this one man . . .": Ibid.

9 "would have influenced . . .": Edelman interview.

9 "To know anything . . .": Guthman, *We Band of Brothers*, p. 330.

9 "a far more decent . . .": *Tulanian* (Tulane University magazine), spring 1998.

9 "I'll go to my grave . . .": Shields interview.
9 things would be different: Bill Clinton writes in *My Life* (p. 122), "If he [Robert Kennedy] had become president, America's journey through the rest of the twentieth century would have been very different."
10 "The central point of scheduling . . .": Bruno, p. 30.
10 "This would be a totally different . . .": Mankiewicz interview.
11 Residents of Harlem mourn RFK: *New York* magazine, July 29, 1968.
11 "by five times more in death . . .": Fusco, p. 4.
11 photographs of RFK in offices: RFKMEM.
11 Pentagon goes on alert: WP, June 6, 1968.
11 "The people of the ghetto . . .": NYT, May 18, 1968.
11 They seemed almost embarrassed: Jean Stein [JSOH] asked a wide range of black leaders why the ghettos had not exploded for RFK. Most seemed embarrassed, and puzzled that there had not been riots for Kennedy as there had been following the King assassination.
11 "blue-eyed soul brother": *Time*, May 24, 1968.
12 "crying, sobbing . . .": Lewis, p. 415.
12 "all those areas . . .": JSOH, Papert, p. 13.
12 "huge, joyous adventure": JSOH, Quinn, p. 15.
12 "Once we thought . . .": NYT, February 10, 1968.
12 "I am dissatisfied . . .": AS, p. 800.
12 "what his life . . .": *Atlantic Monthly*, September 1968.
13 "You never know . . .": Shannon, p. 67.
13 "At some point . . .": *Time*, May 9, 1988.
13 "good Bobby . . .": WP, June 7, 1968.
13 "What came out most . . .": WP, June 4, 1988.
15 "For it is long past . . .": Transcript of RFK's speech at Kansas State University [KSU] at www.ksu.edu/lectures/landon/trans/Kennedy68.html.
15 "There is a failing . . .": RFKCS, p. 338.
15 "We cannot continue . . .": Ibid., p. 378.
15 "We have an ally . . .": RFK speech in U.S. Senate, February 8, 1968.
15 "The front pages . . .": Transcript of KSU speech at www.ksu.edu/lectures/landon/trans/Kennedy68.html.
15 "The rich were getting . . .": Halberstam, p. 79.
16 "I have seen these other . . .": RFKCS, pp. 327–30.
16 "What he did was not really . . .": Nolan interview.

One: No Choice

19 "They would have loved . . .": JSOH, Dumbrow, pp. 1–2.
20 The JFK poverty doodle: Thomas, p. 305.
20 the Tribune of the Underclass: AS, p. 778.
20 RFK wants to keep his brother's hopes alive: vanden Heuvel and Gwirtzman, p. 256.
20 "They're here for . . .": Richard Wade interview.
20 "If my brother . . .": Stein and Plimpton, p. 182.
20 "I am announcing . . .": RFKCS, pp. 320–22.
21 "the nostalgic rhetoric . . .": WP, March 17, 1968.
22 RFK press conference following his announcement: NYT, March 17, 1968; WP, March 17, 1968; Mahoney, p. 342; Newfield, pp. 278–79; Witcover, *1968*, pp. 107–8.

22 "When it was over . . .": Ehrlichman, p. 40.

22 RFK at St. Patrick's Day parade: Jim Stevenson manuscript; White, *1968*, p. 194; NYT, March 17, 1968.

23 RFK invites Jim Stevenson to his apartment: Stevenson manuscript.

23 Instead of the mop-haired . . . : *New Yorker*, "Talk of the Town," June 15, 1968; Stevenson manuscript.

23 "even my driver . . .": Newfield, p. 229.

24 RFK on *Meet the Press:* NYT, March 18, 1968.

24 Reaction to RFK candidacy: NYT, March 17–18, 1968; WP, March 17–18, 1968.

25 "He's the whole . . .": AS, p. 865.

25 "the most vicious . . .": vanden Heuvel, p. 147.

25 Reaction of Greek military junta: WP, March 27, 1968.

25 "I hope somebody . . .": Sullivan, p. 56.

27 Reaction of KSU officials to King visit: Ralph Titus (KSU official) interview.

27 "becoming more nervous . . .": Bruno interview.

27 "You guys better do well . . .": Tolan interview; JFKLOH, Tolan.

27 "I'd like to have you travel . . .": Dutton interview; JFKLOH, Dutton.

27 Mankiewicz brought campaign buttons: Mankiewicz interview.

28 Carpenter flies to Kansas with Ethel Kennedy: Carpenter interview.

28 "Do you think . . .": Carpenter interview.

28 "Honorary Kennedys": Navasky, p. 330.

29 "Let me get this . . .": Walinsky interview; HGP.

29 "I didn't want to run . . .": Witcover, *85 Days*, p. 96.

30 Walinsky memorandum: Provided to the author by Adam Walinsky.

30 "most everyone I respect": vanden Heuvel, pp. 260–61.

30 "We weren't that far . . .": Clymer, p. 105.

31 "You know, we had fourteen people . . .": Walinsky interview.

31 "I'm afraid that . . .": Newfield, p. 128.

31 Ted Kennedy approaches McGovern: JFKLOH, McGovern.

31 Ethel Kennedy enlists the Christmas card: JFKLOH, Mankiewicz.

32 "We know where your kids . . .": Rogers, p. 53.

32 "Do you know what . . .": Ibid.

32 November 26 appearance on *Face the Nation:* vanden Heuvel, p. 283.

32 "If you believe that . . .": AS, p. 838.

33 "President Kennedy was fond . . .": John F. Kennedy, p. ix.

33 "thoughtless folly": Robert Kennedy, *To Seek*, p. 232.

33 "There would surely be nothing . . .": NYT, November 30, 1968.

33 "Eugene McCarthy is *not* . . .": JFKLOH, McGovern.

33 "The support just isn't . . .": Richard Goodwin, p. 481.

34 "under any conceivable . . .": AS, p. 840; Newfield, p. 203. When the statement was made public, Kennedy changed "conceivable" to "foreseeable" at the urging of press secretary Frank Mankiewicz.

34 "shattered the mask . . .": White, *1968*, p. 10.

34 "not going to do . . .": Witcover, *85 Days*, p. 53.

35 "Your friend Bobby . . .": JFKLOH, Walton.

35 "I don't know how . . .": Mankiewicz interview; JFKLOH, Mankiewicz.

35 "What are you going . . .": Walinsky interview.

35 Mankiewicz believes he may have decided: Mankiewicz interview; JFKLOH, Mankiewicz.

35 "We seem to have fulfilled . . .": NYT, February 10, 1968.

35   "I think I have to . . .": Guthman, p. 325.
36   "I know . . .": Ibid., p. 326; RFKCONF, p. 18.
36   "I'm going to run . . .": JFKLOH, Edelman.
36   "Yeah, I think I'll run . . .": JFKLOH, Chavez.
36   McGovern urged Kennedy to wait: JFKLOH, McGovern.
36   "I am actively reassessing . . .": Newfield, p. 218.
36   "a classic political . . .": Newfield, p. 219.
36   "moved with the ruthlessness . . .": Halberstam, p. 66.
37   "My brother thinks . . .": JSOH, Wright, p. 15; Stein and Plimpton, p. 232.
37   He discusses his candidacy with his advisers: JFKLOH, Walinsky, Dutton, Greenfield.
37   "Not that anything . . .": AS, p. 857.
37   "It either showed a lot . . .": Sorensen, p. 140.

Two: *"He's Going All the Way"*

39   RFK arrival at Kansas City airport: Newfield, p. 231; Witcover, *85 Days*, pp. 96–97; *Kansas City Times*, March 18, 1968.
40   "Campaigns attract . . .": Schmertz interview.
40   Kennedy at Topeka airport: Jimmy Breslin in the *New York Post*, March 20, 1968.
40   *Topeka Capital-Journal* editorial: March 17, 1968.
40   "In 1960 . . .": *Topeka Capital-Journal*, March 19, 1968.
40   "How am I doing here?": Slattery interview.
40   Meeting with Docking: *Topeka Capital-Journal*, March 19, 1968.
40   Docking had already told reporters: *Topeka Capital-Journal*, March 17, 1968.
41   Kennedy did not press Docking: Drew Pearson column in *New York Post*, March 22, 1968.
41   "the kind of things . . .": Dutton interview.
41   "curious inability . . .": *Saturday Evening Post*, June 15, 1968.
41   "he just couldn't": Nolan interview; JFKLOH, Nolan.
41   Kennedy is reluctant to discuss feelings: Tolan interview; JFKLOH, Tolan.
41   "What was your reaction when . . .": JFKLOH, Tolan.
41   Briefing from a State Department official: Mankiewicz interview; JFKLOH, Mankiewicz; Salinger et al., p. 23.
42   "What I'm going to say . . .": *Topeka Capital-Journal*, March 19, 1968.
42   "Listen, we've got to make sure . . .": JFKLOH, Walinsky.
42   "Can you *please* help . . .": Carpenter interview.
42   "I'll pretend I'm you": Ibid.
42   "Some of you may . . .": *Topeka Capital-Journal*, March 19, 1968.
43   RFK conversation with Dan Lykins: Lykins interview.
43   Description of students and atmosphere at Ahearn Field House: Witcover, *85 Days*, pp. 101–5. NYT, March 19, 1968. Interviews with Dick Haines, Kevin Rochat, Ralph Titus, Rene Carpenter, Jim Slattery, Charles Reagan, Dan Lykins, George Embrey, and Jim Tolan.
43   Why RFK was cheered: Titus interview.
44   Embrey description of crowd: Embrey interview.
44   "Come on! . . .": Slattery interview.
44   Text of KSU speech: RFKCS, pp. 323–27; complete text at www.ksu.edu/lectures/landon/trans/Kennedy68.html.
46   "Yeah! . . .": Carpenter interview.

46 "a good part . . .": HGP.
46 "My God! He's . . .": Rochat interview.
46 "because Kennedy was . . .": Slattery interview.
47 Crowd reaction as Kennedy leaves: Tolan and Schmertz interviews.
47 "This is Kansas . . .": Eppridge interview; Newfield, p. 234.
47 [Footnote] Nixon at KSU: Reagan interview.
48 Kevin Rochat shakes hands with RFK: Rochat interview.
48 "I think he'll be . . .": HGP.
48 Reaction of reporters: Mohbat interview.
48 Tolan and Bruno had planted an editorial: Tolan interview.
48 "emotion beyond reason . . .": *Village Voice*, March 21, 1968.
48 "the day when . . .": *New York Post*, March 20, 1968.
48 Speech at University of Kansas: RFKCS, pp. 327–30. Robert Kennedy had been delivering versions of his GNP speech since 1967. One of the earliest can be found in a May 5, 1967, speech in Detroit. Newfield, p. 64.
50 "an authentic expression . . .": Walinsky interview.
50 "Yes, of course . . .": JSOH, Lindsay, p. 15; *New York Post*, June 5, 1968.
50 "Could you really *see* . . .": *New York* magazine, March 29, 1969.
50 "I feel free! . . .": Tolan interview; JFKLOH, Tolan.
50 "If the single man plant . . .": Rogers, p. 129.

Three: "Bobby Ain't Jack"

51 "Free At Last": Mankiewicz interview.
51 Role of press in RFK strategy: Dutton interview.
52 "We take the position . . .": *Saturday Evening Post*, June 7, 1968.
52 Kimball on the New Politics: Kimball, pp. 1–2.
52 "Gone is the . . .": *Seattle Post-Intelligencer*, March 27, 1968.
53 Appearance at University of Nebraska: *World-Herald* (Omaha) and *Evening Journal* (Lincoln), March 29, 1968.
53 "Ronald Reagan . . .": Eppridge and Gorey, p. 56.
53 His name is an advantage: HGP.
53 "At least McCarthy . . .": White, *1968*, p. 200.
53 "Please don't leave!": Martin, p. 291.
54 "Sock it . . .": Lawford, p. 156.
54 The boy could have been reaching for a gun: *Los Angeles Times*, June 18, 1968.
54 "any who seek . . .": RFKCS, p. 334.
54 "Who is it . . .": Ibid., p. 332; *Tennessean* (Nashville), March 22, 1968.
55 "the line of . . .": WP, March 28, 1968.
55 "large and generally . . .": WP, March 22, 1968.
55 Harwood background: John Harwood (son) interview.
55 "inner reasons": Nolan interview.
55 "I know that God . . .": *Saturday Evening Post*, June 7, 1968.
55 As long as I . . .": GUGPRO, March 23, 1968.
55 His motorcade into Stockton: Stevenson manuscript.
56 The crowd in Stockton: Ibid.
56 Eppridge photographs: Eppridge interview.
56 "I know you are proud . . .": GUGPRO, March 23, 1968.
56 Florin Shopping Center: GUGPRO, March 23, 1968.

57 San Jose: GUGPRO, March 23, 1968; NYT, March 24, 1968.
57 he noticed a little girl: Witcover, *85 Days*, p. 114.
57 young man sitting in front of a farmhouse: JSOH, Quinn, pp. 16–17.
57 "Did you see their eyes?": CBS, p. 11.
57 "The big thing about them . . .": *Sun-Times* (Chicago), May 7, 1968.
58 "They *hate* me . . .": JSOH, Brinkley, p. 9.
58 "one of the wildest . . .": *Los Angeles Times*, March 25, 1968.
58 "And I tell you here in California . . .": Robert Kennedy, *Unfulfilled*, p. 490.
58 "I want hatred and prejudice . . .": *Washington Monthly*, "And Start Helping the Underclass," March 1988.
58 At a downtown rally: *Saturday Evening Post*, June 7, 1968.
59 "islands of blacks . . .": RFKCS, pp. 336–38; GUGPRO, March 24, 1968.
59 press corps at Greek Theater: JFKLOH, Mankiewicz.
59 "demagoguery": *Time*, April 5, 1968.
59 "when a war becomes . . .": RFKCS, p. 339.
59 "bordering on . . .": WP, March 25, 1968.
59 "a terrifying frenzy": *Life*, June 21, 1968.
60 "a terrible strident tone": Salinger, p. 220.
60 "It's too bad . . .": JFKLOH, Dutton; Dutton interview; WP, March 31, 1968.
60 Mankiewicz worried: JFKLOH, Mankiewicz.
60 Meeting in Indianapolis hotel: Riley and Mahern interviews; Mahern blog—"Indy Pundit," August 20, 2004.
60 Tooley told reporters: *Denver Post*, March 29, 1968.
61 "totalitarian arithmetic": *Village Voice*, March 21, 1968.
61 "RFK Visit Here . . .": *Tennessean* (Nashville), March 22, 1968.
61 Schlesinger memorandum: vanden Heuvel, p. 318.
62 CALL THE ROLL . . . : Witcover, *85 Days*, p. 112.
62 "Kennedy in Sacramento . . .": *Sacramento Union*, March 24, 1968.
62 "We loved . . .": NYT *Magazine*, "The Haunting of Kennedy," June 2, 1968.
62 "It was on . . .": Ibid.
62 "a man who brings with him . . .": Ibid.
63 "The Honorable . . .": *Time*, May 24, 1968.
63 "JFK in '68! . . .": Eppridge and Gorey, p. 21.
63 "And the wind shall . . .": Speeches of John F. Kennedy: Presidential Campaign of 1960—Final report of the Committee on Commerce, United States Senate, pp. 422, 620, 644.
63 "all agreed . . .": Michael O'Brien, p. 435.
63 "a little legal . . .": Ibid., p. 733.
64 Ben Bradlee: JSOH, Bradlee, 3.
64 Arthur Schlesinger: *Newsweek*, June 8, 1988.
64 John Bartlow Martin: JBMP, campaign diary.
64 Pierre Salinger: JSOH, Salinger, p. 11.
65 "Bobby Ain't Jack!": Eppridge and Gorey, p. 21.
65 "We're living in a . . .": Recording of Frost interview, New York Public Library.
66 "You've got to be patient . . .": JFKLOH, Tolan.
66 Tolan believes Kennedy underwent a catharsis and lends his PT 109 tie clip: Tolan interview; JFKLOH, Tolan.
67 "It must be quite . . .": Mohbat interview.

Four: The Era of Good Feelings

72 As soon as Kennedy's plane arrived: Newfield, p. 244; Dutton interview; *Newsweek*, April 15, 1968; JSOH, Burns, pp. 7–8; Witcover, *1968*, p. 143.

72 "You didn't actually . . .": JSOH, Daugherty, pp. 1–2.

72 "You're our next . . .": Ibid.

72 Daugherty rides into Manhattan: Ibid.; Dutton interview; Witcover, *85 Days*, p. 127.

72 Johnson worries about his health: Witcover, *1968*, p. 140.

73 "And then the final . . .": Doris Kearns Goodwin, p. 342.

73 An impromptu celebration: Events and conversations in RFK apartment on March 31: Dutton, Mankiewicz interviews; JFKLOH, Dutton, Mankiewicz, Gwirtzman; NYT and WP, April 2, 1968.

73 Mankiewicz had told Gorey: JFKLOH, Mankiewicz.

73 "That's it! . . .": Lucey interview.

73 "bordering on giddiness" and account of reaction of Mahern, Ted Kennedy, and others in Indianapolis on March 31: Mahern interview; Mahern blog—"Indy Pundit," August 20, 2004; JFKLOH, Burke; Riley interview.

74 "I'm the only candidate . . .": RFKCONF, p. 24.

75 Cardinal Spellman's funeral: vanden Heuvel, p. 334.

75 press conference at Overseas Press Club: NYT and WP, April 2, 1968; Witcover, *85 Days*, p. 133; RFKCP, Media File 3.

75 One reporter described him: Witcover, *85 Days*, p. 133.

75 Jim Stevenson rode with him: Stevenson manuscript; *New Yorker*, "Talk of the Town," June 15, 1968.

75 Words like *rudderless*: Shesol, p. 446; Newfield, p. 245; JFKLOH, Gwirtzman.

76 "It's hard to . . .": *Newsweek*, April 15, 1968.

76 "a lot of trouble": JFKLOH, Buchwald.

76 "When I'm President . . .": Eppridge interview.

76 "the old politics . . .": Newfield, p. 245.

77 White House "unity meeting": AS, p. 869; Sorensen, pp. 146–47; Shesol, p. 442.

77 "mean, bitter . . .": Guthman and Shulman, p. 417.

77 "lies continuously . . .": Ibid., p. 26.

78 "This is why you go . . .": O'Donnell, pp. 360–61; Bruno interview.

78 RFK visit to Brazil's impoverished northeast: AS, p. 697; Richard Goodwin, p. 441; Thomas, p. 310.

78 RFK visit to Mississippi: Edelman interview; Kotz, p. 1; Edelman, pp. 51–53; Hampton et al., pp. 451–52; AS, p. 855.

79 "could see things . . .": AS, p. 799.

80 "You don't know . . .": Thomas, p. 339.

80 In the Senate, Kennedy had addressed poverty: The best expression of Kennedy's views on poverty can be found in his book *To Seek a Newer World*, pp. 19–62.

81 A private poll commissioned by Kennedy: RFKCP, Black Books, Box 6.

81 Ted Kennedy and David Burke meet Gordon St. Angelo: JFKLOH, Burke.

82 A second offer came from the Teamsters: Clymer, p. 111; JFKLOH, Burke.

82 Kennedy's briefing papers described Indiana: RFKCP, Research Division, Boxes 65–66; JBMP; JFKL, Edelman papers.

82 Kennedy invited Martin: Flight to Indiana on April 4 described by Martin: JBMP, campaign diary; Martin, pp. 281–82.

83 The sound track recorded: GUGPRO, April 4, 1968; RFKCP, Media File 3.

83 FBI agent Angelo Lano and threats: JFKLOH, Tolan.
84 Mayor Lugar summoned Riley to City Hall: Riley interview.
84 Tolan was astonished: Tolan interview.
84 speech at Notre Dame: Robert Kennedy, *Unfulfilled Promise*, pp. 177–82.
85 "frenzied": *Muncie Star*, April 5, 1968.
85 Speech at Ball State: Transcript and Tape of RFK April 4 speech at Ball State at library of the Indiana Historical Society; excerpts in *Muncie Star*, March 23, 1969.
87 "a man who has a lot . . .": JSOH, Coles, p. 1.
88 Kennedy hears news of King shooting at Muncie airport: Hanley interview; *Muncie Star*, March 23, 1969.
88 Kennedy moved seats, and conversation with Lindsay: JSOH, Lindsay, pp. 10–11.
89 "Kennedy . . . Kennedy . . .": HGP.
89 Jim Tolan conversations at Weir-Cook Airport: Tolan interview; JFKLOH, Tolan and Nolan.
89 Lewis argued that Kennedy had to attend: Lewis interview; Lewis with D'Orso, p. 405; JSOH, Lewis, p. 6.
89 "Oh, God . . .": JSOH, Lindsay, pp. 10–11.
89 "It was unbearable . . .": Newfield, p. 57.
89 Tolan boarded the plane: Tolan interview; JFKLOH, Tolan.
90 Kennedy asked Frank Mankiewicz: Mankiewicz interview; JSOH, Mankiewicz, p. 25; JFKLOH, Mankiewicz.
90 "I could take my wife . . .": Gigerich interview.
90 "Stay with her . . .": Ibid.
90 As Kennedy was driven to the rally: Dutton interview; JSOH, Dutton, p. 66; JSOH, Barry, p. 22. Dutton does not recall Kennedy writing any notes during the drive but Barry remembers him writing notes on a piece of yellow paper. Since one can see him holding a piece of paper as he spoke at the rally, Barry's account is more credible.

Five: A Prayer for Our Country

91 Two groups of people: For the description and anatomy of the rally crowd I have relied heavily on "Kennedy and King: The Rhetoric of Control," in *Today's Speech*, vol. 16, no. 3, pp. 31–34. The article was written by two Purdue professors, Karl Anatol and John Bittner, who interviewed many of the people in the audience within a month of the rally. Their findings contradict the conventional story that everyone in the crowd was unaware of King's assassination.
91 "the black people . . .": Howard interview.
92 "What are you doing . . .": Anatol and Bittner, "Kennedy and King."
92 "Dr. King is dead . . .": Ibid.
92 The rally's black organizers became nervous: information suppled by Don Boggs, producer of a documentary about Kennedy in Indianapolis.
92 After Dallas, he had embraced risk: Kimball, p. 64.
92 Speech to students in South Africa: AS, pp. 745–46.
93 "I sure hope . . .": Martin, p. 283.
93 Braden at the rally: Braden, p. 154.
93 Mankiewicz gave Kennedy a sheet of paper: JFKLOH, Mankiewicz; Mankiewicz interview.
93 Bill Eppridge unable to shoot: Eppridge interview.

93 "Fear was palpable . . .": Braden, p. 155.

94 "Do they know . . .": NBC News footage of April 4, 1968, Indianapolis rally.

94 The next moment reminded one witness: description of crowd reaction: Anatol and Bittner, "Kennedy and King"; Eppridge and Gorey, p. 31; JSOH, Quinn, p. 5; *Star-Ledger* (Newark, N.J.), June 7, 1995.

94 The speech he had prepared: RFKCP, Media Files, Box 3.

95 June 11, 1963, JFK speech and RFK input: Guthman and Shulman, pp. 200–201; Michael O'Brien, p. 836.

95 "Martin Luther King . . .": There are several versions of what Kennedy said on April 4. Some have cleaned up some of the repetitions and grammar. I have relied on RFKCP, Media Files, Box 3, and RFKCS, pp. 356–57.

97 The speech is so well reasoned: Murphy, " 'A Time of Shame and Sorrow,' " pp. 404–7.

97 "pure Bob Kennedy": Dutton interview; JFKLOH, Dutton.

97 "I agree with . . .": vanden Heuvel, p. 44.

97 "an incredibly powerful . . .": Lewis interview.

98 "one of those . . .": Hamilton, p. 147.

98 "born fighter": Ibid.

98 "You're our last hope": JFKLOH, Tolan; Tolan interview.

98 "We went there . . ." and other post-speech comments: Anatol and Bittner, "Kennedy and King."

99 "a turning point": *Indianapolis Star*, May 15, 1994.

99 "Kennedy broke down . . .": Lewis interview; Lewis with D'Orso, p. 408.

99 "It could have been me": Braden, p. 155.

99 "This is what is going . . .": Garrow, p. 307.

99 He had wept after seeing a photograph: Kimball, p. 76.

99 RFK wept at Democratic convention: Lawford, p. 170.

100 "shook, really shook": JFKLOH, Tolan.

100 "a very, very deep . . .": JSOH, Salinger, p. 10.

100 "an enormous . . .": JFKLOH, Walinsky.

100 "You know, the death . . .": JFKLOH, Walinsky and Greenfield; Walinsky interview.

100 "special horror of . . .": Robert Kennedy, *In His Own Words*, p. 72.

100 "Help us where . . .": RFKCONF, p. 11.

101 King and Kennedy had a testy telephone conversation: Guthman and Shulman, pp. 88–90.

101 "a distant camaraderie . . .": vanden Heuvel, pp. 100–101.

102 King speech at Riverside Church: NYT, April 5, 1967; Lewis, p. 395.

102 He suggested to King: Hampton, p. 453; JFKLOH, Edelman.

103 King's death upset: Martin, p. 284.

103 Kennedy call to Coretta Scott King: Martin, p. 284; JSOH, King, p. 1; Interviews: Mankiewicz and Dutton.

103 Meeting between RFK and black leaders: Tolan interview; JFKLOH, Tolan, Doherty.

105 "the pendulum just . . .": *Time*, May 24, 1968.

105 "a very, very eerie . . .": JFKLOH, Tolan and Dutton; Tolan interview.

105 He strolled into a room: JFKLOH, Tolan, Mankiewicz, Doherty.

106 "You know, that fellow . . .": JFKLOH, Greenfield.

106 "You aren't so . . .": Ibid.

106 Interview with Jack Paar: Jack Paar transcript in RFKCP, Media Files, Box 3.

107 "The reporter became aware . . .": Mailer, p. 51.

107 "No. We'll never stop . . .": JSOH, Barry, p. 21.

107 Speech at City Club: *Plain Dealer* (Cleveland), April 6, 1968; *Miami Herald*, April 6, 1968; text in RFKCP, Media Files, Box 3, and RFKCS, pp. 359–69.

108 Walinsky and Greenfield had written them: JFKLOH, Greenfield.

109 RFK edited City Club Speech: JFKLOH, Tolan; Tolan interview.

109 "Bobby could have been . . .": Stein, p. 193.

109 "What you really are . . .": *Look*, July 9, 1968.

109 "You know, sometimes . . .": Richard Goodwin, p. 530.

110 women in the audience had been in tears: *Plain Dealer* (Cleveland), April 5, 1968.

110 "the best-written speech . . .": JFKLOH, Greenfield.

110 "People think I'm wasting . . .": JSOH, Wright, pp. 23–24.

110 he would persuade the networks to cooperate: Mankiewicz interview.

Six: "Guns Between Me and the White House"

112 "My God! What's happening . . .": Tolan interview.

112 witnessing the civil rights movement: Martin, p. 284.

112 "Well, it's finally . . .": Walinsky interview.

112 After landing Kennedy wants to visit the riot zone: Martin, p. 284.

113 Kennedy goes to New Bethel Baptist Church: Fauntroy interview; WP, April 8, 1968; JSOH, Fauntroy, pp. 26–27.

113 Kennedy took communion: Mankiewicz interview.

114 Fauntroy and Kennedy walk through riot zone: Fauntroy interview; WP, April 8, 1968; NYT, April 8, 1968; JSOH, Fauntroy, pp. 26–27; *New York Daily News*, April 8, 1968; Witcover, *The Making of*, p. 109.

114 Fauntroy asked Kennedy how his campaign: Fauntroy interview.

115 "I'm afraid there are guns . . .": Ibid.

115 "It could have . . .": Braden, p. 15.

115 "There is no way . . .": JSOH, Salinger, p. 8; AS, pp. 900–901; NYT, June 7, 1968; *Houston Chronicle*, June 9, 1968.

115 "I knew they would . . .": O'Donnell, p. 341.

115 Brazil in 1965: AS, p. 698.

115 he imagined that he saw an assassin: JSOH, Huerta, pp. 20–21.

116 "Watch that guy": JSOH, Lyons, p. 4.

116 Some farmworkers: JFKLOH, Chavez.

116 Jerry Bruno recalls: Bruno, p. 117.

116 An underground newspaper: Chester et al., p. 352.

116 "We just want . . .": *Life*, June 21, 1968.

116 "was on our minds . . .": Martin, pp. 297–98.

116 "a partisan band . . .": Lawford, p. 179.

117 "If anything happens . . .": Heymann, p. 473.

117 "Look, you'll notice . . .": Eppridge interview.

117 Some newsmen were concerned: Bruno, p. 113.

117 AP reporter Joe Mohbat: Mohbat interview; JSOH, Mohbat, pp. 4–5.

117 Hays Gorey thought: HGP.

117 John Lindsay believed: JSOH, Lindsay, p. 18.

117 Sylvia Wright engaged: JSOH, Wright, pp. 27–28.

118 "I've got to do something . . ." Rogers, pp. 52–53.

118 The threats spiked: Chester, pp. 311–12.
118 An FBI informant: Mankiewicz interview; JFKLOH, Mankiewicz.
118 "Oh hell . . .": *Look*, July 9, 1968.
119 "I get mixed up . . .": *New York Post*, June 5, 1968.
119 Kennedy felt safest: JFKLOH, Tolan.
119 After Adam Walinsky and Jerry Bruno tricked him: Bruno and Walinsky interviews; Bruno, p. 117.
119 During the tour, Barry and Tolan: Tolan interview.
119 A few days later in Salt Lake City: Tolan and Bruno interviews; JFKLOH, Tolan.
119 "If you want to leave . . .": Robert Kennedy, *Unfulfilled Promise*, p. 693.
120 Kennedy fixed Fauntroy: Fauntroy interview.
120 "out of whatever . . .": JFKLOH, Dutton.
120 "a resident melancholy . . .": *New Yorker*, "Talk of the Town," June 15, 1968.
120 "almost alone . . .": *Sunday Courier and Press* (Evansville, Ind.), May 5, 1968.
121 Kennedy was in Lansing, description of Lansing incident and Kennedy reaction: Witcover, *85 Days*, pp. 147–48; Dutton interview; JSOH, Tuck, p. 19; Dutton, pp. 32–33.
121 "I saw real fear there": Amick interview.

Seven: *"Prophets Get Shot"*

122 "the greatest gathering . . .": *Atlanta Constitution*, April 9, 1968.
123 "great tragedy that began . . .": Chester, p. 17.
123 Hayes was as "concerned": Ibid., p. 18.
123 His staff rejected the Thunderbird: *Atlanta Constitution*, April 9, 1968.
124 "how close the thought . . .": Ibid.
124 "My heart bled . . .": Ibid., April 10, 1968.
124 "It would mean . . .": JSOH, King, p. 2.
124 "perhaps lined with . . ." *Atlanta Constitution*, April 9, 1968.
124 On the night of his brother's assassination: Manchester, pp. 442–43.
125 Minutes later, he was heard weeping: JFKLOH, Spauling.
125 "You Uncle Toms . . .": JSOH, King, p. 5.
125 The last meeting: JSOH, Seigenthaler, p. 43; Stein and Plimpton, pp. 259–60.
126 "a hopeless man . . .": JSOH, Willams, p. 5.
126 Finally, he struggled to his feet: vanden Heuvel, p. 339.
126 "The thing that kept us going . . .": JSOH, Williams, pp. 6–7.
126 "Dr. King may be gone . . .": Lewis interview; Lewis with D'Orso, p. 413.
127 the kind of communications that had previously gone: Palermo, pp. 183–84.
127 He and Ethel arrived around 3 a.m.: Lewis interview; Lewis, pp. 410–11.
127 On the night of his brother's: Manchester, p. 619.
127 The night before coming to Atlanta: JSOH, Lowenstein, p. 7.
128 "who took seats . . .": Wilkins, p. 215.
128 The dignitaries entered the church: NYT, April 10, 1968.
128 Prominent senators: *Time*, April 19, 1968.
128 As Senator McCarthy's wife: McCarthy, p. 393.
129 "What's *she* doing . . .": *Washington Star*, April 10, 1968.
129 Jackie Kennedy, who rewarded: *Time*, April 19, 1968.
129 "Oh, what is the matter . . .": McCarthy, p. 395.
129 "Cover Rockefeller . . .": Ibid.

130 The two heartbreaking moments: JSOH, Lowenstein, p. 8; Abernathy, p. 462; *Atlanta Constitution*, April 10, 1968.

130 Kennedy sat near Evers: Evers and Szanton, p. 225.

131 "If they want to shake . . .": Ibid.

131 "shaking like a leaf": *Atlanta Constitution*, April 10, 1968.

131 "bound to evoke . . .": Ibid.

131 So many joined: NYT, April 10, 1968.

131 He marched with: *Amsterdam News*, April 10, 1968.

131 "No one relates to . . .": *Life*, May 10, 1968.

131 "number one target . . .": Abernathy, p. 459.

131 "if the next person . . .": Ibid.

131 "richest Negro street . . .": *Fortune*, September 1956.

132 "stack them up": *Newsweek*, April 22, 1968.

132 their suburban branches remained open: Halberstam, p. 89.

132 Kennedy removed his jacket: Evers, pp. 225–26.

132 "began to feel . . .": McCarthy, p. 397.

133 reporters considered it noteworthy that: *Atlanta Constitution*, April 10, 1968.

133 "You've got to sit . . .": Ibid.

133 "Kennedy Stirred . . .": Ibid.

133 John Maguire: JSOH, Maguire, p. 16.

133 Harris Wofford: Wofford, pp. 226–27.

134 "*You* think this will change . . .": Evers and Szanton, p. 226.

134 Ralph Abernathy invites Kennedy to the platform: Fauntroy interview; JSOH, Fauntroy, p. 27; McCarthy, p. 398; *Atlanta Constitution*, April 10, 1968.

135 "We wanted him . . .": Abernathy, p. 463.

135 Mays's eulogy: *Atlanta Constitution*, April 10, 1968; copies of the eulogy and all of the MLK service are available at the King Library in Atlanta.

136 Fauntroy noticed Kennedy: Fauntroy interview.

Eight: Like Frank Sinatra Running for President

139 a six-hour meeting at Hickory Hill: Martin, pp. 285–86.

140 These so-called backlash voters: A good discussion of the backlash can be found in Unger and Unger, pp. 343–47.

141 "typifies the audacity . . .": Evans and Novak, *Rapid City Journal*, April 17, 1968.

141 "Indiana is the ball game . . .": Martin, p. 285.

141 Martin objected: JBMP, campaign diary, p. 27.

141 "Indiana can help . . .": Martin, p. 286.

142 Schlesinger memorandum: JFKL, Research Division, Box 65.

142 Washington memorandum: Ibid.

142 speech at Fort Wayne's Scottish Rite Temple: Robert Kennedy, *Unfulfilled Promise*, pp. 186–89; RFKCP, Media Files, Box 3A.

144 Terre Haute: Brown, pp. 60–61.

144 "coon-catcher . . .": Halberstam, p. 92.

144 "I'm so interested in winning . . .": RFKCP, Media Files.

144 "Thus Kennedy follows . . .": *Atlanta Constitution*, April 11, 1968.

144 Kennedy had breakfast with 150 Terre Haute housewives: His remarks can be found in RFKCP, Media Files, Box 3A.

146 he discussed the breakfast with reporter David Halberstam: Halberstam, p. 94.

146 In Ann Arbor, he told: RFKCS, pp. 368–69.
146 Kennedy made his first foray: NYT *Magazine*, "A Test for Bobby Kennedy," May 5, 1968.
147 "I don't think violence or . . .": GUGPRO, April 15, 1968; RFKCP, Media Files, Box 3A.
147 Kennedy delivered the same message: NYT *Magazine*, "A Test for Bobby Kennedy."
149 The first meeting between Wade and Daley, and subsequent meetings and conversations between the two men: Wade interview; JFKLOH, Wade.
150 Some Kennedy advisers . . . were wary of Wade: Ibid.
150 "Make sure you don't ever make a trip . . .": Ibid.
151 Kennedy entered the Gary Memorial Auditorium: Kennedy's April 15 visit to Gary and speech: *Post-Tribune* (Gary, Ind.), April 16, 1968; GUGPRO, April 15, 1968; RFKCP, Media File; Wade interview; JFKLOH, Wade.
152 "Well, I guess that didn't . . ." Wade interview; JFKLOH, Wade.
152 He noticed that a black boy: Lawford, pp. 154–55; Witcover, *85 Days*, p. 149.

Nine: Brave Heart and Christopher Pretty Boy

153 The cabin where they are sitting: Klink interview.
153 A Jesuit Father from the Red Cloud Mission: Father Jim Fitzgerald interview; Father Paul Steinmetz (photographer) interview.
153 He presented her with a framed copy: Klink interview.
154 at the 1963 convention: NYT, September 14, 1963.
154 collected so many tomahawks: Heymann, p. 12.
154 "I wish I'd been born . . .": Ibid., p. 413.
154 "Bob was incensed . . .": JSOH, Tuck, pp. 50–51.
154 He also came away mad: Ibid., p. 52.
155 And while visiting: Vanocur interview; vanden Heuvel, p. 108; JSOH, Vanocur, p. 5.
155 during a trip to Los Angeles: Salinger, pp. 2–4.
155 "the inexcusable and ugly . . .": RFKCS, p. 321.
155 "a little bit of me . . .": Salinger et al., p. 144.
155 "callous sons of bitches": Mahoney, p. 358; Nolan interview.
155 Dutton begged him to cut back: Dutton interview; JFKLOH, Dutton.
156 "When I was Attorney . . .": NYT, March 30, 1968.
156 Dutton snapped: Dutton interview; JSOH, Dutton, pp. 38–39.
156 "Is it not barbaric . . .": Robert Kennedy, *Unfulfilled Promise*, p. 710.
156 "When the United States . . .": *Arizona Republic* (Phoenix), March 30, 1968.
156 "I've waited all my life . . .": NYT, March 30, 1968.
157 "It would be quite a lever . . .": *Brookings Register* (S.D.), May 11, 1968.
157 "I mean, how many . . .": Fitzgerald interview.
157 His official welcoming party included: Cornelius interview.
157 Deloria rode on the press bus: Deloria interview.
158 according to former Pine Ridge chief: Holy Rock interview.
158 Harrison had arranged for key North Dakota Democrats: Harrison interview.
158 "And it was not some quickie . . .": Ibid.
158 "I mean, if you didn't . . .": Cornelius interview.
158 He stopped to speak: *Rapid City Journal* (S.D.), April 17, 1968.
158 "It makes me sad . . .": *Star-Journal* (Lincoln, Neb.), July 7, 1999.

158 He woke a sick boy: Klink, Cornelius, and Fitzgerald interviews.
159 Pretty Boy and Kennedy remained together: Fitzgerald interview.
159 When Kennedy noticed tribal elders: Klink and Fitzgerald interviews.
159 Fred Dutton thought: Dutton interview.
159 John Nolan believed: Nolan interview; JFKLOH, Nolan.
159 "a special response": JFKLOH, McGovern.
160 "a tentative quality": JSOH, Coles, p. 1.
160 "Spiritually, he was an Indian!": Deloria, p. 193.
160 He persuaded Leona Winters: Hearings before the Special Subcommittee on Indian Education, Ninetieth Congress, part 4, pp. 1235–38.
160 "it seems it could spend . . .": *Rapid City Journal* (S.D.), April 17, 1968.
160 Kennedy insisted on going: Lawford, p. 169; Stein and Plimpton, p. 285.
161 "I should have brought . . .": Lawford, p. 169; Stein and Plimpton, pp. 285–86.
161 "Who are the people . . .": Stewart interview; JSOH, Stewart, p. 17.
161 Clinton stopped there: NYT, July 8, 1999.
161 A reporter who returned: WP, October 21, 2004.
161 In fact, statistically: WP, ibid.; *Journal Star* (Lincoln, Neb.), July 7, 1999; *Wall Street Journal*, March 5, 2002.
162 he instructed an aide: Fitzgerald interview.
162 "Look, there are no playgrounds . . .": RFKCONF, p. 37.
162 Like Kennedy, he was dead: Deloria, Klink, Cornelius, Fitzgerald, Steinmetz, Holy Rock interviews.
162 "That I'd made . . .": Tape of Frost interview, New York Public Library.
163 "a man who had put . . .": *Rapid City Journal* (S.D.), April 17, 1968.
163 He rode into town with: Daugherty interview.
163 He had been undeterred: Attempts of Daugherty to put Kennedy on the ballot: Daugherty interview; JFKLOH, Burke.
163 "The hell with it . . .": JFKLOH, McGovern.
163 "Bob, I don't think . . .": Daugherty interview.
163 Kennedy tried to rise: HGP; *Rapid City Journal* (S.D.), April 17, 1968; *Sunday Courier and Press* (Evansville, Ind.), May 5, 1968.
163 "in a discreet way": JFKLOH, McGovern.
163 "the absolute personal honesty . . .": AS, p. 899; Salinger et al., pp. 117–18.
164 This time, McGovern introduced him: JFKLOH, McGovern; JSOH, McGovern, pp. 8–9.
164 "I know there are times . . ." and conversations at dinner: O'Donnell, p. 414; JFKLOH, McGovern; JSOH, McGovern, pp. 8–9.
165 The next morning, McGovern drove Kennedy: JSOH, McGovern, p. 8.
165 "a terribly poignant . . .": JSOH, Brinkley, pp. 11–12.
165 "More than most candidates . . .": JBMP, campaign diary, p. 36.

Ten: "How Does It Look for Me Here?"

166 John Bartlow Martin flew back to Washington: Martin, pp. 287–89.
167 When Kennedy reviewed Martin's schedule: Ibid.
167 "I have come because . . .": *Sun-Commercial* (Vincennes, Ind.), April 23, 1968.
168 Greeting Kennedy at the airport was Jim Osborne: Osborne and Stevens interviews.
168 "Great things . . .": Stevens interview.
168 Osborne feared that no one: Osborne interview.

168 The kitchen could only serve: Ibid.
169 The speech Martin had written: RFKCP, Media File, Box 3A.
169 John Nolan, who had scheduled: Nolan interview; JFKLOH, Nolan.
169 "But those are the audiences . . .": Martin, p. 294.
169 "I know most of you . . .": Witcover, *85 Days*, p. 157.
169 a survey: *Indianapolis News*, May 2, 1968.
169 Kennedy's face tightened: Witcover, *1968*, p. 174; Witcover, *85 Days*, pp. 155–57.
170 "gave up all notion of speaking . . .": *Saturday Evening Post*, June 29, 1968.
170 "remote from . . .": JBMP.
170 "a welcome usually . . .": *Times-Herald* (Washington, Ind.), April 23, 1968.
170 "All of us are . . .": Ibid.
170 slap-happy style captivated Gus Osborne: Osborne interview.
171 the most important foreign policy address of his campaign: RFKCS, pp. 374–79.
172 "The strongest argument against . . .": Robert Kennedy, *Thirteen Days*, p. 39.
172 "spent more time on this moral question . . .": CBS, p. 18.
173 "I can't help remembering . . .": Ibid.
173 "Our struggle against Communism . . .": Robert Kennedy, *Thirteen Days*, p. 30.
173 Jerry Abramson . . . faced: Abramson interview.
174 a reporter noticed him reading: *Times-Mail* (Bedford, Ind.), April 25, 1968.
174 Al Walker presented Kennedy: Walker interview.
175 "a slap in the face": Ibid.
175 "You don't have a prayer . . .": Ibid.
175 Kennedy read them out loud: *Times-Mail* (Bedford, Ind.), April 25, 1968.
175 Dutton had to jump onto the hood: JFKLOH, Dutton.
175 "I don't even know . . .": JFKLOH, Tolan.
175 Arthur Schlesinger called Martin: Martin, p. 292.
176 "Kennedy has taken an unbelievably . . .": *New Republic*, May 11, 1968.
176 "RFK Keeper of the . . .": *Boston Globe*, May 2, 1968.
176 "I run for President . . .": JFKLOH, Mankiewicz.
176 The clearest statement of Kennedy's position: RFKCP, Media Files, Box 3; Robert Kennedy, *Unfulfilled Promise*, pp. 219–22.
177 [FOOTNOTE] A survey of . . .: *North Platte Telegraph* (Neb.) and other newspapers, April 25, 1968.
177 "the difference between . . .": *Newsweek*, May 20, 1968.
177 "I come from . . .": Walinsky interview.
178 Jack Newfield got it right: Newfield, p. 66.
179 "don't want to listen . . .": Witcover, *1968*, p. 174.
179 "a liberal day": Martin, p. 292.
179 "You go up there . . .": JFKLOH, Dutton; Dutton interview.
179 "I'm tired of talking . . .": JFKLOH, Greenfield.
179 "Gene McCarthy doesn't have to prove . . .": Ibid.
180 "'What he [Kennedy] did and said . . .": JBMP, campaign diary, p. 36.
180 "Camus once said . . .": Martin, p. 291; Lawford, pp. 174–75.
181 The audience had been cold: Halberstam, pp. 118–19.
181 "He [Kennedy] spoke . . .": Lawford, pp. 174–75.
181 "*really* cares about . . .": WP, May 2, 1968.
181 "Scotty Reston . . .": Halberstam, p. 119.
181 Jim Osborne was impressed: Osborne interview.
181 Gus Stevens remembers: Stevens interview.
181 "because when Robert Kennedy . . .": Gigerich interview.

182   "I felt I was the only . . .": Amick interview.
182   "he must have touched . . .": Martin, p. 296.
182   "The people [of Indiana] didn't want . . .": JBMP, campaign diary, p. 42.

Eleven: "From You!"

183   Until then, he had been a lackluster candidate: Schaap, p. 109.
183   "snotty, wise-ass kids": Papert interview.
183   After regaining his composure: vanden Heuvel, pp. 43–44.
183   A girl wearing a turtleneck: transcript of Kennedy's appearance at Columbia: RFKCS, pp. 125–26; Papert interview; DVD of the event supplied by Fred Papert (differs slightly from the RFKCS transcript).
185   Fred Dutton, however, believed: Dutton interview.
185   Jerry Bruno later said: WP, March 17, 1993.
185   "We should slow down . . .": *Time*, May 24, 1968.
185   When a bellicose student: *Oregonian* (Portland), April 19, 1968.
185   During a May 2 luncheon: *Indianapolis Star*, May 3, 1968.
186   His exchange: Robert Kennedy, *Unfulfilled Promise*, pp. 676–80; RFKCS, pp. 341–42.
186   when he spoke at the University of Indiana Medical School: Nolan interview; JFKLOH, Nolan; JSOH, Quinn, pp. 37–42 (Quinn made a tape of the event and played it during his interview with Jean Stein); Witcover, *85 Days*, pp. 165–66; NYT, April 23, 1968; RFKCS, pp. 342–44; *Indianapolis Star*, April 27, 1968.
188   As at Columbia: JFKLOH, Tolan; Tolan interview.
189   John Nolan thought: Nolan interview; JFKLOH, Nolan.
189   "Well, you tell me something . . .": RFKCP, Media Files, Box 3; Witcover, *85 Days*, p. 169.
189   he spoke in the quadrangle of Omaha's Creighton University: Salinger et al., pp. 143–44; Witcover, *1968*, p. 208; Witcover, *85 Days*, pp. 193–94.; *World-Herald* (Omaha), May 14, 1968; Steve Bell (ABC) interview; Don Walton interview.
191   "It is we who live . . .": Mahoney, p. 343.
191   "These are my people!": JFKLOH, Dutton.
191   He sat next to reporter Jack Germond: Germond, pp. 79–80.

Twelve: Riding with the Next President

193   "when everything came together": Greenfield interview (during 2005 RFK memorial event).
193   The train had been organized: O'Brien interview.
193   On April 27, Kennedy rode: interview with William Kratville, former Union Pacific employee.
194   "Why don't you get bored . . .": Witcover, *85 Days*, p. 150.
195   "You may not know it . . .": *Life*, Special Edition, June 1968.
195   Pointing to the Nixon signs: Ibid.
195   Hays Gorey was impressed: HGP.
195   Jeff Greenfield noted: JSOH, Greenfield, p. 18; JFKLOH, Greenfield.
195   "You should see us . . .": JFKLOH, Edelman.
195   "Now, you wouldn't want . . .": *Life*, Special Edition, June 1968.
195   "Quick, someone . . .": Eppridge and Gorey, p. 55.

196 "the most spontaneously . . .": WP, June 7, 1968.
196 "Midwestern New Englander": JSOH, Alan King, p. 1.
196 "Top priority!": HGP.
196 Before leaving Kimball: *Life*, Special Edition, June 1968.
196 He told the crowd: *Sydney Telegraph*, April 29, 1968.
197 Ethel Kennedy had organized an elaborate prank: Dutton interview; Oppen-
       heimer, p. 321; JSOH: Dutton, pp. 43–47; Tuck, pp. 2–4.
197 "None of my children . . .": Newfield, pp. 266–67.
197 At the Ogallala station: *Keith County News* (Ogallala, Neb.), April 29, 1968.
197 An article in the North Platte: *North Platte Telegram*, April 26, 1968.
198 After his rally: Ibid., April 28, 1968.
198 Before each stop: Doug German interview; Jerry Micek interview; *Sunday Jour-
       nal and Star* (Lincoln, Neb.), April 28, 1968.
198 "I don't really thrive . . .": Pieper interview.
198 Hays Gorey found him: Eppridge and Gorey, p. 44.
199 Jerry Micek, who headed his campaign: Micek interview.
199 Doug German and Wilbur ("Doc") Kloeppering: German interview.
200 aide Peter Edelman decided: JFKLOH, Edelman.
200 Richard Harwood thought: JSOH, Harwood, p. 7.
200 "he sort of respects . . .": Eppridge and Gorey, p. 55.
201 He looked at their pained faces: JFKLOH, Edelman.
201 "I like him . . .": *Chicago Sun-Times*, May 1, 1968.
201 While he was touring a Ford plant: Tolan interview; JFKLOH, Tolan.
202 "Here we are . . .": NYT, April 28, 1968.
202 So many members of the Johnson cabinet: Ibid.
202 "a grape of hope . . .": JFKLOH, May 3, 1968; Ryle interview; Halberstam, p. 167.
203 he had put his head on his desk: Schaap, p. 124.
203 "For those who have affluence . . .": *Time*, May 24, 1968.
203 The absurdity of Humphrey's Politics of Joy: Royko, pp. 173–77.
204 "Don't let him off . . .": JSOH: Barry, p. 20; Dutton p. 49; Dutton interview.
204 "You just don't have it!": *World-Herald* (Omaha, Neb.), April 28, 1968.
205 "bearing down and drawing on . . .": JSOH, Breasted, p. 12.
205 "it is both compassionate . . .": RFKCP: Media Files, Box 3; Research Division,
       Box 58.
205 During the flight back: JSOH, Breasted, p. 12.
205 AP reporter Joe Mohbat: Mohbat interview; JSOH, Mohbat, pp. 2–4.
205 But then he sat down next to Mohbat and did talk about it: Mohbat interview;
       JSOH, Mohbat, pp. 2–4; JSOH, Quinn, pp. 18–20; Eppridge and Gorey, p. 125.

Thirteen: Mother Inn

206 and locals like Jim Ryle: Ryle interview.
206 "You know, I get a lot of form . . .": Ibid.
207 A mob of teenagers waving: *Greensburg Daily News*, May 3, 1968; JFKLOH,
       Tolan; Ryle interview.
207 Sylvia Wright began calling: JSOH: Wright, pp. 19–22; Harwood, pp. 14–15;
       Lawford, pp. 160–63.
208 After CBS correspondent Roger Mudd: JSOH, Tuck, p. 17.
208 "so big that it took us in": Lawford, p. 160.
208 He changed his mind after hearing him: *Life*, May 17, 1968; *Time*, May 9, 1968.

208 "the old, tired . . .": JSOH, Kraft, p. 20.
208 "an easy man . . .": Stein and Plimpton, p. 319.
209 "wooden as a stick": JSOH, Lindsay, p. 1.
209 "fun enterprise": Lawford, p. 172.
209 "huge, joyous adventure": JSOH, Quinn, p. 15.
209 "a partisan band . . .": *Life*, Special Edition, June 1968.
209 Joe Mohbat sometimes found himself: Mohbat interview.
209 "but it was 12:30 at night . . .": JSOH, Stevenson, p. 8.
210 "No. You have to go out there . . . ": Halberstam, pp. 107–9.
210 "If you were as good . . .": *Look*, July 9, 1968.
210 Kennedy also preferred campaigning: JFKLOH, Tolan; Tolan and Dutton interviews.
211 She was struck by: Glinn interview; JSOH, Glinn, p. 8.
211 "Two little girls . . .": *Chicago Sun-Times*, May 2, 1968.
211 "like a couple of drinks": JFKLOH, Dutton.
211 [Footnote] "He liked kids . . .": JFKLOH, Nolan.
211 He liked sending aides: Dutton interview.
212 Some of the energy flowing: Eppridge interview.
212 Joe Mohbat, who spent more time: Mohbat interview.
212 "The important thing . . .": JFKLOH, Chavez.
212 "No. No. No . . . ": JSOH, Barry, p. 19.
212 "I remove myself . . .": *New York* magazine, June 17, 1968.
213 Comedian Alan King warned: JSOH, King, p. 5.
213 Folk singer John Stewart: Stewart interview; JSOH, Stewart, pp. 4–5.
213 The way the crowds swarmed: JBMP, campaign diary, p. 35.
213 "he had to see the people . . .": Dutton interview; JSOH, Dutton, p. 99.
214 Kennedy's television spots: RFKCP, Media File, Box 3; JFKL, audio-visual archives.
214 After debating the merits of campaigning: JFKLOH, Tolan; Tolan interview.
214 Slow-moving motorcades: Bruno interview.
215 "one of the most incredible . . .": Witcover, *1968*, p. 197.
215 "I'm *going* to win . . .": Bruno interview.
215 Kennedy was supposed to cover: Newfield, pp. 260–61; Palermo, p. 203; Witcover, *85 Days*, pp. 173–77.
215 Reporters in the press bus: *Life*, June 21, 1968.
216 White neighborhoods sat jammed: JFKLOH, Mankiewicz.
216 After riding through Hammond: Wade interview.
216 noticed three children in pajamas: JSOH, Drayne, p. 8.
217 When a woman told him that her mother: JSOH, Douglas, p. 3.
217 "it all came out . . .": JSOH, de Segonzac, pp. 1–3.
217 "Well, I've done all I could . . .": Witcover, *Making of*, p. 112.
218 "I like Indiana . . .": Newfield, p. 261.
218 But throughout dinner he kept returning: Witcover, *Making of*, p. 112; Witcover, *1968*, p. 199.
218 He had won: HGP; Eppridge and Gorey, p. 65; *Newsweek*, May 20, 1968; NYT, May 9, 1968.
219 "I've proved I can really . . .": Witcover, *85 Days*, pp. 180–81.
219 "The way Kennedy won . . .": *Newsweek*, May 20, 1968.
219 "an unusual coalition . . .": NYT, May 9, 1968.
219 Columnists Evans and Novak: vanden Heuvel, p. 348 (footnote).
219 "went a long way . . .": *Newsweek*, May 20, 1968.
220 They concluded on the basis of the returns: vanden Heuvel, p. 349.

220   Kennedy debunkers such as Ronald Steel: Steel, pp. 174–75.
220   The same is true of Roger Dooley: Dooley, p. 126.
221   "In the seventy precincts . . .": vanden Heuvel, p. 349.
221   "carried the Southern-oriented . . .": NYT, May 9, 1968.
222   Kennedy's strong showing in the pro-Wallace counties: Chester et al., p. 293.
222   Jim Tolan believed: Tolan interview.
222   Art Buchwald reached: JFKLOH, Buchwald.
223   "Equally important . . .": NYT, May 15, 1968.
223   "crushed the argument . . .": *Time*, May 23, 1968.
223   "They [the delegates] don't care . . .": O'Donnell, p. 409.
223   "could not recall a more . . .": WP, May 14, 1968.
223   "the best damn speech . . .": O'Donnell, p. 410.
223   "I'm not asking favors . . .": NYT *Magazine*, June 2, 1968.
224   "He knew just what . . .": O'Donnell, pp. 410–11.
224   But he wanted to win the nomination as badly: *Newsweek*, May 27, 1968.
224   "break his neck": Eppridge and Gorey, p. 44.

Fourteen: "This Is Peanuts"

227   He received a cool reception: JFKLOH, Edelman; Witcover, *85 Days*, p. 200.
227   That evening he attended: JFKLOH, Edelman.
228   "Let's face it . . .": Witcover, *85 Days*, p. 206.
228   Over dinner in Portland with folk singers: Stewart interview; JSOH, Stewart, p. 9.
229   When Kennedy delivered his usual call: WP, April 19, 1968.
229   "I've got a problem here . . .": Witcover, *Making of*, p. 113.
230   "How about giving me some jokes?": JSOH, Drayne, p. 10.
230   One of the most poignant came: CBS, pp. 8–9; JFKLOH, Edelman; Edelman interview.
230   "I'm home!": Tolan interview; JFKLOH, Tolan.
231   On the flight to Los Angeles she organized: JSOH: Lindsay, p. 18; Tuck, pp. 15–16; Wright, pp. 40–41.
231   "I just felt that . . .": JFKL, Media Archives, tape of RFK gala.
232   "So do not ask . . .": *New York* magazine, June 17, 1968.
232   They poured drinks, took off jackets: JSOH: Wright, pp. 41–45; Tuck, pp. 15–17.
233   Before leaving the Benson: JFKLOH, Dutton; Dutton interview.
233   McCarthy had told speechwriter Richard Goodwin: Richard Goodwin, p. 509.
234   Kennedy had come to see McCarthy as: Newfield, p. 191.
234   "I have not been able to understand . . .": Chester, pp. 301–3.
234   He belittled Indiana voters: WP, May 26, 1968.
234   "It is necessary that . . .": Ibid.
235   Kennedy heard about the comment when Dick Tuck: JSOH, Tuck, pp. 31–32.
235   "Do you think it's . . .": Lawrence O'Brien, p. 241.
235   "I think there's some stage . . .": Dutton interview; JSOH, Dutton, pp. 51–52.
235   He stomped into the hall: Dutton interview; JSOH, Dutton, pp. 51–52; Walinsky interview; JFKLOH, Edelman.
236   The day before the primary Kennedy flew to Roseburg: Halberstam, pp. 187–88; *New York* magazine, June 17, 1968; Witcover, *1968*, pp. 223–24; Witcover, *85 Days*, pp. 218–19.
237   But columnist Joseph Alsop; JFKLOH, Alsop.
237   As he stood on the backseat: *Los Angeles Times*, May 29, 1968.

237 As he was boarding his chartered plane: Ibid.

237 "That's a lot of malarkey . . .": JSOH, Harwood, p. 11.

237 "I sometimes wonder . . .": Eppridge and Gorey, p. 73.

238 "No. I have a program . . .": Ibid.

Fifteen: Resurrection City

239 "a body blow": *Los Angeles Times*, May 29, 1968.

239 A *New York Times* editorial: NYT, May 30, 1968.

239 At an airport press conference: NYT, May 19, 1968; *Los Angeles Times*, May 30, 1968.

240 Daley and Wade had met as planned: Wade interview; JFKLOH, Wade.

241 In a *Saturday Evening Post* column: *Saturday Evening Post*, June 15, 1968.

241 The most unpleasant confrontation: NYT, April 20, 1968; JFKLOH, Mankiewicz.

241 "There was this guy screaming . . .": JSOH, Stewart, p. 2.

242 On May 15 he spoke at Los Angeles Valley College: Tolan interview; JFKLOH, Tolan.

242 "built close to the ground": Chester et al., p. 314.

242 Kern County sheriff Roy Gaylen: AS, pp. 790–91; JFKLOH, Chavez, Edelman; vanden Heuvel, p. 103.

243 "Don't tell them . . .": JFKLOH, Edelman.

243 As in Oregon, his California campaign had drifted: NYT, May 10, 1968; RFKCP.

244 Unruh wanted to mount a traditional California campaign: Tolan interview; JFKLOH, Tolan.

244 Some of the native Californians: JFKLOH, Steven E. Smith; Newfield, p. 278.

245 Journalist Theodore White, who traveled with him: White, *1968*, p. 208.

245 "I find it hard to talk about . . .": RFKCONF, p. 24.

245 "I think I probably have to win . . .": Robert Kennedy, *Unfulfilled Promise*, p. 583.

246 People filled the streets: *Los Angeles Times*, May 30, 1968; *Village Voice*, June 13, 1968; Newfield, p. 275; Witcover, *85 Days*, pp. 232–35.

246 A boy poked his head: Stewart interview.

246 "We're all right . . .": Chester et al., p. 335.

246 "nobody special": JSOH, Peter Smith, pp. 11–12.

247 On orders from: JSOH, Barry, p. 15.

247 "If I died in Oregon . . .": Chester et al., p. 336.

247 Hays Gorey, who was in the audience: HGP; Eppridge and Gorey, p. 80.

248 "Don't tell me . . .": JSOH, Lindsay, p. 13.

Sixteen: "The Last of the Great Believables"

249 When Robert Kennedy whistle-stopped: *Sacramento Union*, May 31, 1968; Martin, pp. 300–301; Lawford, p. 172; *Fresno Bee*, May 31, 1968; JSOH: Marian Schlesinger, pp. 2–5; Arthur Schlesinger, pp. 1–2; AS, p. 908.

250 Dave Murray of the *Chicago Sun-Times*: HGP, letter from Murray to Gorey.

250 "meeting its responsibilities to freedom . . .": NYT, September 14, 1960.

250 This may explain why Cesar Chavez estimated: Library of Congress, Chavez oral history.

250 They sang: Stewart interview; JSOH, Stewart, pp. 10–12.

252   "It's going to be a very disorganized . . .": JSOH: Seigenthaler, pp. 32–39; Brown, pp. 2–5; Dutton, pp. 59–60. Dutton interview.

253   The roughest questions came from Curtis Baker: JSOH, Baker, pp. 55–56.

254   "Well, I'm glad I went . . .": JSOH, Seigenthaler, p. 38; vanden Heuvel, p. 374.

254   As they walked into the lobby: JSOH: Berkeley, p. 9; Seigenthaler, p. 38.

254   speech at a Commonwealth Club luncheon: Robert Kennedy, *Unfulfilled Promise*, pp. 597–602.

256   Hector Lopez, an Oakland community activist: JSOH, Lopez, pp. 1–6.

256   "like a volcanic cone . . .": White, *1968*, p. 202.

256   "trying to touch . . .": JSOH, Lopez, p. 5.

256   The Black Panthers who had heckled Kennedy: AS, p. 909; vanden Heuvel, p. 375.

256   Kennedy invited him: JSOH, Baker, p. 8.

257   But Kennedy was curiously detached: Thomas, p. 286; AS, p. 910; vanden Heuvel, pp. 376–77; Dutton interview; JSOH, Dutton, pp. 84–87.

257   "That's a very interesting question . . .": JFKLOH, Mankiewicz.

257   "What you've got to do . . .": JSOH, Tuck, pp. 34–35.

257   Reporters scoring the debate: Newfield, p. 282.

258   He told Dutton and Newfield: JFKLOH, Dutton; Newfield, p. 283.

258   He offered a better explanation: Tolan interview; JFKLOH, Tolan.

258   "racist appeal": Steel, p. 185.

258   The plan also struck him: Walinsky interview.

259   He responded by saying: Robert Kennedy, *Unfulfilled Promise*, pp. 620–21.

259   "It was not so demagogic . . .": AS, p. 911.

260   "Meeting the Urban Crisis": Robert Kennedy, *Unfulfilled Promise*, p. 121.

260   "You know, if anything happens . . .": Richard Goodwin, p. 534.

260   Jim Tolan, for example, considers it noteworthy: Tolan interview.

260   John Lewis remembers: Lewis with D'Orso, p. 414.

261   George Plimpton recalled: JSOH, Plimpton, p. 12.

261   Hays Gorey would write: HGP.

261   Jules Witcover described it: Witcover, *1968*, p. 245.

261   While canvassing in Delano: JFKLOH, Chavez.

261   Earlier, Hays Gorey had reported that: HGP.

261   During this week, Richard Harwood told: Thomas, p. 377.

261   Explaining his decision: JSOH, Harwood, pp. 2–3.

261   Theodore White collapsed: White, *1968*, p. 209.

262   He woke to news: NYT, June 4, 1968.

262   "This is going to be the best thing . . .": JFKLOH, Tolan; Tolan interview.

262   Tolan warned Bobby and Ethel to expect fireworks: Tolan interview; JFKLOH, Tolan; WP, June 7, 1968; Eppridge and Gorey, p. 86; JSOH: Harwood, p. 3; Dutton, p. 55.

262   "in a state beyond fatigue": Newfield, p. 286.

262   But while driving to the airport: WP, June 7, 1968.

262   A man standing next to the platform: JSOH, Plimpton, p. 12.

263   "You had a little trouble . . .": Newfield, p. 287.

263   Still, spectators hurled themselves: *Life*, June 21, 1968.

263   A five-year-old black girl: Ibid.; Lawford, pp. 151–52.

263   Kennedy told Tolan and Hannon: JFKLOH, Tolan.

264   Ashen-faced, shaking, and racked with nausea: Grier, p. 217; JSOH, Harwood, p. 12.

264   He held a flower: Clooney, p. 32.
264   "I know you think so . . .": HGP; Eppridge and Gorey, p. 92.

Seventeen: "So This Is It"

265   Kennedy spent a smoggy: White, *1968*, p. 211; *Life*, June 21, 1968.
265   Speechwriter Richard Goodwin: Richard Goodwin, p. 535.
266   They were late: Robert Blair Kaiser, p. 15.
266   His campaign had rented: JFKLOH, Greenfield.
266   Minutes after arriving: Daugherty interview.
267   The next day: *Rapid City Journal* (S.D.), June 5, 1968.
267   Senator George McGovern also telephoned: O'Donnell, p. 417.
267   Kennedy called Daugherty back: Daugherty interview; recording of telephone call supplied to author by Daugherty.
267   When Warren Rogers of *Look:* Rogers, p. 147.
267   He poked his head into a room: Lawford, p. 174; Martin, p. 303.
268   He said, "Have a drink . . .": HGP.
268   He told aide Peter Smith: JSOH, Smith, pp. 7–8.
268   Someone said, "Maybe people . . .": *New York Post*, June 5, 1968.
268   During an impromptu hallway press conference: HGP; Newfield, p. 291.
269   "I've got to spend that time . . .": Richard Goodwin, p. 537.
269   Moments before heading downstairs: O'Donnell, p. 418.
270   "I'm going to get Humphrey . . .": Rogers, pp. 149–51.
270   Kennedy retreated to a corner: Newfield, p. 297.
271   "You let me down today . . .": Lewis with D'Orso, p. 415.
271   He stopped for another conversation: JSOH, Kraft, pp. 13–14.
272   He addressed them for about fifteen minutes: Robert Kennedy, *Unfulfilled Promise*, pp. 401–2; WP, June 6, 1968.
272   Then he broke his own rule: Rogers, p. 154; Witcover, *1968*, pp. 252–53.
273   As Kennedy was heading: Moldea, p. 35.
273   "I had been in the infantry . . .": *People*, June 7, 1968.
273   When the shots rang out: Eppridge and Gorey, p. 106.
274   Five others were wounded: JSOH, Harwood, p. 9.
274   The most dramatic: WP, June 6, 1968.
275   He asked the busboy: Eppridge and Gorey, p. 106; *Guardian*, January, 13, 2007; JSOH: Benson, pp. 7–8; Quinn, p. 32. Richard Goodwin, p. 538; WP, June 5, 1968.
275   The most shocking thing: HGP; JSOH, Hamill, p. 16; Eppridge and Gorey, p. 129.

Postscript

276   For the members: *Village Voice*, June 13, 1968.
276   For Walter Fauntroy and Hosea Williams: JSOH, Fauntroy, p. 28; Fauntroy interview.
276   For his press corps, the campaign ended: HGP.
277   For filmmaker Charles Guggenheim: JFKLOH, Guggenheim.
277   For the aides who had arranged and typed: RFKLCP.

279 "the first new Democrat . . .": Clinton, p. 122.
279 But when Clinton signed a welfare reform act: Edelman, pp. 6–7.
279 During the November 2005 commemoration: author's notes.
280 "A Slow Demise . . .": WP, June 20, 2007.
280 "Indian Reservation Reeling . . .": NYT, June 9, 2007.
280 Charles Quinn of CBS: JSOH, Quinn, p. 27.
281 "Soon the dam will break . . .": Guthman and Shulman, p. xvii.

Bibliography

Abernathy, Ralph David. *And the Walls Came Tumbling Down: An Autobiography*. New York: Harper & Row, 1989.

Beran, Michael Knox. *The Last Patrician: Bobby Kennedy and the End of American Aristocracy*. New York: St. Martin's Press, 1988.

Bloom, Alexander, ed. *Long Time Gone: Sixties America Then and Now*. New York: Oxford University Press, 2001.

Braden, Joan. *Just Enough Rope*. New York: Villard, 1989.

Brown, Stuart Gerry. *The Presidency on Trial: Robert Kennedy's 1968 Campaign and Afterwards*. Honolulu: University Press of Hawaii, 1972.

Bruno, Jerry, and Jeff Greenfield. *The Advance Man*. New York: Morrow, 1971.

CBS Television Network. CBS News Special: *Some Friends of Robert Kennedy*. June 7, 1968.

Chester, Lewis, Godfrey Hodgson, and Bruce Page. *An American Melodrama: The Presidential Campaign of 1968*. New York: Viking Press, 1969.

Clinton, Bill. *My Life*. New York: Knopf, 2004.

Clooney, Rosemary, with Raymond Strait. *This for Remembrance: The Autobiography of Rosemary Clooney, an Irish-American Singer*. Chicago: Playboy Press, 1977.

Collier, Peter, and David Horowitz. *The Kennedys: An American Drama*. New York: Macmillan, 1969.

Clymer, Adam. *Edward M. Kennedy: A Biography*. New York: Morrow, 1999.

Deloria, Vine, Jr. *Custer Died for Your Sins: An Indian Manifesto*. New York: Macmillan, 1969.

Dooley, Roger. *Robert Kennedy: The Final Years*. New York: Macmillan, 1969.

Edelman, Peter. *Searching for America's Heart: RFK and the Renewal of Hope*. Boston: Houghton Mifflin, 2001.

Ehrlichman, John. *Witness to Power: The Nixon Years*. New York: Simon & Schuster, 1982.

Eppridge, Bill, and Hays Gorey. *Robert Kennedy: The Last Campaign*. New York: Harcourt Brace, 1993.

Evanier, David. *Roman Candle: The Life of Bobby Darin.* New York: Rodale, 2004.

Evers, Charles, and Andrew Szanton. *Have No Fear: The Charles Evers Story.* New York: Wiley, 1997.

Fleming, Karl. *Son of the Rough South: An Uncivil Memoir.* New York: PublicAffairs, 2005.

Fusco, Paul. *RFK Funeral Train.* New York: Umbrage Editions, 2001.

Garrow, David J. *Bearing the Cross: Martin Luther King Jr. and the Southern Christian Leadership Conference.* New York: Morrow, 1986.

Germond, Jack W. *Fat Man in the Middle Seat: Forty Years of Covering Politics.* New York: Random House, 1999.

Gitlin, Todd. *The Sixties: Years of Hope, Days of Rage.* New York: Bantam Books, 1987.

Graves, Earl G. *How to Succeed in Business Without Being White: Straight Talk on Making It in America.* New York: HarperBusiness, 1997.

Grier, Roosevelt "Rosey." *Rosey: An Autobiography: The Gentle Giant.* Tulsa, Okla.: Honor Books, 1986.

Goodwin, Doris Kearns. *Lyndon Johnson and the American Dream.* New York: Harper & Row, 1976.

Goodwin, Richard N. *Remembering America: A Voice from the Sixties.* Boston: Little, Brown, 1988.

Gould, Lewis L. *1968: The Election That Changed America.* Chicago: Ivan R. Dee, 1993.

Guthman, Edwin O. *We Band of Brothers.* New York: Harper & Row, 1971.

Guthman, Edwin O., and Richard Allen, eds. *Collected Speeches.* New York: Viking Press, 1993.

Guthman, Edwin O., and Jeffrey Shulman, eds. *Robert Kennedy: In His Own Words: The Unpublished Recollections of the Kennedy Years.* New York: Bantam, 1988.

Halberstam, David. *The Unfinished Odyssey of Robert Kennedy.* New York: Random House, 1992.

Hamilton, Edith. *The Greek Way.* New York: Norton, 1930.

Hampton, Henry, Steve Froyer, and Sarah Flynn, eds. *Voices of Freedom: An Oral History of the Civil Rights Movement from the 1950s through 1980s.* New York: Bantam, 1990.

Heymann, C. David. *A Candid Biography of Robert F. Kennedy.* New York: Dutton, 1988.

Hilty, James W. *Robert Kennedy: Brother Protector.* Philadelphia: Temple University Press, 1997.

Jamieson, Kathleen Hall. *Eloquence in an Electronic Age: The Transformation of Political Speechmaking.* New York: Oxford University Press, 1988.

Johnson, Rafer. *The Best That I Can Be: An Autobiography.* New York: Doubleday, 1998.

Kaiser, Charles. *1968 in America: Music, Politics, Chaos, Counterculture, and the Shaping of a Generation.* New York: Grove Press, 1988.

Kaiser, Robert Blair. *"RFK Must Die!"* New York: Dutton, 1970.

Kennedy, John F. *Profiles in Courage.* New York: Harper & Brothers, 1964 (memorial edition).

Kennedy, Maxwell Taylor, ed. *Make Gentle the Life of This World: The Vision of Robert F. Kennedy.* New York: Harcourt Brace, 1998.

Kennedy, Robert F. *The Enemy Within.* New York: Harper & Brothers, 1960.

———. *The Unfulfilled Promise: The Speeches and Notes from the Last Campaign of Robert F. Kennedy, 16 March 1968 to 5 June 1968.* San Diego: M. J. Aguirre, 1986.

———. *Thirteen Days: A Memoir of the Cuban Missile Crisis.* New York: Norton, 1969.

———. *To Seek a Newer World.* Garden City, N.Y.: Doubleday, 1967.

Kimball, Penn. *Robert Kennedy and the New Politics.* Englewood Cliffs, N.J.: Prentice-Hall, 1968.

King, Coretta Scott. *My Life with Martin Luther King, Jr.* New York: Holt, Rinehart and Winston, 1969.

Kotz, Nick. *Let Them Eat Promises: The Politics of Hunger in America.* Englewood Cliffs, N.J.: Prentice-Hall, 1969.

Lawford, Patricia, ed. *That Shining Hour.* Hanover, Mass.: private publication of the Kennedy family, 1969.

Lewis, John, with Michael D'Orso. *Walking with the Wind: A Memoir of the Movement.* San Diego: Harcourt Brace, 1998.

Macafee, Norman, ed. *The Gospel According to RFK: Why It Matters Now.* Boulder, Colo.: Westview Press, 2004.

Mahoney, Richard D. *Sons and Brothers: The Days of Jack and Bobby Kennedy.* New York: Arcade, 1999.

Mailer, Norman. *Miami and the Siege of Chicago.* New York: Donald I. Fine, 1968.

Manchester, William. *The Death of a President.* New York: Harper & Row, 1967.

Martin, John Bartlow. *It Seems Like Only Yesterday: Memoirs of Writing, Presidential Politics, and the Diplomatic Life.* New York: Morrow, 1986.

McCarthy, Abigail. *Private Faces/Public Places.* Garden City, N.Y.: Doubleday, 1972.

McGinniss, Joe. *The Selling of the President 1968.* New York: Trident Press, 1969.

Moldea, Dan E. *The Killing of Robert F. Kennedy: An Investigation of Motive, Means, and Opportunity.* New York: Norton, 1995.

Murphy, John M. "'A Time of Shame and Sorrow': Robert F. Kennedy and the American Jeremiad." *Quarterly Journal of Speech* 76 (1990): 404–7.

Navasky, Victor S. *Kennedy Justice.* New York: Atheneum, 1971.

Newfield, Jack. *Robert Kennedy: A Memoir.* New York: Dutton, 1969.

O'Brien, Lawrence F. *No Final Victories: A Life in Politics—from John F. Kennedy to Watergate.* Garden City, N.Y.: Doubleday, 1974.

O'Brien, Michael. *John F. Kennedy: A Biography.* New York: St. Martin's Press, 2005.

O'Donnell, Helen. *A Common Good: The Friendship of Robert F. Kennedy and Kenneth P. O'Donnell.* New York: Morrow, 1998.

Oppenheimer, Jerry. *The Other Mrs. Kennedy: Ethel Skakel Kennedy: An American Drama of Power, Privilege and Politics.* New York: St. Martin's Press, 1994.

Palermo, Joseph A. *In His Own Right: The Political Odyssey of Senator Robert F. Kennedy.* New York: Columbia University Press, 2001.

Rogers, Warren. *When I Think of Bobby: A Personal Memoir of the Kennedy Years.* New York: HarperCollins, 1993.

Royko, Mike. *Boss: Richard J. Daley of Chicago.* New York: Dutton, 1971.

Salinger, Pierre. *P.S.: A Memoir.* New York: St. Martin's Press, 1995.

Salinger, Pierre, Edwin Guthman, Frank Mankiewicz, and John Seigenthaler, eds. *An Honorable Profession: A Tribute to Robert F. Kennedy.* Garden City, N.Y.: Doubleday, 1968.

Sandbrook, Dominic. *Eugene McCarthy: The Rise and Fall of Postwar American Liberalism.* New York: Knopf, 2004.

Schaap, Dick. *R.F.K.* New York: New American Library, 1967.

Schlesinger, Arthur M., Jr. *Robert Kennedy and His Times.* New York: Random House, 1978.

Shannon, William V. *The Heir Apparent: Robert Kennedy and the Struggle for Power.* New York: Macmillan, 1967.

Shesol, Jeff. *Mutual Contempt: Lyndon Johnson, Robert Kennedy, and the Feud That Defined a Decade.* New York: Norton, 1997.

Sidorenko, Konstantin. *Robert F. Kennedy: A Spiritual Biography.* New York: Crossroad, 2000.

Sorensen, Theodore C. *The Kennedy Legacy.* New York: Macmillan, 1969.

Steel, Ronald. *In Love with the Night: The American Romance with Robert Kennedy.* New York: Simon & Schuster, 2000.

Stein, Jean, and George Plimpton. *American Journey: The Times of Robert Kennedy.* New York: Harcourt Brace Jovanovich, 1970.

Sullivan, William C. *The Bureau: My Thirty Years with Hoover's FBI.* New York: Norton, 1979.

Taraborrelli, J. Randy. *Jackie Ethel Joan: Women of Camelot.* New York: Warner Books, 2000.

Thomas, Eva. *Robert Kennedy: His Life.* New York: Simon & Schuster, 2000.

Unger, Irwin, and Debi Unger. *Turning Point: 1968.* New York: Charles Scribner's Sons, 1988.

vanden Heuvel, William, and Milton Gwirtzman. *On His Own. Robert F. Kennedy, 1964–1968.* Garden City, N.Y.: Doubleday, 1970.

White, Theodore H. *The Making of the President 1960.* New York: Atheneum, 1961.

———. *The Making of the President 1968.* New York: Atheneum, 1969.

Wilkins, Roger. *A Man's Life: An Autobiography.* New York: Simon & Schuster, 1982.

Wills, Garry. *The Kennedy Imprisonment: A Meditation in Power.* Boston: Little, Brown, 1981.

Witcover, Jules. *85 Days: The Last Campaign of Robert Kennedy.* New York: Putnam, 1969.

———. *The Making of an Ink-Stained Wretch: Half a Century Pounding the Political Beat.* Baltimore: Johns Hopkins University Press, 2005.

———. *1968: The Year the Dream Died.* New York: Warner Books, 1997.

Wofford, Harris. *Of Kennedys and Kings: Making Sense of the Sixties.* New York: Farrar, Straus and Giroux, 1980.

Acknowledgments

Robert Kennedy's 1968 campaign was covered by a number of talented journalists. Jack Newfield, Jules Witcover, David Halberstam, and Hays Gorey have all written excellent books about Kennedy and the campaign that have proven invaluable, as have biographies of Robert Kennedy by Arthur Schlesinger, who was an eyewitness to some of the events he described, and Evan Thomas, who found and interviewed a number of Kennedy's friends and aides overlooked by earlier authors.

I am also grateful to Jim Stevenson, who permitted me to read and quote from his unpublished account of his experiences covering the Kennedy campaign, and to Jean Stein, who allowed me to read and quote from the hundreds of interviews she conducted for *American Journey*, her oral history of the Kennedy campaign. These interviews are exceptionally vivid and poignant because many were conducted within months of the assassination. Some of this material appeared in her book, but much of it appears here for the first time. Interviews with Jeff Greenfield, Adam Walinsky, Peter Edelman, Frank Mankiewicz, John Nolan, and Jim Tolan conducted for the oral history archives of the Kennedy library were also conducted soon after Kennedy's death and were indispensable. Jim Tolan advanced many of

Kennedy's most memorable appearances that spring. His 295-page oral history is one of the longest and most detailed in the Robert F. Kennedy Oral History Archives, and many of his observations appear here for the first time. The Hays Gorey papers at the University of Utah and John Bartlow Martin's campaign diary at the Library of Congress were also important sources.

I conducted over a hundred interviews, in person and by phone. The late Fred Dutton, who spent more time with Robert Kennedy during those eighty-two days than anyone else, spent several hours with me despite his failing health, and expanded on many of the points raised in his two oral histories. AP reporter Joe Mohbat traveled with Kennedy throughout the entire campaign, often riding with him in motorcades. Before speaking with me, Mohbat had not been interviewed about his experiences for decades, and his testimony was fresh and heartfelt.

The majority of my interviews were with Kennedy campaign workers and journalists in Indiana, South Dakota, Kansas, and Nebraska who had seldom, if ever, been questioned about the campaign. Some had spent only a short time in Kennedy's company, riding with him in a motorcade or on a train, introducing him at a rally, or hearing him speak. I interviewed some by telephone and met others in person while retracing Kennedy's campaign in South Dakota, Nebraska, and Indiana. They were generous with their time and memories, and I am particularly grateful to Jim Osborne, Gus Stevens, Mike Riley, and Shirley Amick in Indiana, Frank German in Nebraska, and Johnson Holy Rock in South Dakota. I am also grateful to Don Boggs, who has produced a documentary film about Kennedy's April 4 speech in Indianapolis and shared his research with me; the staff of the King Center in Atlanta; and Sharon Kelly, Steve Plotkin, James Hill, and Laurie Austin at the John F. Kennedy Library in Boston. I am indebted to George Hodgman for his insightful comments and graceful editing. I was sorry to lose him as my editor several months before the book went into production, but was reassured by the perceptive final edits performed by his able successor, David Patterson. As always, I am indebted most to Kathy Robbins for her enthusiasm, encouragement, and wise counsel.

Index

About the Author

Thurston Clarke has written eleven books of fiction and nonfiction, including *Pearl Harbor Ghosts* and *California Fault*, a *New York Times* notable book. His articles have been published in *Vanity Fair*, *Glamour*, *The New York Times*, and *The Washington Post*. He is the recipient of a Guggenheim Fellowship. He lives in Willsboro, New York, with his wife and three daughters.